The Senjūshō

Buddhist Tales of Early Medieval Japan

Translated by

Yoshiko Dykstra

Kanji Press
HONOLULU

© 2014 YOSHIKO DYKSTRA
All rights reserved
Printed in the United States of America
ISBN 978-0-917880-04-9

This publication is printed on acid-free paper and
meets the guidelines for permanence and durability
of the Council of Library Resources.

Print-ready copy prepared by Kanji Press.

DISTRIBUTED BY

UNIVERSITY OF HAWAI'I PRESS
2840 Kolowalu Street
Honolulu, Hawai'i 96822
www.uhpress.hawaii.edu

CONTENTS

INTRODUCTION	v
The *Senjūshō*	1
Section One	4
Section Two	29
Section Three	55
Section Four	74
Section Five	93
Section Six	125
Section Seven	166
Section Eight	201
Section Nine	257
SELECTED BIBLIOGRAPHY	293

INTRODUCTION

The present work is a translation of the 121 stories contained in the *Senjūshō (A Collection of Selected Tales)*, which dates from the Kamakura period (1185–1333).[1] For many years the collection was attributed to the itinerant poet-priest Saigyō (1118–1190), but scholars have since disproved this claim.[2]

Numerous story collections, or *setsuwashū*, were compiled in the Heian (794–1185) and Kamakura periods, including Minamoto Akikane's *Kojidan* (1212-1215), Tachibana Narisue's *Kokonchomonjū* (1254), and Fujiwara Nobuzane's *Imamonogatari* (1239–1240).[3] They narrate old stories and events and include gossipy tales handed down by generations of aristocrats. A common feature of *setsuwashū* is an admiration and appreciation for the tastes and values of the nobility, which were in decline as the courtly Heian era gave way to the plebeian, samurai-dominated Kamakura. In addition to these texts, collections of Buddhist tales, or *bukkyō setsuwashū*, were produced, among them the *Konjaku monogatarishū* (early twelfth century), Taira Yasunori's *Hōbutsushū* (early Kamakura), Kamo Chōmei's *Hosshinshū* (1216),

---

1. The Matsudaira text contains an additional eight stories without titles. A partial translation of the *Senjūshō* is given in Jean Moore's "*Senjūshō*: Buddhist Tales of Renunciation," *Monumenta Nipponica* 41, no. 2 (1986): 127–174.
2. For a study of Saigyō and his legendary tales, see Taniguchi Kōichi, "Saigyō monogatari no keisei," *Bungaku* 46, no. 10 (1978).
3. 古事談; 古今著聞集; 今物語.

Keisei's *Kankyonotomo* (1222), and Mujū's *Shasekishū* (1279–1283).[4] Although Buddhist collections were compiled mainly to enlighten and educate the masses, they, too, betray a longing for *ōchōbunka*, or aristocratic culture.[5] Thus the *Senjūshō* adopts the didactic tone typical of Buddhist story collections even as its compiler saw fit to include many sentimental anecdotes and *waka* poems that harken back fondly to earlier times. The principal theme of the work, however, is expressed in the stories of men and women renouncing secular life to attain religious enlightenment. The protagonists include noble lords and ladies, samurai warriors, priests and monks, nuns, and courtesans.

Modern studies of the *Senjūshō* agree that Saigyō did not compile the work; numerous discrepancies between Saigyō's dates and the dates of the poems and poets in the tales convincingly show that Saigyō could not have been the author.[6] (For example, some of the poems quoted are adopted from those in the *Shinkokinshū*, which was compiled in 1201, after Saigyō's death.)[7] The author or compiler, whether singular or plural, of the collection remains a mystery. The date of the *Senjūshō* is not known for certain, but it lies somewhere between 1143 and 1255.[8]

The purpose of the *Senjūshō* is clearly expressed in the preface, which states that its compiler collected useful stories of holy men and women who, through their often eccentric and unorthodox experiences, inspired others to embrace the Way. The stories are divided into nine sections to coincide with the Nine Realms of the Pure Land of Amida Buddha. Some tales narrate miracles performed by gods and deities, such as those enshrined at Ise, Kasuga, and Kashima, and reflect the

4. 今昔物語集; 宝物集, 発心集; 閑居友; 砂石集. For a comparative study of the *Senjūshō* and the *Kankyonotomo*, see Yasuda Takako et al., *Senjūshō*, vol. 1 (Tokyo: Gendai Shichō Shinsha, 1987), 51–67.

5. For contemporary nostalgia for the *ōchōbunka* 王朝文化, see Nomura Hachirō, *Kinko jidai setsuwa bungakuron* (Tokyo: Meiji Shoin, 1935).

6. For a study of the *Senjūshō* and its attribution to Saigyō, see Nishio Kōchi, "Saigyōteki ningen to Saigyō gonomi no ningen: Senjūshō no katakusei," *Bungaku* 38 (April 1969): 66–67.

7. For discrepancies in the *Senjūshō*, see Nishio Kōichi, *Senjūshō* (Tokyo: Iwanami Shoten, 1975), 356–364; Yasuda Takako et al., *Senjūshō*, vol. 1, 4–11.

8. For the dates of the *Senjūshō*, see Konno Tōru, "Senjūshō no seiritsu nitsuite," *Kokugo kokubun* 25 (December 1956): 6; Kobayashi Tadao, "Senjūshō ni kansuru ichikōsatsu," *Kokugakuin zasshi* (September 1940).

assimilation of Buddhism and Shinto (*honjisuijaku*) at the time.[9]

The *Senjūshō*'s general theme is based on the doctrine of *yuishiki*, or consciousness only, which asserts the futility of life and encourages abandonment of the secular to pursue the Way.[10] Many of the stories are adopted from Buddhist story collections such as the *Shūiōjōden* (1123), compiled by Miyoshi Tameyasu, which tell of high-ranking priests of famous temples hiding their identities and quietly living as wandering beggars and recluses: The story of the priest Genpin is a prime example.[11] The tales also reflect another contemporary trend—that of the wandering recluse, or *hyōhaku inseija*,[12] which can be found in the earlier *Hosshinshū* and *Kojidan* collections. Other *Senjūshō* tales recount more personal matters and unusual events: One protagonist, purportedly Saigyō, visits the rock chamber of Shō and reminisces about Priest Gyōson (8-32), exchanges poems with a courtesan of Eguchi (9-8), happens upon a nun who was once his wife (9-10), and tries to create a man out of bones (5-15). Other stories tell of men abandoning their wives and children to follow the Way. This may appear selfish from a Western point of view, but the narrator praises their decisiveness and religious zeal.

Establishing a relationship or friendship with a buddha, bodhisattva, or eminent monk is a common occurance in Buddhist tales. The *Senjūshō* has such stories in abundance (for example, story 7-7, "Monk Musō"). In Japan, being introduced or given the chance to meet someone new is highly valued because that person may become an important teacher or guide in one's life.[13]

The *Senjushō* differs from earlier Buddhist collections such as the *Nihonryōiki* and the *Hokkegenki*[14] because its narrator appends critical

---

9. For a study on general thought in relation to the *Senjūshō*, see Nomura Hachirō, *Kamakura jidai bungaku shinron* (Tokyo: Meiji Shoin, 1922).

10. For the *Senjūshō* theme of *yuishiki* 唯識 in relation to the *Kankyonotomo*, see Kojima Takayuki, "Setsuwa bungaku," in *Kenkyū shiryō nihon koten kenkyū*, vol. 3 (Tokyo: Meiji Shoin, 1984), 259–268.

11. For Genpin, see *Senjūshō* 1-8, 2-4, 2-8, 5-1, 7-9, and 9-11.

12. 漂白隠世者. For studies on *intonja* 隠遁者 or *inseija* (retired recluses), see Numanami Seiho, "Inton no shisōteki haikei," *Dōmei Daigaku Ronsō* 35 (December 1976); Itō Hiroyuki, *Inton no bungaku* (Tokyo: Kasama Shoin, 1975).

13. This idea was developed into *ichigo-ichie* 一期一会, "one meeting in a lifetime," by the tea master Sōji (1544–1590), who wrote the *Yamagami Sōjiki* 山上宗二記.

14. 日本霊異記; 法華験記.

comments and an appraisal to each tale, making it an example of tale criticism, or *setsuwa-hihyō*, as well as a contributor to the development of the *zuihitsu* (essay) genre.¹⁵ These comments may seem sentimental, repetitious, and didactic, but they reveal the narrator's understanding of the suffering endured when one must choose between art—the Way of Poetry—and life, between religious aspirations and secular ambitions. Perhaps this is why the eminent *haiku* poet Bashō (1644–1694) always kept a copy of the *Senjūshō* at his side—this coupled with the fact that he believed its author was Saigyō, for whom he had a deep admiration, and that he had visited the *utamakura*¹⁶ mentioned in the stories. So prevalent was the belief that the renowned Saigyō had compiled the *Senjūshō* that the work became popular enough to warrant a mention by the Portuguese missionary João Rodrigues in his grammar of the Japanese language, published in 1620.¹⁷

There are primarily two types of *Senjūshō* texts available: the Kōhon, or popular, versions and the Ryakuhon, or abridged, versions.¹⁸ The Kōhon versions include the Hashimoto Shinkichi text, which lacks sections 1, 2, and 3; the Matsudaira text, upon which the present translation is based; the Yōmei bunko text; the Shoryōbu text; the Naikaku bunko text; and the Shōkōkan text. The block-printed versions include those printed in 1651, 1687, and 1810 and are represented by the *Dainihon bukkyō zensho*, the *Meicho bunko*, and the *Saigyō senshū*. As for the Ryakuhon versions, the Kokkai toshokan, the Tōdaiji, the Saga, and the Kokatsuji texts make up this category.

For this book I have supplied kanji for names and terms when necessary. Macrons are omitted in well-known place names such as Tokyo, Osaka, and Kyoto. The pinyin system is used for romanization of Chinese names and terms. For romanization of Japanese names and terms, including *waka* poems, I used modern Japanese readings: "i" for

---

15. Nisho Kōichi, *Senjūshō* (Tokyo: Iwanami Shoten), 333.
16. 歌枕: places famous for the poems they inspired. Bashō visited *utamakura* in the *Senjūshō* to sympathize with Saigyō. For a study on Bashō and Saigyō, see Itō Hiroyuki, "Senjūshō ni okeru tonsei shisō," *Bukkyō Bungaku Kenkyū* 5 (1974): 173–176.
17. Michael Cooper, ed., *They Came to Japan: An Anthology of European Reports on Japan, 1542-1640* (Ann Arbor: Center for Japanese Studies, University of Michigan, 1995), 255.
18. Kōhon 広本; Ryakuhon 略本. For a study of the various texts, see Yasuda Takako et al., *Senjūshō*, vol. 1, 68–79.

"hi," "wa" for "ha," "o" for "uo." The illustrations reproduced here are by the popular Edo writer and artist Ihara Saikaku (1642–1693) and can be found in texts owned by the Nara Women's University.

My work has benefited greatly from a recent and complete study, *Senjūshō zenchūshaku*, compiled by professors Yasuda Takako, Umeno Kimiko, Nozaki Noriko, Kōno Keiko, and Morise Yoshie;[19] without the profound studies of these scholars, spanning more than forty years, this translation would not have been possible. I am grateful to Dr. George Tanabe, professor emeritus at the University of Hawai'i, who provided valuable insight on the interpretation of some Buddhist terminology. My deep appreciation goes to Dr. Michael Cooper, former editor of *Monumenta Nipponica*, who read this translation several times and graciously made innumerable suggestions and valuable comments. I am also grateful for the efforts and enthusiasm of Dr. Matthew Stavros, the editor of *Pre-Modern Japanese Studies*. Finally, this book is dedicated to my late husband, Dr. Andrew H. Dykstra, who had always encouraged and supported my translation of classical Japanese literature.

---

19. Yasuda Takako, Umeno Kimiko, Nozaki Noriko, Kōno Keiko, and Morise Yoshie, eds., *Senjūshō zenchūshaku*, 2 vols. (Tokyo: Kasama Shoin, 2003).

THE SENJŪSHŌ

Preface

I have not yet emerged from the long sleep between life and death,[1] only dreaming of delusions that occur from morning to night. I regard the moon's reflection on the water as the real moon and a reflection[2] seen in a mirror as reality. Although I have found no boat to cross the sea of suffering in life and death, I do not count myself among the sheep being led to the slaughterhouse.[3] I have spent some forty years watching from a distance the smoke arising from Toribe and Funaoka,[4] and my hair has become as white as frost. I do not know what will happen to me in the future. Death may approach me even today. This life is like a futile game in a dream.

If I am to play the game, I may as well enjoy it while following in the footsteps of sages past. So I have gathered their words and tales into a collection, which I have entitled *Senjūshō* (A Collection of Selected Tales), and have kept it by my side as a guide to the Way of the Law.[5]

I have divided this work into nine chapters, deliberately leaving out one to mimic the Nine Realms of the Pure Land,[6] and included eighty stories instead of one hundred,[7] in the manner of the Eighty Pleasant Features of a Buddha.[8] Being ignorant and common, I fail to see the truth just as a blind man is unable to see even with his eyes open, and

---

1. That is, we repeat many cycles of life and death without rebirth in the Buddha's Pure Land. *Nagaki nemuri* 長き眠り (long sleep) refers to the long duration of sufferings in the life-death cycles.
2. I have translated *kage* 影 (shadow) as "reflection."
3. The slow pace of sheep led to a slaughterhouse implies people ignorant of their imminent death.
4. Both Toribe 鳥部 (or Toribeno 鳥部野) and Funaoka 舟岡 were burial grounds near the capital of Kyoto. Toribe was located in the area between the temples of Kiyomizu and Nishiōtani in the east of the city. Funaoka was in contemporary Kita ward. The smoke rising from the two places refers to funerary pyres.
5. *Chishiki* 智識 (knowledge) and *zenchishiki* 善智識 (good knowledge) signify those people, objects, incidents, and the like that might facilitate future enlightenment. The terms often refer to good teachers or someone who guides and leads others to the way of buddhahood. In the text, I have translated them as "a guide to the Way."
6. *Kuhon no jōdo* 九品の浄土: nine kinds of rebirth in the Pure Land. These depend on an individual's buddha nature (*kikon* 機根).
7. The Matsudaira text contains 121 stories in 9 chapters.
8. *Hachijūzuikō* 八十随好, or *hachijūzuigyō* 八十随形, meaning the eighty good features of the buddhas in the *Yakushi hongankyō* 薬師本願経 (*Daizōkyō* 大蔵経, Kyōshūbu 経集部, p. 405).

my mind is too distracted to overcome delusions. Praying for the help of the gods,[9] I have included tales about them in each chapter.

1-1 Holy Man Zōga

Holy Man Zōga[10] had a strong desire for the Way since his youth. He confined himself to the Konpon Chūdō Hall on Mount Hiei[11] for one thousand nights, praying to attain the Way, but his mind and heart were not in accord with his prayers.

One day he visited the Grand Shrine of Ise[12] and prayed to the Great Deity. Finally, he had a revelation and in a dream heard the words, "If you want to attain the Way, abandon your desire for fame and fortune." Surprised, Zōga woke up and with great determination declared, "I will leave all desire to follow this revelation." He immediately removed all his clothes, including his priestly robe, gave them to beggars, and returned home naked from Ise. The people who saw him on the way thought it most extraordinary and said to each other, "So he has gone insane." Others felt too embarrassed to look at him, but Zōga utterly ignored the spectators.

He proceeded to climb Mount Hiei for four days, begging for food along the way. Finally, Zōga arrived at the home of Master Jie. Seeing his extraordinary appearance, some of his colleagues concluded, "So the holy man has become deranged." Others avoided him, saying, "How embarrassing!"

Master Jie quietly invited Zōga into his chambers and gave him some advice. "I understand your wish to abandon the desires for fame

---

9. This phrase reflects the Buddhist-Shinto syncretism typical of the time.

10. Zōga 増賀 died in 1003 at the age of eighty-seven. When he was ten, he entered Enryakuji Temple, northeast of Kyoto, where he became a disciple of Master Jie 慈恵大師 (912–985), the eighteenth Tendai *zasu* 天台座主, or director of the Tendai School 天台宗. Zōga engaged in various Tendai practices, including the *shikan* 止観 (cessation of thought) concept by abandoning fame and fortune. He appears in many tale collections including the *Honchōhokkegenki* 本朝法華験記 (III, 83); the *Konjaku monogatarishū* 今昔物語集 (10-18, 12-33, 19-10); the *Hosshinshū* 発心集 (1-5, 2-3); the *Ujishūi monogatari* 宇治拾遺物語 (no. 143), and the *Shasekishū* 沙石集 (10-1). For a study on Zōga, see Yasuda Takako, "Zōga shōnin setsuwa," in *Sugiyama kokubungaku*, no. 6.

11. Konpon Chūdō Hall 根本中堂 was and continues to be the central structure of Enryakuji Temple, founded by Priest Saichō 最澄 (later Master Dengyō 伝教大師, 767–822).

12. The Grand Shrine of Ise (伊勢神宮) enshrines Amaterasu Ōmikami 天照大神, the progenitor of the Japanese imperial family. This tale reflects Shinto-Buddhism syncretism.

and fortune. But dress yourself properly and correct your manners. Detach yourself from desires only in your mind."

"If I completely abandon my desires, my manners will be duly corrected. Oh, how happy I am now," Zōga cried and stood up to run toward the gate. Master Jie followed him outside the gateway and tearfully watched him leave. Some time later, Zōga finally reached Mount Tōnomine[13] in Yamato province and settled in the ruins of the hut of Zen Master Chirō.[14]

Truly, the two desires for fame and fortune are lamentable problems that arise from the three poisons of anger, avarice, and ignorance. A man often repeats lies to prolong his life, which he assumes to be something true and eternal. If he is born into a samurai family, he learns the Way of Archery from his youth. Swinging his three-foot-long sword while running around a battlefield at risk of losing his life, he wishes to surpass all others in his desire for fame and fortune.

When a courtesan paints her eyebrows as narrow as willow leaves, dresses herself in a fragrant robe, and makes her appearance as alluring as a lingering autumn breeze,[15] she has only the two wishes for fame and fortune. This is also true of a priest in a black robe with rosary beads in his hand. He wishes to be respected by other monks and priests by rising to a higher official position and being invited to imperial Buddhist meetings. He has not yet left behind the desire for fame and fortune.

There is no hope for those ignorant of the Law. But even others who are aware of the Law and have profound knowledge of the *yuishiki* and

---

13. Tōnomine 多武峰 is a peak located in Nara prefecture, in the southern part of present-day Sakurai-shi. The temple of Myōrakuji 妙楽寺 on its summit enshrines the relics of Fujiwara Kamatari 藤原鎌足 (614–666). Myōrakuji later became Dansan (Danzan) Shrine 談山神社山. Among the many ascetics on the mountain was Fujiwara Takamitsu, who lived there in a grass hut after taking the tonsure as described in the *Tōnomine shōshō monogatari* 多武峰少将物語.
14. Master Chirō 智朗禅師, a relation of Emperor Montoku 文徳 (827–858), took the tonsure and studied both the Tendai and Shingon 真言 teachings. He also appears in *Senjūshō* 3-9, *Kankyo no tomo* 閑居の友 1-5, and *Shasekishū* 4.
15. A typical expression used when referring to a woman who wishes to attract a man's attention.

shikan concepts[16] are still drifting in the sea of life and death. Although they try to abandon these desires, they are unable to do so because it is difficult to break long-accustomed habits.

It was quite unusual that Zōga abandoned his desires immediately after his revelation. Thanks to the help of the Great Deity of the Ise Shrine, he maintained his strong conviction. His mind, which had been clouded by anger, avarice, and ignorance, and his heart, which had been deluded by the two desires, must have been purified by the waves of the Isuzu River[17] and made to disappear in the splendid light of Amaterasu. This is most wonderful and should never be forgotten by later generations.

1-2 A Revelation at Gion Shrine[18] and a Poem

Some time ago, a man living in a hut at Shirakawa[19] was devoted to the Law and practiced the Way as an ascetic. Because someone had stolen his inheritance earlier, he had no other recourse but to confine himself to Gion Shrine and pray to the gods for a solution to his problem. At dawn on the seventh day, he heard a noble voice from the inner shrine reciting a poem:

Nagaki yo no
Kurushiki koto o
Omoe kashi
Kari no yadori o
Nani nagekuran

---

16. *Yuishiki* 唯識, or "consciousness only," a concept propagated by the Hossō 法相 Sect in Japan, regards all phenomena in this life and world as nothing but the provisional illusions produced in one's mind. The concept appears frequently in the *Senjūshō* (1-1, 5-1, 5-4, 5-5, 5-14, 6-3, 6-6, 7-9). The idea of *shikan* 止観 (cessation of thinking, an abbreviation of *maka shikan* 摩珂止観), the main practice of the Tendai School, emphasizes concentration of mind to dispel delusions and illusions. The *shikan* idea appears in the *Senjūshō* (2-4, 9-3, 9-5).
17. The Isuzu River 五十鈴川 runs through the city of Ise.
18. Some titles in the original text have subtitles printed in smaller fonts. In this text I have either placed them in brackets or incorporated them into the main titles. Gion Shrine 祇園社 is known today as Yasaka Shrine. Its principal deities are Susanoo and Kushinada Hime.
19. Shirakawa is in northeastern Kyoto.

> Think of the sufferings
> In this long life,
> Why are you
> Lamenting in this
> Temporary life?

Surprised, the man woke up and realized that the poem was a revelation from the gods. He carefully reflected on its meaning and thought, "This life is most futile. A man I see in the evening may die the next morning. People alive in the morning may become a handful of white ashes in the evening. Happiness does not last long, while sorrow may soon disappear. We may enjoy happiness for a moment but suffer sadness in the next minute. Everything in this life is just as transient as a gesture of our hands. It is most regrettable that we attach ourselves to transient things and fail to be mindful of the sufferings in our future life."

As soon as he understood the poem's meaning, the man cut his hair and took the tonsure there and then. Without telling his wife and child, he gathered bamboo wood at Shirakawa, built a simple hut, and lived there while reciting the Buddha's name day and night. Unattached to life and content with the bare minimum to survive, he did not go out begging for alms in the village. As he was totally devoted to the singular act of reciting the Buddha's name, the neighbors were impressed and began to help him.

Several days passed before his wife and child heard about him and they finally came to see him. They tried to persuade him to return home, but he disregarded them and concentrated only on his practice. So his helpless wife and child left without him, but soon his wife kindly sent him some things for his daily needs, and so he was able to live more comfortably in the hut.

Meanwhile, the thief [of the inheritance] heard about him and thought, "Alas, I never believed he was so serious about this. Indeed, I should have realized the futility of this life." So he immediately returned everything he had stolen to the ascetic's wife, shaved his head, and went to see the ascetic at Shirakawa.

Hearing his visitor's explanation, the ascetic felt overwhelmed and tearfully asked him, "Where are you going? If you like, you can stay here and recite the Buddha's name with me."

"Where shall I go? Practicing the Law with you is exactly what I want," the man replied. He stayed with the ascetic in the hut and they became close friends. Since that time, they recited the Buddha's name day and night. Their chanting sounded so noble that it often consoled their elderly neighbors when they had difficulty sleeping during the night.

Two years passed, and finally, at dawn on the fourteenth day of the third month, the first ascetic breathed his last while sitting, facing west.[20] The second man, placing his head on his companion's lap, also passed away as if sleeping. In the morning, many people came to establish a relationship with the enlightened ascetics and copied their images, which, so they say, still exist.

Such a story overwhelms us with tears. If someone stole our possessions, we would usually want to recover them and would constantly strive to do this by praying to the gods and buddhas. At the same time, we develop hatred toward the thief and wish him evil. Thus, by attaching ourselves to such futile matters, we waste not only our present life but also our future one. But the first ascetic believed in the gods'

---

20. In a person's last moments, sitting while facing west was the way to ensure rebirth in Amida's Western Paradise (*saihō jōdo* 西方浄土).

revelation and instantly detached himself from worldly affairs, taking the tonsure and leaving his wife and child. This was most noble and praiseworthy.

After stealing the first man's possessions, the second ascetic could have enjoyed the stolen goods when he heard of the other man taking the tonsure. Instead, he realized his mistake, and he, too, left secular life and joined the other to practice the Law. This was most remarkable.

In old examples found in India, China, and Japan, we often read of someone renouncing the world because of his sad experiences, but rarely do we hear about a person abandoning secular life because he had received a fortune. So these two ascetics finally fulfilled their earnest wish for enlightenment. Moreover, it is most gratifying that a buddha revealed himself as a deity to help sentient beings. "They say the true entity of Rushana Buddha of Everlasting Enlightenment[21] is manifested as Daimyōjin, Great Bright Deity, to help sentient beings. We should also be especially thankful to Nyorai of Supreme Enlightenment,[22] who appears in this world, which is as insignificant as dust, to save us sentient beings."[23]

1-3 A Monk with No Relations Returns a Robe

Some time ago, a poor monk wandered about the capital. Covered in mud from head to foot, he appeared very shabby as he begged for alms at each house, wearing an old straw mat. But he was very good-natured and honest, and he would never take even a tree branch without the

---

21. Vairocana 廬遮那仏, the Sun Buddha and the principal image of the *Kegonkyō* 華厳経 sutra, symbolizes infinite knowledge illuminated by the Buddha's light. His appearance as a Japanese *daimyōjin* 大明神, or great bright deity, is an example of the concept of *honji-suijaku* 本地垂迹, or Buddhist-Shinto syncretism. This buddha is also the master of the Lotus Flower World; seated on a lotus, he is identified with the Great Buddha of Nara and the Dainichi Nyorai 大日如来 of *mikkyō* 密教, or esoteric, teachings.
22. Tathāgata 如来, or the one who has obtained enlightenment, comes from the World of Truth to this world to help sentient beings.
23. The sentence implies the concept of *wakōdōjin* 和光同塵: to soften the light of buddhas who will become the same as the dust, the common people. It means that buddhas and bodhisattvas hide their prestige to associate with common sentient beings. It is related to *honjisuijaku* theory.

owner's permission. People were sympathetic and helped him to survive from day to day.

A man once invited him to his house and offered him an unlined kimono, saying, "Why not wear this?" The monk politely replied, "I thank you for your kindness. A man like me with no relations can survive only with the help of others, so I will accept this when I need it. But since I am accustomed to wearing straw mats, wearing something as fine as this kimono would be wasted on me. When you throw away some straw, I would be grateful to have some of it." In this way the monk declined the offer and did not touch the robe, and so the man was unable to give it to him.

The monk ate very little, and if someone invited him to eat more, he would say, "No, thank you. I already have had enough." He never kept anything for the future. All he did was recite the Buddha's name and passages from the sutras. Thus he was completely devoted to the Way, although he seemed to know little about Buddhist doctrines.

The monk once visited Holy Man Geisai,[24] who in all sincerity asked him, "Please tell me something from a sutra to inspire me." The monk gazed at a morning glory blooming by his side, but a light wind soon blew the dew on its petals to the ground. Seeing this, the monk tearfully recited a poem:

Miruya ikani
Adanimo sakuru
Asagao no
Sakidatsu kesa no
Shiratsuyu

Don't you see
The *asagao* that bloomed
In vain this morning,
And the white dew
That has already fallen from it?

Then he said to Geisai, "Look at this morning glory that opened in

---

24. Priest Geisai 迎西 (d. 1135) appears in another *Senjūshō* tale (2-8) and also in the *Kōyasan ōjōden* 高野山往生伝 (*Nihon shisō taikei*, p. 699).

vain this morning. Alas, the dew has fallen before the flower. What do you think of this? Isn't this truly a noble teaching of the Buddha?" The monk then left, and no one knew where he went.

What the holy man said was most noble. Living in this dreamlike life, we attach ourselves to futile things such as fame and fortune, instead of practicing the Way in mountains and forests. But having abandoned worldly affairs, this man was seeking virtuous merit while living as an indigent monk. How truly commendable! It accords with the old saying, "He hid his virtue by begging alms." We all would like to know more about such a high-minded man who took the tonsure and wandered about as a beggar.

The monk's interpretation of the poem is also extraordinary. The morning glory was often cited as an example of the futility of this life. He noticed the dew that had fallen before the flower was scattered and wondered about the passing wind that had blown away the dew. His insight was quite remarkable.

The morning glory reopens in the morning just as the sun invariably sets in the evening. Time passes as fast as an arrow in this short life.[25] Why, then, should anyone spend his fleeting life desiring futile things while the wrinkles on his forehead and his white eyebrows go unnoticed? He vainly seeks worldly fame and wealth like a child begging his parents for something.

The meaning of the above poem is a basic teaching of the Buddha. Most of us think we understand everything, but in fact we understand nothing. If only we had a mind like this monk's, even for a short while.

The monk appears in the *Ōjōden*, compiled by Gōsotsu,[26] and I rewrote the story in a simple style since I could not resist mentioning him. I was moved to tears when reading that he finally fulfilled his wishes near Higashiyama in the capital.

Sadly and endlessly we repeat birth and death in the Twelve

---

25. The expression in the text means "time passes quickly" and is borrowed from old Chinese legends. The white horse 白駒 gallops away and the three-legged sun crow 金烏 (with three feet in the sun) does not remain. The combination of the white horse and golden crow appears in another *Senjūshō* tale (7-1).

26. Gōsotsu 江師, or Ōe Masafusa 大江匡房, died in 1111 at the age of seventy-two. He was a poet and the compiler of the *Zoku honchō ōjōden* 続本朝往生伝, biographical records of enlightened people of Japan, although this text does not appear to record anything concerning the monk. A similar tale appears in *Hosshinshū* 1:10.

Karmic Relations and transmigrate through the Twenty-Five Worlds.[27] We have come from the delusional existence of our previous lives and may return to the same existence in our future lives. As sentient beings, we will be related to others and associated as parents and children, masters and disciples, lords and servants, while we attach ourselves to this or that person. As regards death, we ignore the fact that everything is caused by previous karmic relations, and we think our sadness lasts for only one generation in this life, and we wet our sleeves with tears of blood.

Isn't it truly foolish to regard whatever has passed as spring dreams? But the sufferings caused by separation [death] cannot be likened to a dream. Relationships with our friends may return to us like echoes in a valley, but separation is different from such echoes. His son's death caused Confucius[28] much suffering, while Gankai's death at a young age filled his father with sadness.[29] Thus not even sages and holy men of the past could escape the sufferings of separation. In our country, Jittoku, a shogun of the Right, lost his father when he was young, and in his old age Kyōgoku Great Minister Munesuke[30] grieved for his son's death. On such occasions, everyone believes unbearable sufferings afflict only him and no one else. But we should realize death comes to everyone who passes through the cycle of birth and death. We should calmly contemplate and practice the Way before wrinkles appear on our forehead and our eyebrows turn white.

---

27. The Twelve Karmic Relations (*jūni innen* 十二因縁) refer to the various karmic relations through which one repeats life and death, while the Twenty-Five Worlds (*nijūgou* 廿五有) refer to the realms through which all sentient beings transmigrate.
28. Confucius 孔子, or 仲尼 (551–479 B.C.), the great Chinese philosopher, wept at the death of his son Li 鯉 in the *Lunyu* 論語 (*Shinshaku kanbun taikei*, p. 238).
29. Yan-hui 顔回 (514–483 B.C.), a most virtuous disciple of Confucius, died before his father, Yan-lu, who grieved for his son in the *Lunyu* (*Shinshaku kanbun taikei*, p. 238).
30. Jittoku is unidentified. Kyōgoku Daisōkoku Munesuke 京極大相国宗輔 was Fujiwara Munesuke (1077–1126), but his son Toshimichi died after him, thus contradicting the text. It has been suggested that Kyōgoku Daisōkoku may have been Fujiwara Morozane 藤原師実 (1042–1101), whose son Moromichi died before his father in 1099 at the age of thirty-eight (*Senjūshō zenchūshaku* I, p. 51).

1-4 Empress Shichijō and a Long Poem

When Empress Shichijō[31] passed away, many of her servants and attendants left and the palace became desolate. Some shaved their heads [to take the tonsure] and others changed into black mourning robes. When people expressed their condolences to Lady Ise,[32] who had served the empress for a long time, she composed a long poem[33] in reply:

> Since the empress has left us, the palace has become like a desolate sea with wild waves. I, Ise, have lived here for a long time and now

---

31. Fujiwara Onshi 藤原温子 (872–907), was a daughter of Prime Minister Fujiwara Mototsune. She became a *nyōgo* (imperial concubine) of Emperor Uda.
32. Ise 伊勢 (d. 939) was a daughter of Fujiwara Tsugikage 藤原継陰. She was called Ise or Ise no Go because her father was governor of Ise. She gave birth to a son of Emperor Uda. She was one of the Thirty-Six Immortal Poets, and her poems appear in her private collection, the *Iseshū* 伊勢集. Blessed with beauty and poetic talent, Ise associated with many noblemen. Various stories about her appear in many tale collections including the *Yamato monogatari* 大和物語 (no. 147) and the *Konjaku monogatarishū* (24-31, 30-2). In *Senjūshō* 8-22 there is an outrageous tale of her as the wife of a supervisor or superintendent at the Hachiman Shrine at Otokoyama and of her producing several children.
33. The poem appears in the *Kokinshū*, or *Kokin wakashū* 古今和歌集 (19 *zattai*, 1006, *Iseshū* no. 462).

feel as if I am a pearl diver of Ise Bay[34] who has lost her boat. Sad and helpless, my tears, falling like a sudden shower, turn red like the crimson autumn leaves, which are scattering like the people who are leaving the palace. Only the pampas grass remains in the palace garden, swaying and beckoning toward the sky, while the crying geese fly away as they watch us from afar.[35]

Those who read her reply empathized entirely. Not many days had passed since they lost the empress on whom they had depended, and their sleeves were still wet with their tears. It was quite natural for them to feel as sad and helpless as the lady who had expressed such grief in her reply.

Among those who read Lady Ise's poem was a man of the Third Rank called Kuniyuki.[36] From the moment he read it, he wished to renounce the world. Finally, he cut his hair, left his wife and children, and disappeared. No one heard of him or saw him again. This was most extraordinary. Until then, he did seem eager to leave secular life. Finally he abandoned his family, who were so difficult to leave, and renounced the secular world. His conviction and decision were indescribably strong and noble.

Indeed, your wife, children, treasures, and even a throne will not accompany you when you depart this life[37] but will instead interfere with your future deliverance while making you wander and suffer through the bad realms.[38]

It is truly fearful that the attachment to this short life will obstruct your salvation in the much longer future life. There is a saying: "Practicing no evil deeds, giving alms, and avoiding indulgence are your only companions in this and the next life." This tells us that observing the *śīla* commandments, giving alms, and avoiding indulgence are the only help you have during the hard journey to the Land after Death.

---

34. Ise was famous for its female pearl divers.
35. The departing geese refer to the ladies who will also leave the palace and view it from the outside.
36. Kuniyuki is unidentified.
37. This sentence suggests the journey during the period between this life and the next (*chūu* 中有).
38. *Akushu* 悪趣, the bad realms, include the three worlds of hell, animals, and hungry ghosts.

But it is very difficult to accumulate merits by obeying the *śīla* commandments and giving alms while at the same time leaving behind love and obligations to which we have become accustomed for so long.

Was it not admirable that Kuniyuki suddenly renounced the world? It was most noble that he never reappeared at his home, and this was indeed proof of his strong devotion to the Way. It was even more impressive that Lady Ise showed him how to attain his wish for salvation.

1-5 A Monk on Mount Utsu

Once when I was wandering through the eastern provinces, I wanted to see the cherry blossoms on Mount Utsu,[39] and so I went deeper into the mountains. There, I saw a monk in his forties practicing Zen meditation in a shabby hut. It was built in the dark shadow of a tree near a lonesome narrow path bordered with thickly grown vines.

Wondering where he came from, I became curious to learn the karmic reason for his leaving secular life. So I approached the hut and asked him questions.

He replied, "I am from Sagami province.[40] Born to a warrior family, I should wear a three-foot-long sword and carry a quiver of arrows on my back. But as I thought of the futility of life, which must end in death, I became frightened. From time to time, I calmly practiced Zen meditation, but it was not easy to abandon this life.

"Meanwhile, my wife, with whom I had lived for a long time, passed away and I lost interest in this life. So immediately, I shaved my head and confined myself to this mountain. Before I came here, I lived at a temple in Matsushima.[41] But I soon became weary of the people who talked to me about various things, and so I secretly left them. Since then I have been living here like this for about two years. At first I survived by begging for food in the village, but now as my mind becomes clearer and purer, I have no appetite and eat only a few times a month."

After listening to him, I was so impressed and envious that I immediately asked him if I could stay with him. The monk said rather

---

39. Mount Utsu is located between Shizuoka city and Shita-gun in Shizuoka prefecture.
40. Present-day Kanagawa prefecture.
41. Present-day Miyagi prefecture. Saigyō 西行, too, had lived in Matsushima (*Senjūshō*, 3-1).

coldly, "That would be useless, as both you and I would stray from the Way. It would be hard for us to lead each other to the Way. You should find your own place somewhere, and visit me again."

At first I thought his answer was cold, but I now believe I was careless to ask him such a favor. So without deciding to reside nearby, I left him after promising to see him again. I did not mean to break my promise, but, after a while, I wandered around the northeastern provinces for some time and then took a different route back to the capital. Since then, I have not had a chance to visit him again.

The monk's way of renouncing the world was most pure and noble. I had heard of some wise men in distant countries, such as India, Tibet, and China, who renounced the world, but no one in my own country had ever done this, and so I was not familiar with their thinking. But when I actually witnessed this monk as he gazed at the pure moon in a cloudless sky while listening to the wind blowing through the pine branches on the summit, I was moved and envied him. I even shed tears when I read about such recluses who purified their minds by living by the sea or deep in the mountains. Seeing such a recluse in reality was so touching that I could not suppress my joyful tears. I still think of him enviously as I wonder into which paradise he was reborn.

What kind of practice is Zen meditation? How should you experience the truth of the Buddha's teachings in your mind and heart? Abandon everything,[42] concentrate on your mind only, and eventually abandon your mind as well? I wonder if you know the *kōan*[43] that says, "The running mud cow in the sky and the neighing wooden horse in heaven."[44] Will you keep it in your mind while you practice meditation? How will you be able to keep the saying in your mind? Should you observe such a *kōan*? The really important thing is you can

---

42. The sentence means to leave behind everything around you, including the situation, knowledge, perception, and cognition, and to concentrate only on your mind and enter the state of *munen musō*, no-thinking 無念無想.

43. In Zen teaching, *kōan* 公案 include old sayings, words, and actions of famous Zen masters and are used by ascetics while practicing meditation. There are 1,700 *kōan* used in the Rinzai School of Zen.

44. This sentence often appears in Zen writings and means something unrealistic. "A cow made of mud will be dissolved in water" denotes delusions, while "a wooden horse without life" means to transcend thinking and perception and enter the state of *mushin* 無心, no-thinking or no-mind. More famously, *kōan* are like riddles that admit no logical solution (e.g., "What is the sound of one hand clapping?").

18 THE SENJŪSHŌ

follow any means to practice the Way as long as you uphold your true devotion to the Way.[45]

There is another saying from a sage of olden times: "Delusion is like an old sly rat while enlightenment is like a kitten."[46] If you carefully practice meditation, you will realize that it is an action of thought, one of the Three Karmic Actions,[47] and is far superior to building innumerable stupas. So no matter what kind of good deeds you accumulate, everything depends on how you maintain your mind and heart.

1-6 A Visit to Uemura Village in Echigo Province

I once went to Uemura village in Shita in Echigo province.[48] The village was by the sea and had a deep harbor. Many people gathered at the morning market by the port and traded various things, including food from the sea and mountains, textiles such as silk, and even people[49] and horses. Some were still young and innocent, some older and stronger, and some aged with white hair. Elderly men, carrying *azusa* bows[50] on their bent backs, had no idea how long they would last; they might die that very day or the next. As I watched them, telling all kinds of lies to sell their goods to survive for a short while, I could not help but shed tears.

---

45. Here the author is not so strict in following Zen teaching and advocates pursuing the Way by any methods or means to attain buddhahood.
46. The quotation is unidentified. Here illusions and delusions are compared to an old sly rat 老鼠, while perception of the truth is likened to an innocent cat 猫 or kitten that drives away delusion.
47. The Three Actions (*sangō* 三業), or tri-karma, include the deeds of the body, of words, and of thoughts.
48. This village is unidentified. Echigo province is present-day Niigata prefecture.
49. People were sold as slaves. The first account of selling a person or child appears in the article of the fifth year (677) during the time of Emperor Tenmu in the *Nihonshoki* 日本書紀. A *Konjaku* tale (29:24) tells of a man selling a woman who belonged to his master; see Yoshiko Dykstra, *The Konjaku Tales*, Japanese Section 3, Intercultural Research Institute Monograph 28 (Osaka: Kansai Gaidai University, 2003), 253–255. A *Shasekishū* tale (9:9) narrates how a son sold himself to support his mother; see Robert Morrell, *Sand and Pebbles (Shasekishū): The Tales of Mujū Ichien, a Voice for Pluralism in Kamakura Buddhism* (Albany: State University of New York Press, 1985), 239.
50. Bows made of *azusa* wood 梓弓 have strong elasticity. The curved bow here suggests the curved backs of elderly men.

Priest Kūya[51] sadly thought his quiet place in the mountains too noisy and went down to Shijō in the capital, which was more boisterous with many passers-by. But believing it to be an ideal place to settle, he built a hut with hanging straw mats and lived there. As I recall him, I cannot suppress my tears.

What shall we compare this life to? It has been likened to the white wake vanishing behind a rowboat in the morning or to the evening lightning faintly illuminating the autumn fields. Deceived by the white wake and the faint lightning, I have passed many years since youth with my heart unchanged; I have gained no merit chanting the Buddha's name, and I am trapped by the demon of futility. It is most regrettable that, at my last moments in the evening when I depart this life like the dew on Mount Hokubo,[52] my wife, children, and parents,

---

51. Kūya, or Kōya, 空也 (903–972) was a son of Emperor Daigo (r. 897–930). As he wandered through various places, he repaired roads and temples and built bridges while propagating the recitation of Amida's names, and he always lived among people in towns. He was also known as the founder of the *odori-nenbutsu* 踊り念仏, dancing while chanting the Buddha's name, and was popularly called Amida Hijiri 阿弥陀聖, or Holy Man of Amida. He built the Rokuharamitsuji 六波羅蜜寺 Temple in Kyoto.

52. This is a reference to Mount Beimang in Luoyang, Henan, China, which was known as a burial ground.

whom I have loved so much, cannot accompany me. Those who are left after me will do nothing except dispose of my body on heaped firewood in a field and then helplessly watch me vanish as a column of smoke rising into a drifting cloud in the sky. In the morning, they will return to the field and see only my white bones blown by the autumn wind in the pampas grass.

So, like you and others, I live this transient life. Someone much attached to this futile life composed a song: "Having no visitors, why should I wait for them like wisteria blossoms clinging to a pine tree?" Resenting this futility, another replied: "Seeing you is like a string of pearls made of tears. As soon as the string is broken, I grieve with more tears." This is all because we attach ourselves entirely to this temporary life.

Attachment is truly the most futile thing of all. Once we are born in the human world, we can find the Way, although it is often difficult to learn. Once we find the Way, we should by all means familiarize ourselves with it. By severing the Twelve Rings of Karmic Relations and severing the bondage of the Twenty-Five Worlds of Life and Death,[53] we should all attain enlightenment.

Reluctant to follow the Way, we soon fall into the bad realms, from which we may emerge after extremely long periods of time. Thanks to our practice of the Ten Good Deeds and observance of the Five Śīla Precepts in our previous lives, we are reborn into the human world. But in the Degenerate Age of the Law, the light of Buddha is faint in the wind and scarcely lasts long enough to illuminate the Way for us through the long, dark nights. When the Buddha's holy water, which cleanses away our delusions, is exhausted, we return to this life. Since missing the boat to cross the sea of life and death, we again head to the bad realms. It is tragic to repeat this cycle of life and death.

Wandering through the Six Realms and Four Births,[54] we are no different from carts circling a garden. When we stop for a while in this

---

53. The karmic relationships (*innen* 因縁) are divided into twelve kinds (*jūni-innen*) in which life and death are repeated like rings. All sentient beings transmigrate into the twenty-five kinds of worlds/realms (*nijūgo-u*) owing to their ties to each other.
54. *Rokudō* 六道, the six realms, are heaven 天, humans 人, *asura* 阿修羅, animals 畜生, hungry ghosts 餓鬼, and hell 地獄. *Shishō* 四生, the four births, include birth by womb, by egg, from wet substances (how insects are born), and by provisional entities like buddhas and heavenly beings.

life, we are bound to suffer from birth, age, sickness, and death while attached to the futility of life. While repeatedly floating and sinking in this futile life, we end up neither floating nor sinking. We simply reappear in different shapes and forms. Truly, the saddest fate is transmigrating endlessly through the cycles of life and death.

1-7 A Former Emperor's Grave

During the Annin period (1166–1169), I traveled through distant western provinces for ascetic practices and lived for a short while in the Miosaka grove in Sanuki province.[55] I built a hut with oak leaves in a place deep in a mountainous grove where everything appeared very desirable all day long—small branches burning in a fire, breezes softly passing over treetop blossoms, cries of cuckoos as if calling out to someone, quails walking among *yomogi* bushes. I felt painfully lonely at dawn when I heard monkeys crying out in the tall pine trees. Although this was not to be my home for long, I felt my mind and heart were well purified. I could have stayed there longer, but I decided to leave as I wanted to detach myself from all worldly feelings.[56]

Wishing to visit the former emperor's[57] grave, I went to Shiramine.[58] I soon arrived at a grave surrounded by a nailed wooden fence in a small pine grove. When I recognized it as the emperor's tomb, I felt so sad that I became tearfully confused. Still, that was exactly what I saw.

Emperor Sutoku once lived and ruled in the Seiryōden and Shishinden halls in the imperial palace and was served by many officials. Three thousand beautifully dressed ladies with [long] black hair attended him in his entourage as they vied with one another to win his attention. He was in charge of all political affairs, and he also held

---

55. The ruins of Saigyō's hut are in present-day Kagawa prefecture (Sakaide-shi, Tamakoshi-chō).
56. Here the protagonist's desire to stay at that lonely place was itself an attachment and thus ran contrary to the Way.
57. Emperor Sutoku 崇徳 (1119–1164), popularly called Shin-in 新院 (new cloistered emperor), was the first son of Emperor Toba (1103–1156).
58. Emperor Sutoku's grave, Shiramine-ryō 白峰陵, is in present-day Kagawa prefecture (Sakaide-shi). For a study of the Shiramine legend and other collections, including the *Kojitan* 古事談, the *Hosshinshū*, and the *Hōgen monogatari* 保元物語, see Umeno Kimiko, "About the Shiramine Legend in the *Senjūshō*," in *Sugiyama kokubungaku*, no. 7 (March 1983).

flower-viewing parties every spring and moon-viewing feasts in carriages following one after another under the autumn moon.

At that time, who would have imagined that the emperor would be eventually buried under weeds on a remote mountain? The ceremonial conch shells and gongs and the priests chanting the Hokke-sanmai[59] rite were not heard there. The only sound came from the strong wind blowing through the pine trees on the summit, where not a single bird was to be seen. As I gazed at all this, I could not stop shedding tears. I knew, of course, that whatever begins must end, but I had never really realized this so strongly.

Thus we should never attach ourselves to the secular world. Even a lord [such as the former emperor] could not avoid suffering. Regardless of rank and position, whether we live in palaces or in straw huts, we are unable to keep material possessions and live forever, so we should not yearn for higher rank and office. In our previous lives, we may have been kings and lords of certain countries, but we cannot remember anything about that. The only noble and worthwhile thing is to attain buddhahood through difficult ascetic practices. While pondering various things, I tearfully composed a poem:

Yoshiya kimi
Mukashi no tama no
Yuka totemo
Kakaran ato ha
Nani ni kawa sen

Oh, my lord,
Once you lived
In a palace with pearled floors,
But after becoming like this
What can you do?[60]

---

59. The Hokke-sanmai 法華三昧 rite, which is based on the *Hokekyō* 法華経, includes walking around the image of the principal buddha of the temple, paying respect to the buddha while seated, reciting sutras, and performing penitential rites to realize the Middle Way, *chūdō* 中道, propagated in the Tendai teachings.
60. The poems in which Saigyō mourns the death of Sutoku while in Sanuki province appear in the *Sangashū* 山家集 (2, Zatsu, nos. 1353 and 1355).

There is nothing new about a person's rise and fall in the secular world, but I was especially moved as I gazed at his grave.

Regarding the former emperor, around the seventh month of Hōgen 1 (1156), when the cloistered Emperor Toba[61] passed away, the sky was covered with clouds, the atmosphere of the flowery capital became oppressive, as if it were wrapped in darkness, and the people grieved. Within ten days of the emperor's demise, Emperor Go-Shirakawa and Former Emperor Sutoku began to compete for the throne.[62] Their strife upset both heaven and earth. One evening, the Ōi Hall of the former emperor's palace was set on fire and black smoke filled the building. As the imperial army of Go-Shirakawa was gaining the upper hand, the defeated Sutoku and Minister Uji of the Left secretly rode out of the palace. Unfortunately, some hostile samurai followed them and without hesitation aimed and shot arrows at them. As I watched this, I repeatedly regretted that I had come to the capital only to witness such a tragic event.

Later, I learned that the former emperor was moved to Ninnaji Temple after being found on a mountain, while Minister Uji was shot to death and interred at the Hannyano burial ground in Nara.[63] When I heard that some imperial messengers were sent out to Nara and dug up the minister's grave to inspect his body,[64] I felt nothing but disgust for this sordid, mundane life. Doesn't anyone know how futile this life is? Our fragile bodies are exposed to many dangers in this transient life, but we vainly spend our time pretending that we know everything. When suddenly caught by the demon of futility in our last moments, we loudly cry for help as we traverse the bad realms. This is most sad and regrettable.

Suppose we have a life free from rising and falling, and even from death—when we learn of the splendor of buddhahood, how can we not aspire to the Way? Needless to say, our secular life in reality is full

---

61. For the death of Toba-in, see William R. Wilson, trans., *Hōgen monogatari* (Ithaca, NY: Cornell University Press, 2001), pp. 5–7.
62. Go-Shirakawa 後白河 (1127–1193), the fourth son of Emperor Toba, and Sutoku fought for the throne and this conflict developed into the Hōgen Revolt 保元の乱, involving Regent Fujiwara Tadamichi 藤原忠道 (1097–1164) and his brother, Lord Uji 宇治の左府, or Fujiwara Yorinaga 藤原頼長 (1120–1156), Minister of the Left.
63. Hannyano 般若野 was located to the south of present-day Narazaka.
64. See Wilson, pp. 80–82.

of rising and falling as death approaches every second. Let us calmly reflect on the past. Were the days in our past different from our dreams? Indeed, were they not dreams? All things—including happiness, sadness, success, failure—all are events in the provisional forms and shapes of this transient world.

1-8 Priest Gyōga Cuts Off His Ear

At one time Sōzu Gyōga[65] was living in Yamashina Temple[66] in the Nara capital; he had been a posthumous disciple of Daitoku Byōbi.[67] Incomparably learned, he greatly helped others in the Way of the Law. One evening, when he was staying in one of the temple's three living quarters,[68] a monk who looked to be in his forties and with a most respectful appearance secretly came to see him and tearfully said, "What I am going to tell you is something very unusual, and perhaps my wish may not be granted. But after much consideration, I have concluded that you are the only person who can help me, so with hesitation I will ask you for a favor. I have a terrible abscess on my back and it will kill me. I want to live but I won't be able to survive with this pain. So I consulted a very famous doctor, and he told me, 'Unless you bring me a holy man's left ear, your pain will never stop, no matter how many of the Seven Rare Treasures[69] you accumulate.'

"I thought, 'What sort of a holy man would cut off his own ear and

---

65. *Sōzu* 僧都 is a high-ranking priestly title after *sōjō*, or abbot. Gyōga 行賀 (729–803) studied under Eigan of Kōfukuji Temple and Byōbi 平備 of Gangōji Temple; on an imperial order he went in 757 to China, where he studied both Hossō and Tendai teachings for seven years. After returning to Japan, he became a *bettō*, or director of administration, of Kōfukuji Temple. His stories appear in *Genkō shakusho* 元亨釈書 16, and *Honchō kōsōden* 本朝高僧伝 4.

66. Kōfukuji Temple in Nara 興福寺 is the headquarters of the Hossō Sect in Japan and one of the seven great temples in the old capital, Nara. It is the tutelary temple of the Fujiwara clan.

67. *Daitoku* 大徳, great virtue, is a title given to an eminent priest. Byōbi, a scholarly priest whose birth date is unknown, wrote many books including the *Yuishikironhasoku* 唯識論羽足. A posthumous disciple, or *itei*, is someone who admires and follows a deceased master's teaching and who becomes a disciple after his death.

68. The three priests' living quarters in the east, west, and north surrounded the lecture hall of the temple. Today, only the foundation stones remain.

69. The seven treasures, *shichihō* 七宝, generally include gold, silver, lapis lazuli, *shako* shells, crystal, coral, and agate, but they can vary according to the sutra.

give it to me?' and I remained tearfully depressed. Then someone said to me, 'That holy man [Gyōga] is so merciful he might help you, if you ask him.' So I have come here and I am asking you for this favor." The monk wept bitterly as he finished speaking.

Feeling much sympathy, Gyōga asked him, "What kind of boil do you have? Let me see it." The monk removed part of his robe, and the abscess looked so horrible that even Gyōga would not look at it twice. So he said to the monk, "In this case, it's easy to do what you ask," and with that he cut off his left ear with a knife and gave it to the monk, who left tearfully joining the palms of his hands as if praying to Gyōga in gratitude.

Completely ignoring the pain, Gyōga was concerned only about the poor monk's future. He associated with no one, left the Way of Learning, and confined himself to Miwa[70] with a pure heart. He

---

70. Mount Miwa, where Priest Genpin 玄賓 also lived, is in Nara prefecture (in present-day Sakurai-shi). Miwamyōjin Shrine on the mountain is introduced in *Senjūshō* 9-1.

recalled Priest Genpin[71] of olden times and his poem, "I will not soil the color of the robe that I have washed in a pure stream," and he spent days and months in confinement.

Some time later, while Gyōga was falling asleep, he dreamed of the Eleven-Faced Kannon[72] standing by his pillow and saying to him, "I will now return to you the ear that you gave me the other day. You are indeed a merciful man. Do not wake up before I give it back to you." To his surprise, Gyōga woke up and found his left ear just where it had been. How wonderful! He was overwhelmed by the bodhisattva's miracle and felt as if he were still dreaming. This was indeed a most impressive and noble occurrence.

We recall from ancient China that Priest Genjō Sanzō[73] went to India, where he mercifully licked a smelly sick man from head to foot on a mountain. The sick man instantly changed into Bodhisattva Kannon and gave him a copy of the *Shingyō*.[74] But apart from this, I have heard of nothing like Gyōga's story either in China or in Japan. Priest Sanzō licked the sick man in spite of his bad odor while Gyōga cut off his ear in spite of the pain. Both deeds were most extraordinary. One happened in ancient times, while the other occurred in later generations; one took place in a big country, while the other came about in a smaller country; one was an incarnation of a bodhisattva, while the other was only a man, and so we cannot compare the two. But I think

---

71. Genpin, a man of the Yuge clan in Kawachi, died in 818 in his eighties. He was summoned to the capital to cure Emperor Kanmu's illness in 805 and was appointed Great Abbot, but declined and retired to Bitchū province instead. He lived on Mount Miwa before Gyōga. His stories appear in *Gōdanshō* 江談抄 1-46, *Hosshinshū* 1-1, and *Kojidan* 3-7. He is often quoted in the *Senjūshō* (2-4, 2-8, 5-1, 7-9, 9-11).

72. The Kannon 観音 has the power to save all sentient beings whose conditions are reflected in its eleven faces.

73. Xuang Zhuang 玄奘 (602–664) went to India in 629, brought back many Buddhist writings, and translated them. For his life story in a picture scroll, see *Genjō Sanzō e* 玄奘三蔵絵, in *Zoku Nihon emaki taisei* 7, pp. 156–159. For the story of the sick man, see *Daizōkyō* 大蔵経 50, shidenbu 2, p. 224; Tale 6-6, in Dykstra, trans., *The Konjaku Tales*, Chinese Section, pp. 35–41).

74. *Hannyashingyō* 般若心経 (*Prajñāparamitā-sūtra*), or Wisdom Sutra, one of the most important sutras of Mahāyāna Buddhism, is based upon the doctrine of Śūnyatā (Kū 空), negating all the phenomena of this world. The single-page summary of the sutra, *Daihannya-haramittashingyō* 大般若波羅蜜多心経 (*Mahāprajñāpāramitā-hṛdaya-sūtra*), has seven Chinese translations. The translations by Genjō and Kumārajīva are the ones most popularly read. An English translation of the Sanskrit text by M. Muller is found in *Manual of Zen Buddhism* by D. T. Suzuki.

Priest Gyōga was as admirable as Prince Satta, who gave himself to a hungry tiger in ancient times.[75] That was why the Great Holy Kannon showed a most marvelous revelation. This was doubly remarkable.

[Gyōga] hid himself after cutting off his ear for the poor monk in order to spread the Law in this life and to save others, although he was only a man. When I try to write about him, I cannot see my writing brush clearly as my eyes become clouded with tears. My mind with its various thoughts is as confused as the deranged legs of a spider seeking its way in a withered field. I only hope that the god of Usa Shrine[76] will help me in his mercy as spring rain moistens and softens my strained mind like the distressed spider. And with the god's blessing, the rain of mercy will fall and permeate all of us with a sense of compassion.

Truly, we are helpless while we are attached to this dreamlike world. I remember a poem: "Hearing the sound of hail hitting bamboo leaves, I don't feel like sleeping alone." I would like to ask others if their thoughts, like mine, are deepened in the evening. Feeling resentment against someone who failed to visit me, I wait like the light purple wisteria blossoms hanging from a pine tree. I seek in vain the shadow of my visitor at the bottom of the bamboo water pipe as the flow of the water is reduced. As I hear the helpless sound [of the water pipe], the smoldering fire in my heart is not yet extinguished, and it rises to make me choke on the smoke blown by the wind. Thus I tearfully spend my time until my eyebrows become as white as frost while my forehead is lined like the waves of the Four Seas. I see in the mirror that I have lost my youthful looks.

When I want to talk with my friends, I cannot hear them well. As I look up to see the flowers on the tree tops, I cannot see them clearly. My back becomes bent as old age and death approach. But ignoring all these, I vainly spend my days in this futile life. How will I answer after my death, when I am asked at the judgment in King Enma's court about

---

75. The story of Prince Mahāsattva, Śākyamuni's name in a former life, appears in *Shishū hyakuinnenshū* 私聚百因縁集 1-3, 2-4; *Sanbōekotoba* 三宝絵詞 1-11; Edward Kamens, trans., *The Three Jewels: A Study and Translation of Minamoto Tamenori's Sanbōe* (Ann Arbor: Center for Japanese Studies, University of Michigan, 1988), pp. 144–146.

76. The sound of *usa* (depression) is associated with Usa Shrine 宇佐神宮 in present-day Ōita prefecture. The shrine is the headquarters of all the Hachiman shrines 八幡宮 (eight-banner shrines) of Japan. The mind confused with miscellaneous thoughts is compared with a lost spider's eight legs, implying *hachiman* (eight banners). Buddhist and Shinto syncretism is reflected in this story.

the merits I accumulated in life? If I had accumulated good deeds, my answer would be satisfactory; otherwise, I would be sadly regretful. Looking at the crystal mirror in King Enma's court, I may well only see reflections of myself in anger or attached to greed and amorous affairs. There are many buddhas everywhere in this life, and many flowers blooming in the wild fields, but have I ever offered a single branch or flower to the Buddha for my future life while I was alive in this one? There are many teachings of the Law, but I never studied them. I lack the talent of learning, yet I can draw pictures of them.

It is most regrettable that we indulge ourselves only in futile affairs with women while at the same time wishing to elevate our minds as high as the summit of Mount Fuji. Alas, our minds are clouded by the volcanic smoke of Mount Asama,[77] and thus we spend days and months wastefully only to meet suffering in the end.

With his firm, merciful heart, Priest Gyōga severed his ties to life and death thanks to the merit gained by cutting off his ear and left the burning house of the Three Worlds.[78] It was most noble of him to pity those of us who remain in the flames of [delusion].

I heard that this [story of Gyōga] appeared in the *Yūshinshū*.[79] Because I want to be associated with him, I decided to record Gyōga's story. But I am very much afraid that I failed to write in a fine style and employed only common language. I hope that I have not left out anything important in my rewriting. I also hope that people after my death will not criticize my writing. Even if I fall to the bottom of hell, I will never forget this merciful priest. Please, buddhas of the three generations of past, present, and future, consider my single-heartedness and bless me with a heart of mercy, however small.

---

77. Mount Asama, or Asamadake 浅間だけ, an active volcano located between Nagano and Gunma prefectures, is an *utamakura*, or a place appearing in poems. Asama is also related to *asamashii* (wretched, pitiful).

78. The phrase means the "world of delusion through which all sentient beings transmigrate." *Sangai* 三界, the three worlds, are the worlds of greed, color (flesh and sex), and non-color. The burning house, or *kataku* 火宅, refers to this confused life.

79. Unidentified.

2-1 Sōzu Ichiwa and the Kasuga Deity's Revelation

Long ago Monk Ichiwa[1] lived in Kōfukuji Temple.[2] Thanks to his knowledge and virtue, he rose to the high rank of senior monk. Later he retired to a mountain village called Toyama.[3] According to the *Yūshinshū*,[4] which gives a brief account of Ichiwa, Kōfukuji Temple annually held a most splendid Buddhist service called the Yuimae Meeting.[5] Imperial envoys attended and a most eminent holy monk representing the Eight Buddhist Schools performed the ceremony. The *engi*[6] recitation, written by Kanshōjō,[7] was the revelation of an awesome deity,[8] and the Nyoi liturgical wand,[9] held by the principal lecturer, originally belonged to Abbot Shōbō.[10] So it was the greatest

---

1. Ichiwa 一和 (890–970), a scholarly monk of the Hossō School and the Yuimae Lecturer in 950, studied under Sōzu Zōri. He first lived in Tōin and later moved to Tōbokuin. His biographies appear in the *Genkō shakusho* (4), the *Tōgoku kōsōden* 東国高僧伝 (5), the *Honchō kōsōden* (9), and the *Kasuga gongenkenki* 春日権現験記 (8-4).
2. For Kōfukuji, see *Senjūshō* 1-8.
3. Toyama is in present-day Kyoto (Fushimi-ku, Hino-chō). Many recluses lived there since it was not far from the villages; Kamo Chōmei 鴨長明, the author of the *Hōjōki* 方丈記 also lived there.
4. *Yūshinshū*, not extant, appears in *Senjūshō* 1-8, 2-1, 4-5, and 9-6, and also in *Kankyonotomo* 1-10. The work might have been a Buddhist tale collection like the *Hosshinshū*, the *Kankonotomo*, or the *Senjūshō*.
5. One of the Three Meetings 三会, including Saishōe 最勝会 of Yakushiji and Gosaie 御斎会 of Daigyokuden. In the Yuimae Meeting 唯摩会 of Kōfukuji, the *Yuimakyō* 唯摩経, the *Vimalakīrti* sutra, was recited and explicated by a principal lecturer who was an expert in the Eight Schools, which in the Heian period (794–1183) comprised Gusha 倶舎, Jōjitsu 成実, Ritsu 律, Hossō 法相, Sanron 三論, Kegon 華厳, Tendai 天台, and Shingon 真言.
6. *Engi* 縁起 are texts narrating the origins and the miraculous tales of temples.
7. Sugawara Michizane 菅原道真 (845–903), a son of Koreyoshi, served Emperor Uda (r. 887–897) and later became Minister of the Right during the reign of Emperor Daigo (897–930). But he was exiled to Kyushu as a result of Fujiwara Tokihira's slander. Known for his scholarship and calligraphy, he is one of the Three Holy Calligraphers along with Kūkai and Ono Dōfū 道風. He edited the *Sandai jitsuroku* 三代実録. His anthologies include the *Kanke bunsō* 菅家文草.
8. This refers to the Kasuga Deity and suggests Buddhist-Shinto syncretism.
9. The diamond-shaped head of a *nyoi* 如意 made of wood, bamboo, bones, or iron is attached to a wand one to three feet long and held by lecturers when preaching and reciting sutras.
10. Shōbō 聖宝 studied the teachings of the Sanron, Hossō, and Kegon schools and built Daigoji Temple. He became an abbot in 906 and died in 909 at the age of seventy-eight.

joy and honor for those of the Way to be selected as the meeting lecturer.

One year, Ichiwa was expecting to be selected as lecturer, but, against his wishes, Monk Shōen[11] was chosen instead. Greatly disappointed, Ichiwa tried to console himself by thinking that everything was based upon the karmic relations inherited from his previous lives. But still feeling greatly upset, he left the temple without telling his disciples and began pursuing the Way while traveling. Carrying a bamboo basket on his back containing a Buddhist image[12] and a sutra, he secretly left the temple's three living quarters, visited the four worship halls of the Kasuga Shrine,[13] and tearfully recited the sutra as his parting offering.[14] Ichiwa must have felt very sad to leave the temple because he had lived there for a long time and had close friends there. With no particular destination in mind, Ichiwa headed toward the northeastern provinces and finally reached Narumi Beach in Owari province. When the tide receded, he visited the Atsuta Shrine.[15] While he was reciting his sutra at the shrine, a strange Shinto priest appeared and said to him, "You have left your temple on account of your resentful feelings. It is quite natural for those who are distressed to have constant resentment against things in this life. But you cannot have everything as you like in this life. Even though you wish to go to Ebisu Castle in the far northeast, you may find someone unpleasant there.[16] Then where else would you go? So make haste, return to your temple and attain your aim."

"You speak about something unexpected. Why do I, a beggar-ascetic,

---

11. Shōen 性延 (891–966) was a lecturer in 949 (*Dainihon bukkyō zensho*, 65, p. 28), but no records show his appointment as the principal lecturer of the Yuimae Meeting.

12. A *honzon* 本尊 is a principal icon, either painted or sculpted. *Jikyō* 持経 refers to a person's preferred sutra.

13. For the three living quarters of Kōfukuji, see note 4 of story 1-8. The four worship halls (established in 768) are all included in the main hall of the Kasuga Shrine in Nara. The present main hall was constructed in 1863.

14. Reading or reciting a sutra at a Shinto shrine is regarded as an offering to a *kami* deity.

15. Atsuta Shrine 熱田神宮 in Nagoya enshrines the Atsuta Great Deity and the Kusanagi no tsurugi sword, one of the three imperial regalia.

16. The "far northeast" is indicated as Michinoku 陸奥国 (also Oku or Mutsu), which corresponds to the premodern provinces of Iwaki (present-day Fukushima), Iwashiro (central and southern Fukushima), Rikuzen (Miyagi), Rikuchū (Iwate), and Mutsu (eastern Aomori). The people in these regions were regarded as Ebisu.

hold resentments against anything?" Ichiwa replied, lowering his head. Then the Shinto priest laughed scornfully as he quoted an old poem:

Tsutsume domo
Kakurenu mono ha
Natsumushi no
Miyori amareru
Omoi narikeri

He tries to conceal his heart,
Yet he cannot hide
His overwhelming feelings
Like a firefly's shining light
On a summer night.[17]

"You are most foolish, so let me explain. Were you not resentful because Shōen took the position of lecturer at the last Yuimae Meeting? But selection of the lecturers for the meeting had already been decided and recorded in Taishaku's tablet,[18] and they included Shōen, Ichiwa, Gisō, and Kanri in that order. Now forget your hard feelings and return quickly to the temple. Although you have heartlessly left me, I have not yet abandoned you and have shown you this revelation. The old bones of Mount Kasuga[19] have become quite tired now."

When he heard this, Ichiwa felt most touched and immediately started back. During his return journey he recalled the Kasuga deity's help and wet his grass pillow with his tears like evening dew. He cleansed his troubled heart with each shower in the autumn fields and his tear-stained robe was repeatedly rinsed in the shower. This was truly heart-moving.

After reading about Ichiwa, I could not stop my tears. Everyone has difficulty in overcoming resentment. Ichiwa must have felt very sad leaving the place he had long called home. As I think of the deity's

---

17. The poem appears in *Gosen wakashū* 後選和歌集 4, no. 209; *Yamato monogatari* 大和物語 no. 40; *Wakan rōeishū* 和漢朗詠集 1, *hotaru*, no. 191.
18. Taishaku 帝釈, the Indian deity Indra, incorporated into Buddhism, resides in the palace on top of Mount Sumeru (Shumisen).
19. A reference to the Kasuga Deity.

revelation, "Although you have heartlessly left me, I have not abandoned you and have shown you this revelation," I wring my wet sleeves.

Originally when the Buddha appeared in this world, his teachings were so widely spread that even those in hell greatly benefited.[20] But unfortunately, we are far removed from the time of the Buddha. Born into darkness and far from the dawn of the Three Meetings of Bodhisattva Miroku, we are deluded by our dreams in the morning and evening, which vanish like bubbles by the riverside.

It is most gracious that [the Buddha] appeared as the [Kasuga] deity in order to save us as well as Ichiwa. He wandered about seeking an ideal place, like smoke from burning salt on the beach, wafting to the sky, or plover's footprints on the sand. When he finally finds a certain beach to settle on, he might see there someone unpleasant. Then where else can he go? Unless it is in the Pure Land of Amida, he will never be happily settled, and unless he associates with the holy people of that paradise, he will never find anyone compatible as a friend. Truly, the teachings of the deity's revelation deeply touch my heart.

It is most regrettable that we ourselves remain in this world of suffering, conceive resentful feelings, and confuse ourselves. The Taishaku record on the selection of the lecturers seems most extraordinary. It is really regretful that, unlike Ichiwa, ignorant people never aspire to be lecturers at the Yuimae Meeting, and they are destined to be born untalented and of a lowly status. This most celebrated meeting is held annually on the tenth day of the Kanna [godless] month.[21]

I am still deeply moved by Ichiwa. He tried to retire to a place where he heard no birds flying and had nothing to rely on except his principal Buddhist image; he had no one to speak to but the wind passing over the pines.

---

20. The passage refers to the time of *shōhō* 正法, the True Law of the Śākyamuni Buddha, which lasted one thousand years; during that period his teaching was well understood and practiced by believers. In the following millennium of the *zōhō* period 像法, the Imitative Law, people were still able to understand the teaching but could not obtain enlightenment. The last period, *mappō* 末法, the Degenerate Law, would last for ten thousand years when only conceptual understanding of the Law remains and the people are in confusion until the future Buddha Maitreya 弥勒仏 descends from the Tosotsu Heaven 都卒天 to the human world and gives the Three Meetings (*san'e* 三会) to save sentient beings. Some scholars believe the Mappō period in Japan began in 1052.

21. The Yuimae Meeting is held October 10–16.

2-2 Hōgan Shin'yo of Shōren'in Temple

Once when I was wandering around Chikuzen province,[22] someone told me this story. A strange monk lived in the mountain village of Onono in the Mikasa district of this province.[23] He did not appear to be of lowly birth,[24] but he was unshaven and looked very poor and haggard. He did not eat much and was always tearfully depressed while reciting the Buddha's name. When he watched the villagers hunting and fishing, he cried bitterly, saying, "Be sure to recite the Buddha's name!" With that, he retreated to his place on the mountain and lived there for a year. Since he did not come down to the village for some time, the sympathetic villagers wondered if he had died, and so they went to see him.

They found no one at his dwelling but discovered several of his writings on pieces of board, which said, "In olden days when I was a

---

22. The two provinces, Chikuzen and Chikugo, were together called Tsukushi 筑紫, a general name for Kyushu.
23. The place is near present-day Dazaifu 大宰府 in Fukuoka prefecture.
24. Here *omoikudasu* 思下 means "scornfully regarded" or someone born into a lowly status.

Buddhist student of the Tendai School on Mount Hiei, I wanted to be the abbot[25] of the three thousand monks there, but now I wish to receive Amida Buddha's coming on the Onono mountain."

Yono naka ha
Ukifushi[26] *shigeki*
Kuretake no
Nado irokaede
Midori naruran

In this life
Of good and bad fortunes,
Why am I unable to change the color [of my robe]?
It remains as green as
The *kuretake* bamboo.[27]

The ninth day of the third month of Kyūju 2 (1155) by Hōgen Shin'yo,[28] Shōren'in.[29]

In the same handwriting, there was another poem:

Kokoro kara
Kurahashi yama no

---

25. *Sanzen no kanshu zasu* 三千の貫主 (the head of the three thousand monks) was referred to as *zasu* 座主, the chief abbot of the Tendai School of Enryakuji Temple 延暦寺 on Mount Hiei 比叡山.
26. *Uki*, "float" or "up," and *fushi* (*fusu* 伏す), "prostrate" or "down." *Fushi* 節 also refers to joints of the bamboo.
27. The poem means that the protagonist, in spite of his taking the tonsure, wonders why he cannot change the color of his secular robe (mind) into the black of priestly robes; it remains unchanged like the forever green *kuretake* bamboo くれ竹. This implies his frustration at failing in the Way. The *kuretake* bamboo planted in the imperial garden suggests his noble birth.
28. *Hōgen* 法眼, or *hōgen kashōi* 法眼和尚位, is one of the titles of high monks that is below *hōin* 法印 and above *hōkyō* 法橋. The name Shin'yo does not appear in the lineage of the abbots of Shōren'in Temple (*Shōren'in monzeki keifu*).
29. Shōren'in 青蓮院 is a Tendai temple in the east of Kyoto. It is one of the three *monzeki* 門跡 (temples with close ties to the imperial family) along with Higashiyama Gosho and Enryakuji Temple. The seventeenth abbot, Seson, established the Shōren'in style 青蓮院流 of calligraphy.

Yo wo watari
Towa mu to mo sezu
Nori no michi wo ba

I have never sincerely
Sought the Way of the Law
While crossing through
This life as dark as
Mount Kurahashi.[30]

To this day the villagers miss him and wonder if news of the monk has reached someone in the capital. Since his calligraphy was so splendid, they divided his writing into pieces and each took one or two characters.

When I heard this story, I could not stop my tears falling like the flow of the Koromogawa River in Michinokuni.[31] Shin'yo was the eighth son of Former Emperor Toba[32] and Lady Fujitsubo, a daughter of Shuri-daifu Toshitsuna of Fushimi.[33] After his mother passed away, Shin'yo was sent to Mount Hiei[34] at the age of seven to pray for her repose. Excelling in his learning and practice and regarded as most extraordinary in this degenerate age, he eventually rose to the rank of *hōgan*. But when he reached the age of eighteen he disappeared around the twentieth day of the ninth month. When the news was received from Mount Hiei, the lamenting emperor issued an order to search for his son throughout the country, but he passed away before Shin'yo was found.

---

30. Mount Kurahashi 倉橋 is in Nara prefecture, in the southeastern part of present-day Sakurai-shi. The sound of *kura* relates to *kurai* 暗い, meaning "dark."
31. The Koromogawa River 衣河 flows to the north of Hiraizumi-cho, Nishiiwai-gun, Iwate-ken. The *michi* of "Michinoku" relates to another term, *michi* 満ち, "full," i.e., "full of tears." The river also reminds us of the tearful experiences of the past battles of Zenkunen 前九年役 (1052–1062) and Gosan'nen 後三年 (1083–1087).
32. Emperor Toba's eighth son was Priest-Prince Kakukai 覚解 whose relationship to Shin'yo 真誉 is unknown.
33. Tachibana Toshitsuna 俊綱 (1028–1094) was popularly called Fushimi Shuri-daifu 伏見修理大夫. His father was Regent Fujiwara Yorimichi 藤原頼通 (992–1074). Excelling in poetry, Toshitsuna often held poem-meetings in his elegant mansion in Fushimi. His stories appear in *Ujishūi monogatari* 3-14 and *Jikkinshō* 十訓抄 7-25.
34. Mount Hiei always refers to Enryakuji Temple, located at the summit of the mountain. The temple, the headquarters of the Tendai School in Japan, was founded by Saichō in 788.

How sad it was that Shin'yo had been wandering around until he was found in Ono village. What was in his heart and mind while wandering at an age less than twenty? I felt my heart breaking as I thought of him. He must have had such a hard time with so little food. How did he reach Tsukushi? He surely was exhausted when he arrived there with his tired feet in worn-out footwear. I feel most sorry for him. In this hard life, he lamented that he was not accustomed to his black priestly robe after receiving the tonsure. While treading the dark path without finding the true path, he finally expressed his suffering in his poems. He must have had a pure heart to do that. Even without much food, he pitied those who committed sinful deeds [such as fishing and hunting] and he tearfully told them to recite the Buddha's name. Indeed, this was something most noble.

As I deeply ponder this matter, I realize how fortunate we are to be born into the human world[35] and to have learned Shaka Buddha's teachings after having left the sufferings of the bad realms.[36] I feel doubly noble to think that, unless we have a heart as pure as Shin'yo's, we will not be able to escape the sufferings of the life and death cycle. I tearfully wish the buddhas of the three generations of past, present, and future to bless us with one tenth of Shin'yo's pure heart.

I wonder if Shin'yo is still living in this life or was reborn in the Pure Land. If he is still alive, I wish I could meet him. If he has passed away leaving only his name, may he have pity on me as a friend in the Pure Land. When he climbed the mountain in his youth, I would have accompanied him.

2-3 Receiving the Tonsure at His Wife's Death in Hirano, Harima Province

Some time ago, a monk lived in a shabby hut facing the sea at the foot of a mountain in Hirano, Harima province.[37] He used to recite the Buddha's name from morning to night.

---

35. *Ningai* 人界, or the human world, one of the six realms (see note 54 of story 1-6), is regarded as superior to the other non-heavenly realms and so gains greater benefit from the Law.
36. The final three of the six realms comprise *akushu* 悪趣, bad or evil worlds.
37. Harima province 播磨国 was in the southwestern part of present-day Hyōgo prefecture. Hirano may be in the present-day cities of Miki or Himeji.

When someone asked him why he received the tonsure, he replied, "I was very close to my wife, and after I lost her I worried as I wondered where she was and what kind of suffering she was going through. I became very sad and decided to pray for her repose. So I left behind my rice paddies and have become just as you see me, single-mindedly reciting the Buddha's name." The monk did not go down into the village but managed to survive thanks to food brought by sympathetic villagers.

The monk one day suddenly appeared in the village and announced, "I will be delivered toward dawn tomorrow, so I have come here to bid you farewell as I will not see you again. I cannot begin to express my gratitude for your kindness." He seemed most pitiful, but none of the villagers believed him. They found him dead at dawn the next day, and a strange cloud floated in the sky. The monk passed away as if sleeping. His hands were joined in prayer and he faced west. His hut was filled with an unusual fragrance.

I was deeply touched when I heard the story. Once people get married, they pledge themselves to each other, hoping their love will last until their old age[38] and even in the world after death. A Chinese emperor[39] pledged that he and his lover would fly together in heaven like a pair of birds with their wings side by side, while on earth they would be like a pair of branches. In this country, we have a saying: "A couple like a pair of quails."[40] But, alas, how futile it is to make such a deep pledge and then forget it after the departure of one's partner. A man's mind is so changeable that his thoughts often wander to other women, ignoring the pledge he once made to his wife and ceasing to pray for her repose. So it was extraordinary that this monk devoted his life to praying for his wife. It is most wonderful that the monk attained enlightenment. How could his wife fail to be delivered when he, who had prayed for her, successfully attained enlightenment himself? Truly, we think of our dear ones even at the cost of our own lives when alive,

---

38. The expression *kairō dōketsu no chigiri* 階老同穴の契り refers to a married couple who will grow old together and will be buried in the same grave.

39. The Tang emperor Xuan Zong 玄宗 (685–762) greatly loved his concubine Yang Gui-fei 楊貴妃. The sentence is based upon a poem by Bo Ju-i 白居易, also known as Hakurakuten 白楽天 (772–846); see *Hakushibunshū* 白氏文集, vol. 12, and Arthur Waley, *The Life and Times of Po Chu-I* (New York: Macmillan, 1949).

40. Similar expressions appear in the *Ise monogatari* 伊勢物語 (no. 123) and the *Kokinshū* (no. 972).

but why do we forget the sufferings of our departed ones once they are dead? It is most lamentable.

I wonder where the monk came from and what kind of a man he was. Even though I heard he was poor in appearance, this makes me admire even more his inner self. He must have had such a pure heart from the time he received the tonsure until the end of his life.

2-4 A Monk of Karin'in [Yamashina Temple] Renounces the Secular World [41]

Some time ago, Lord Sotsu-dainagon Tsunenobu[42] lived in the mountain village of Tanakami.[43] One evening after the twentieth day of the ninth month, a haggard monk of about sixty years of age came to the lord to beg for alms. Since his features were very pleasant and noble, the lord retained him and treated him well. Late that night, the lord took him to a quiet place and asked him, "Who are you and why are you doing this?" The monk did not say much but gave a vague reply: "I have become like this because I have no means." The lord did not believe him and further pressed him.

Finally, the monk tearfully explained in detail: "Actually, I was living in Karin'in of Kōfukuji Temple. I had attended Buddhist services at the imperial palace for many years and advanced in rank and position as desired. But, alas, perhaps owing to the karma of my previous lives, I began to feel lonely in my old age, and so I lived with a woman. I hid her for a while, but eventually my secret was discovered. Since the monks could not keep anyone like me, I was driven from the temple and am as you see me now. Unable to separate from the woman, I have

---

41. Yamashina 山階 refers to Kōfukuji Temple (*Senjūshō* 2-1), and Karin'in 花林院 is a building in its compound. Many *Senjūshō* stories have titles that include the term *hosshin* 発心, "to resolve to accomplish something," usually meaning to pursue the Way. I have translated the term as "receiving the tonsure," "abandoning the secular world," or "renouncing secular life."

42. Sotsu-dainagon (chief grand councilor) Tsunenobu 経信 (1016–1097), the sixth son of Minamoto Michikata, excelled in poetry and playing the *biwa*. He was regarded as the founder of the Katsura School of *biwa* and was also called Grand Councilor Katsura. His writings include the *Dainagon Tsunenobu kyōshū* 大納言経信卿集. He appears in other *Senjūshō* tales (8-27, 8-31, 8-32).

43. Tanakami is in present-day Shiga prefecture (Ōtsu-shi).

brought her with me. This is what they call 'life bondage.'" The lord was very moved by his story and said, "In that case, I will take care of you and your woman. You can stay here."

"I am very happy to hear that," answered the monk.

The lord retired to his chamber, but as soon as dawn broke, he hurried to the monk's room. The monk had gone, leaving behind a poem written in splendid calligraphy:

Uchiyakeni
Tanakami yama no
Yamasabite
Norino michi shiba
Atoshi nakere ba

How sad to see
Desolate Mount Tanakami!
The trace of the path to
The Way of the Law
Is likewise disappearing.

It was moving that the monk had disappeared, leaving the poem behind him.

Later, when the lord checked on the affairs of Kōfukuji—including the list of [previous] abbots—Abbot Genkaku[44] tearfully explained, "For many years Sōjō Yōgen[45] of Karin'in wished to retire. He often secretly confined himself in a certain place, but the people of the temple stopped him from doing this as they missed him.

"About five months ago, following a rumor about his becoming the new abbot, Yōgen completely disappeared to his disciples' great disappointment. No one has heard of his whereabouts, but he must still be wandering around somewhere." Since there could be no mistake about his features and appearance, the monk who had come to the lord must have been Yōgen. The lord was said to be tearfully upset.

When I heard this story, I felt so sad that I did not know what to do. I had vaguely heard of Genpin[46] of the old Nara capital, who was determined to abandon the noisy life of the city and who sought pure mountain streams to [cleanse and] keep the color of his priestly robe unsoiled.[47] Among all the other tales about recluses who left the secular world, Genpin's story sounds especially noble. And this story of Yōgen is also extraordinary.

In general, even after abandoning secular life, people try to preserve their names after death. [Yōgen], however, tried to hide his true intention and identity by telling others he had left the temple because of frivolous carnal desire. Thinking of him telling such a lie touches my heart so much that I recall exactly what the *Shikan* says: "Show the craziness and hide the truth."[48] I hear that those who left the secular world in China and Japan followed this plan. Yōgen must have had such a pure heart, concentrating only on the Way while others despised him

---

44. Genkaku 玄覚 twice served as *bettō* 別当, or abbot, of the Kōfukuji Temple (1125–1129 and 1132–1138) and died at the age of 40.
45. Unidentified.
46. Genpin 玄賓 also appears in *Senjūshō* 1-8.
47. This sentence can be traced to a poem by Genpin in which he asserts that he will not soil his priestly robe, which has been cleansed in the pure stream of Mount Miwa. The same poem appears in the *Hosshinshū* 1, *Fukurozōshi* 袋草子 1, *Kojidan* (no. 203), and *Zoku kokin wakashū* 続古今和歌集 (8, no. 801).
48. *Makashikan* (cessation and contemplation), the fundamental teaching of the Tendai Sect, was taught by Chi-yi in China in 594. The passage is in the seventh volume of the work *Iwanami bunko* II, *Kankyonotomo*, 3-1. Also refer to *Senjūshō* 1-1.

as an insignificant man. Also, while wandering around here and there, he must have left any place that he did not like. That, too, sounds very noble.

Imitating the recluses of the past and wishing to renounce the world, I also wandered various provinces when I was physically strong and still had energy. While visiting many famous temples and attractive places, I forgot my worries and was convinced that spending one's life in this manner could not be so sinful. How could those wise and talented men, with their strong conviction to renounce the world, fail to purify their hearts and minds?

[During my travels, I saw] the snow piled on the summit of the white mountain of Koshi[49] and the *hahaki* plants of Ōiso Grove[50] softly swaying in the faint breeze. The pampas grass of Sano Field[51] trembled in the breeze and the dew on the tip of the grass agitated like my deranged heart. The hanging bridge of Kiso and the boat-bridge of Sano[52] were so attractive that I was overcome at their sight.

The ever-changing red autumn leaves on a mountain in Ōsaka Barrier,[53] Narumi Beach printed over with plovers' footprints, Mount Fuji in summer with the eternal snows on its summit in the pattern of *kanoko* deer dots, the beaches of Ōiso and Koiso, Kiyomigaseki

---

49. Koshi no shirayama こしの白山, the white mountain of Koshi, is located in present-day Ishikawa, Toyama, and Fukui prefectures. It is one of the three spiritual mountains, together with Fuji and Tachiyama (Tateyama); see *Shūi wakashū* 拾遺和歌集, 4, winter section, 249.

50. *Hahaki*, or *hōkigusa*, is one meter tall and was used to make brooms. *Ōiso no mori* refers to the grove behind Okuishi Shrine 奥石神社 in present-day Shiga prefecture (Ando-chō, Gamō-gun).

51. *Sano no hara*, or Sano field 佐野の野原, could correspond to several modern-day locations; see *Senjūshō* 7-14.

52. The following places where the author visited are all *utamakura*. The hanging bridge of Kiso is in present-day Nagano prefecture (*Sankashū* 山家集, nos. 1415, 1432). The boat-bridge of Sano is in present-day Sano in Gunma prefecture. "Boat-bridge" refers to a bridge of boards placed over boats lined up in a river (*Sankashū*, no. 223).

53. An old barrier in present-day Shiga prefecture was important as it guarded the approach to the capital Kyoto from the northern provinces. It was one of three old barriers that also included Fuwa 不破 and Suzuka 鈴鹿.

Barrier, and Ukishima Field[54]—all these places I could not overlook or pass by.

I wonder if Yōgen, at the age of sixty, was unable to visit these places. I am deeply concerned and wonder in what kind of place he is resting and purifying his heart. Oh, how I wish I had some strength to renounce [this secular life]!

2-5 A Man Pursues the Way after Listening to a Sermon at the Urin'in

Some time ago, a couple lived in the eastern part of the capital. Although their status was low, they were not all that poor. One day, the man went to Urin'in Temple[55] to listen to a sermon. The preacher delivered such a good sermon that many people were tearfully moved and raised their voices. The man became so devoted that he received the tonsure on the spot by cutting off his top knot and, without returning home, left for Higashiyama.[56]

The man set up a shabby hut on the inner mountain of Higashiyama and quietly recited the Buddha's name. He went down to the village from time to time to beg for food. Once he obtained enough, he did not ask for more. At night, he walked around the village, loudly reciting the Buddha's name. No one awakened by his invocation failed to feel pity and to sympathize with him.

Some people asked him, "Why do you walk around at night when you are tired and need sleep?" The man replied, "Well, if I walk around during the day, I may see a woman and child who will make me recall

---

54. Narumi Beach 鳴海潟 is in present-day Nagoya. Fumi 踏み or *fumitsukuru* ("made steps" or footprints) in the text is associated with another term, *fumi* 文 (letter or poem) (*Shin-kokin wakashū*, 648, 1726). The names Ōiso and Koiso refer to the beach in Kanagawa prefecture facing Sagami Bay (*Genshinshū* 元真集, no. 204). Kiyomigaseki 清見が関 was an old barrier in present-day Shizuoka prefecture (*Shika wakashū* 詞花和歌集, no. 213). Ukishima Field 浮嶋が原 is between Suzukawa and Numazu in Shizuoka prefecture (*Sankashū*, no. 1307).
55. Urin'in 雲林院 was in Murasakino in the north of the city and was originally a detached palace of Emperor Junna (r. 823–833). In the reign of Emperor Go-Daigo (r. 1318–1339) Urin'in belonged to the Daitokuji Temple of the Zen School.
56. The Higashiyama area to the east of Kyoto was known for the Toribe (Toribeno) graveyard, where many recluses lived; some aristocrats also had villas there.

the woman and child I left behind and I will become very disturbed. But at night I see no one and my mind becomes calm and clear. And in my hut, I cannot sleep as I constantly think of the futility of life. So I walk around during the night. Besides, if someone who hears me reciting the Buddha's name comes to feel noble and concentrates on the Way, then I benefit others. That is why I do this during the night." Those who heard him shed tears and revered him, and then left.

Three years passed. When the man did not appear in the village for three days, the villagers were concerned and went to his hut. There they found him dead, facing west with his hands joined in prayer. They grieved and quickly informed other villagers, who came to pray for the man.

This was most unusual. Usually lowly people do not think about the futility of life; their only concern is their present affairs and they ignore the next life. But this man, deeply affected by the Law, abandoned his wife and child and never saw them again. He did not go out during the day because his mind would have been disturbed. This shows his strong devotion to the Way. It is very moving that he could not sleep during the night because he constantly thought of the futility of life. Pursuing the Way without sleep is very difficult for anyone who has left secular life. By doing so, this lowly, ignorant man was even more extraordinary.

It is sad that a person who was alive yesterday might not be here today. People who are proud of themselves in the morning may be turned into white bones in the evening. And others who are enjoying the flowers disappear, just as blossoms are scattered by the wind. Foolishly attached to the futile affairs of this life, many of us vainly spend our years until our hair becomes white, just as the withered grasses of the autumn fields die away. Ignoring all of this, some continue to indulge themselves with sleep and futile dreams. Monk Sendō[57] once said, "Practice the Way as if to brush off the fire from your head," while

---

57. Sendō 善導 (Ch. Shan-dao, 613–681) was a great master of the Chinese Pure Land School and propagated the *nenbutsu* 念仏 practice, that is, the recitation of Amida's name. One of his writings, the *Kanmuryōjubutsukyōsho* 観無量寿仏経疏, greatly influenced the Japanese Pure Land School.

Sōzu Eshin[58] recommended, "Practice without sleeping." This lowly, devout man followed their teachings exactly.

Even if you have abandoned the world, your mind may not be at rest. You have dyed the color of your robe [receiving the tonsure], but your heart does not follow the Way. Since your body and mind do not pursue the Way together, all your practices will end in vain. As the Buddha once said, "Be a master of your mind, never follow your mind as master." When I think of these things, I shed many tears.

2-6 Master Jikei's Skull Recites the Lotus Sutra

When I was living in Retsu village[59] in the Hiraizumi district of Michinoku[60] province, I went to Mount Sakashiba. The appearance of the trees, rocks, and flowing streams on the mountain was indescribably beautiful.

After walking some ten *chō*[61] from the village, I came to a stone pagoda one *jō*[62] in height. Surrounded by a fence and neatly trimmed grass, it looked most impressive. When I asked the man accompanying me about it, he replied, "Some time ago, there was a brave samurai general who had a daughter who wanted to read the *Hokekyō*.[63] But since she had no one to teach her how to read it, she lamented for a long time.

---

58. Eshin 恵心, or Genshin 源信 (942–1017), a monk of the Tendai School, studied under Ryōgen on Mount Hiei and established the Pure Land School in Japan. Because he lived in Eshin'in of Yokawa, he was also called Sōzu Yokawa. His writings include the *Ōjōyōshū* 往生要集 and the *Ichijōyōketsu* 一乗要決.
59. Both Retsu village and Mount Sakashiba are unidentified.
60. Michinoku (Mutsu) province was in the northeastern region. Hiraizumi 平泉 district is present-day Hiraizumi. It was an important military base to control the Ezo (Emishi 蝦夷) people in the north, who were hostile toward the Yamato Imperial Court at the end of the eighth century. Hiraizumi was prosperous for three generations, between the time when Fujiwara Kiyohira 藤原清衡 (1056–1128) established his residence there and when Minamoto Yoritomo 源頼朝 (1147–1199) destroyed it.
61. One *chō* 町 equals 109 meters.
62. More than three meters.
63. *Myōhōrengekyō* 妙法蓮華経, or the Lotus Sutra. Kumārajīva's translation of the *Saddharma-puṇḍarīka sūtra* in A.D. 406 became the most influential scripture in East Asian Buddhism and the basic sutra for the Tendai and Nichiren sects in Japan; see Leon Hurvitz, trans., *Scripture of the Lotus Blossom of the Fine Dharma* (New York: Columbia University Press, 1976).

"One day, the daughter heard a voice coming from the ceiling of her room, saying, 'If you find and bring a copy of the sutra, I will teach you how to read it.'

"Although she thought this rather strange, she obtained a copy. As soon as she placed it before her, she again heard the awesome voice coming from the ceiling, and it began to teach her. After eight days, she finished learning to read the sutra. Feeling very curious, the daughter searched the ceiling and found a white skull covered in moss but with a fresh tongue.[64] She was convinced that the skull with the tongue must have taught her. Greatly overwhelmed, she reverently said to the skull, 'May I ask who you are?'

"'I am the skull of Master Jikei[65] of Enryakuji Temple. I was deeply moved by your devotion, and so I came here to teach you. Now send me to Mount Sakashiba.' Feeling very noble and grateful, she carried the skull to the mountain, buried it, and built a stone pagoda for it. (Until

---

64. The first story of a skull and a fresh tongue reciting the *Hokekyō* appears in the *Ryōiki* 霊異記 (810–824, 3-1).

65. Jikei Taishi 慈恵大師, or Ryōgen 良源 (912–985), a man of Asai in Ōmi province, studied at Enryakuji Temple of Mount Hiei and became the eighteenth Tendai *zasu*; see *Senjūshō* 1-1 and 5-3.

recently, the villagers there heard a noble voice reciting the sutra.) Later the daughter became a nun, lived in a hut on the mountain, and passed away some twenty years ago. Her hut is still there and you can see it." I followed my companion to the inner part of the mountain and saw the ruins of an old hut with an entrance about three *ken*[66] wide. When I saw this, I was too moved to speak.

This was indeed extraordinary. Born a woman in a remote place where no one could teach her, the daughter wished to read the sutra in the morning and evening, and asleep or awake she lamented her lack of a teacher. Such an unusually noble heart moved the great master so much that he graciously appeared as a skull to help her. In ancient China, a poor man grieved over his inability to read the sutra. A beautiful woman appeared, became his wife, and helped him with the sutra. As soon as he finished reading it, his wife turned into Bodhisattva Kannon and disappeared. When I recall this story in the *Meiki* of Shin,[67] I feel uplifted.

This is just one of many examples from the olden days, but in the present time such a story sounds unrealistic. I especially envy the nun, who must have led a serene life with a pure heart. I wonder into which Pure Land she was reborn. Untalented people like us have left home [to attain the Way] and dyed our robes. But, alas, we vainly spend years with little devotion and do not live deep in the mountains. This is truly sad.

I wonder if Master Jikei had decided to save people in a world lacking the Buddha when he appeared in a remote province on Mount Sakashiba where the Law was hardly known. Even though the villagers heard a voice reciting the sutra, their hearts were unmoved and they lived only for fighting and killing. This is most sad. Under such conditions, how could those [ignorant] people have been saved? As I think of the daughter who became a nun in these circumstances, I want to know more about her, such as her name, her character, and her lineage. I spent months and years in vain without finding anyone who knew about her. Since the villagers were ignorant of the Law, they were uncertain about the wonder that had happened some twenty years earlier. If the woman's younger brother is still alive, I wish I could visit him.

....

66. One *ken* equals six feet.
67. A similar story appears in the *Kankyonotomo* (2-5). The *Meiki* of Shin is unidentified.

2-7 A Zen Monk of Neither Coming Nor Going

I once heard that three woodcutters found a shabby hut made of branches in a dark place in the valley of a remote mountain in Harima province. Inside the hut, they found a dead monk wearing his black robe and lying on the grass-covered floor. Birds had pecked out his eyes. They also found a fine writing box with a brush and an ink stone. A poem was written on the trunk of a large tree by the hut and it read:

> Shishō tomo ni
> Shishō ni arazu
> Murai muko
> Ni shite hon rai
> Jakujō nari

> Life is not life
> Death is not death,
> Neither life nor death
> Is coming or going,
> Only original silence remains.[68]

I was told no villagers had gone to look for the deceased monk.

I felt most concerned for him. What sort of a monk had he been? Living in a deep valley, he must have been wrapped in meditation while clearing his mind, listening to the wind blowing from the summit and passing through the pines. I wonder how long he lived in the hut. I believe he lived there for a long time since it looked so old. As I pondered how he had spent his fragile life, I felt his life must have been very austere yet very noble indeed.

His mind must have been extremely clear as he understood the phrase, "Neither life nor death is coming or going." Some people say that practicing meditation is very difficult in these degenerate times, but I would not agree, especially when I remember the poor man of

---

68. The poem means that the Buddha's dharma body is free of the transience of coming and going and is forever impermanent. "Silence" means enlightenment, or nirvana, that is, the quiet state of mind free of the delusions of the secular world.

Kataokayama dying without any chance of seeing buddhas.[69] On the contrary, this might be the right way to obtain the buddhas' salvation by meditation.

It was indeed noble that the monk possessed nothing but a writing box. There are many ways to renounce secular life. I feel especially envious of those who live by the beach or deep in the mountains. But alas, since I have no means to survive alone, I have spent months and years unable to lead a solitary life deep in the mountains. In short, I still deplore my life with its strong attachment to myself. Why do I regret it? If I didn't, wouldn't I clear my mind by living deep in the mountains? And what does "Only original silence remains" mean? What is silence? I wonder what the monk means when he says in his poem, "Neither life nor death is coming or going."

2-8 Priest Kōsai Served Lord Narimichi

Some time ago, when Grand Councilor Narimichi[70] lived in Higashiyama, a strange monk came and told him, "I would like to serve you." The lord said to him, "Your request is quite unusual because monks usually serve priests. Why do you want to serve me? But if you really want to, you may." So the monk was hired and the people in the mansion found him very honest and good natured. They called him Shōbō, or Holy Monk.

The monk did not practice mind concentration in particular but the lord treated him well enough to give him robes occasionally. He put them on for a few days but soon lost them. People wondered about this and began to say to each other, "I wonder if he has a woman to whom he gives away these robes?" and "Maybe so, but it is strange; he certainly does not seem to do so." Finally, the rumors reached the lord, who again gave him another robe, and said, "Why have you lost all the robes I gave you? From now on, don't lose them." The monk gratefully accepted the robe.

---

69. The story of this poor man often appears in various Buddhist tales including the *Shōtoku taishi denryaku* 聖徳太子伝略 (*Dainihon bukkyō zensho*, 71 *maki*, p. 135).

70. Dainagon Narimichi 大納言成通, son of Fujiwara Munemichi (1097–?), was one of the first imperial poets appearing in the *Kin'yō wakashū* 金葉和歌集. It is not known whether his mansion was in Higashiyama.

One day, people noticed the monk hurriedly leaving the mansion. They secretly followed him to the vicinity of Hosshōji Temple[71] and saw him take off his robe and give it to a poor beggar who appeared to be very cold. The people were surprised and impressed, and they immediately reported this to the lord.

The lord and his staff now began to treat the monk respectfully, assuming that he might have been someone important. As a result, the monk began to feel uneasy and finally disappeared a few days later. Everyone, including the lord, missed him and felt sad, but remained helpless as they had no way to look for him.

Some twenty days later, the lord was invited to a poetry contest to compete with Lord Reizei, Middle Councilor Toshitada.[72] While the lord was thinking how to compose poems to impress the emperor at the contest, the monk suddenly appeared and told him, "I have

....

71. Hosshōji 法勝寺, built by Emperor Shirakawa 白河 in 1077, was in the vicinity of present-day Okazaki in Kyoto's east.

72. Toshitada 俊忠 was a son of Fujiwara Tadaie, who belonged to the Mikohidari School 御子左一流 of poetry founded by Nagaie 長家, the sixth son of Regent Michinaga 道長. Toshitada was the father of Fujiwara Shunzei 藤原俊成 and died at the age of fifty-three in 1123. He might have been referred to as Lord Reizei 冷泉 since he was living in the old mansion of his grandfather, Fujiwara Teika 藤原定家. The Reizei School of poetry founded by Fujiwara Tamesuke 藤原為相 followed the Teika style within the Mikohidari School.

returned because I composed these poems for you," and he recited these two poems:

Mino omoni
Furu shirayuki no
Katamo naku
Kieya shina mashi
Hitono tsurasa ni

My life of suffering,
Caused by others,
May soon vanish just as
The falling white snow
On the surface of the water.[73]

Uramu nayo
Kage miegata no
Yūzuki yo
Oboroke naranu
Kumo ma matsu mi o

Think no ill of me,
For I am waiting until
The cloud that hides
The evening moon
Passes away.[74]

As soon as the monk finished reciting the poems, he made ready to leave, but the lord held on to his sleeves and asked him, "Who are you? I want to know because I really appreciate you."

"I am Kōsai of Hatsuseyama,"[75] replied the monk and, shaking free

---

73. The poem appears in the *Kin'yō wakashū* 8 (Love 2, no. 452) by Narimichi, with the caption "Poem Composed on Winter Love."
74. The poem appears in the *Kin'yō wakashū* 8 (Love 2, no. 483) by Ichinomiya Kii, with the caption, "Poem Composed When Someone Did Not Come in the Evening."
75. The *Honchō kōsōden* states that Kōsai 迎西 was alive in 1132–1135. He lived on Mount Kōya 高野山 for a long time and died there, not in Hasedera Temple 長谷寺 at Hatsuseyama 泊瀬山 as narrated in this tale.

his sleeves, he left. Since then, no one has seen him.

Usually people want to leave behind their names so they will be remembered, but this monk, Kōsai, tried to remain anonymous, as if hiding his devotion to the Way. He lived as a servant in a place where a monk usually would not work and secretly gave his robes to the poor. This was truly wonderful.

Even though people may wish to leave secular life, they are in fact unable to do so. The monk's decision to obtain complete detachment from his secular life was indeed noble. I will not criticize his poems since they were included in the *Kin'yō wakashū*[76] under the name of the grand councilor. Kōsai must have had a clear and elegant mind [to compose these poems]; he must also have had a merciful heart, although he was unaware of this, which makes him appear so much more touching and noble.

If we calmly compose ourselves, we know that even ants and worms are living beings and that we should not ignore them. We might have been born as the sparrows that flew off frightened by the sound of the rattles set up by Monk Genpin,[77] who tried to scare the birds away from the rice fields. Or birds alarmed by the sound of clappers as their flapping wings touched them. Or geese that flew off into the distant northern sky after picking up grain in harvested fields. We might have been fish caught and cooked in delicious dishes. We might have neighed loudly while pulling heavy carts in this futile life. So animals and birds are related to us, for they share the same mind. They themselves must have been born once as human beings and been affected by various feelings of passion and grief as they deplored separation in their lives. They might have been our merciful lords or the parents who cared for us. So it is a great and foolish mistake to regard them as unrelated to us. Whoever we may be, if we try to be kind to animals and birds, then we will cultivate a merciful mind and gradually reciprocate the bountiful mercy of the Great Master Shaka.

Does it make any difference to be reborn in this or that form? Although we know about the cycle of birth and death, we pay little attention to the reality. O buddhas of the three generations, please

---

76. One of the eight imperial anthologies compiled by Minamoto Toshiyori 源俊頼 by order of Former Emperor Shirakawa in 1127; it is also called the *Kin'yōshū* 金葉集.

77. For Genpin, see *Senjūshō* 1-8 and 2-4.

help us to abandon hatred and widely spread the pure buddha heart among us.

It is truly sad that although we happened to be born as human beings, we ignore the Buddha's teachings, spend months and years creating karmic causes for whatever we do, and waste all the good deeds accumulated in our past lives. It is no use regretting this now. Perhaps we have not truly regretted our sinful deeds?

All sins are like dew on grass that vanishes as the sun, the Buddha's blessing, appears. Regarding the Buddha's blessing, it must be sought in our own hearts and minds. It is in our hearts, and nowhere else. The Buddha's blessing means to seek only the Way. So if we keep the buddha mind, our past sins will eventually disappear. Upholding the original, pure buddha nature is never difficult. If we are enlightened, everything, including the rising wind and waves, is a sacred teaching.

I heard that Kōsai finally died at Hasedera Temple after wandering in various places. As I think of his noble heart, it is difficult to suppress my tears. When writing about him, my tears drop into the ink and it is this that makes my writing so poor. But I hope people of later generations will forgive me and not criticize my poor writing after my death.

3-1 Monk Kenbutsu

Some time ago, I traveled to the northern provinces with a *hijiri* monk.[1] We arrived at a place between a mountain and the sea in the Inayatsu district of Noto province.[2] Far from villages, it had a rough beach with huge rocks. Greatly moved by the forbidding ambiance, we stopped to view the scenery.

We saw a rock chamber among the trees by a high cliff near the beach. We quickly approached it and found a monk in his forties sitting there. Wearing only one robe, he appeared very serene with a pure heart. I felt drawn to him and asked, "I suppose for you this is a pleasant place to live. May I ask who you are?" Faintly smiling, the monk recited a poem:

Naniwagata
Mura tatsu matsu mo
Mienu ura wo
Koko sumiyoshi[3] *to*
Tare ka omowamu

I wonder
Who would think this
A pleasant place to live,
Where you see no pine groves
As in Naniwa Bay?

Impressed by his poem, I replied with my own poem:

Matsuga ne no
Kishi utsu nami ni
Arawarete
Koko sumiyoshi to
Omou bakari zo

---

1. Saigyō 西行 often traveled with a monk named Saijū 西住; see *Senjūshō zenchūshaku*, ed. Senjūshō Kenkyūkai, I, p. 221.
2. Located in the northern part of present-day Ishikawa prefecture.
3. *Sumiyoshi* 住吉 means "a nice place to live." It is also the name of a place by Naniwa (Osaka) Bay. The pine grove at Sumiyoshi, a traditional poetic subject, is also called Suminoe no matsu すみのえの松, "the pines of Sumino Bay."

> I do think this
> Is a pleasant place
> With the waves
> Pounding the pine roots
> As they cleanse your heart.

My poem seemed to please the monk. I asked him, "Who are you? And do you always live here?"

He then said, "Well, people call me 'the *hijiri* of Matsushima[4] waiting for the moon.' I come and live here only ten days a month and during this time I do not take any food." I was very surprised by his answer as I realized that he was the well-known Monk Kenbutsu[5] and respectfully introduced myself: "People call me Saigyō."

"Yes, I have heard of such a person," he replied.

Although reluctant to leave him, I asked him some questions on Buddhist texts and then tearfully departed. On our return home, we again visited the rock chamber but found no one there. So we spent four days making a detour to Matsushima, where we stayed at [Kenbutsu's] temple for two months.

When I think of Monk Kenbutsu, I cannot suppress my tears. Leaving serene Matsushima, which was quiet enough to calm his mind, he deliberately traveled across mountains to a distant place in Noto to deepen his thoughts while listening to the wind blowing through the pines; there he purified his heart by the beach, where the waves washed the shore. Taking no servants or food, he spent ten solitary days there. In the warm seasons of spring and summer, it must have been easier, but living in a rock chamber in a northerly place under the winter sky must have been very difficult. His strong heart and incomparable determination overwhelm me with tears.

We both share a human heart and mind, so why is the difference between the holy man in the rock chamber and me as great as a mountain? It is quite common for those aspiring to the Way and escaping

---

4. Matsushima 松島 (Pine Island) in Miyagi prefecture is famous for its picturesque bay with more than 260 small islands covered in pine trees. Saigyō and other poets, including Bashō 芭蕉 (1644–1694), visited and admired the place.

5. The name Kenbutsu 見仏 means "seeing Buddha"; his birth date is unknown. The monk lived at Matsushima Temple, where he recited the Lotus Sutra during the reign of Emperor Toba 鳥羽 (r. 1107–1123) and died at the age of eighty-two.

from the secular world to live in quiet temples. But Monk Kenbutsu left Matsushima, where he heard only the occasional cries of birds and the wind passing through the roof to the garden. And then he stayed at the lonely beach of Noto, where the cold wind blew on the sleeves of his skimpy hemp robe. Indeed, it is deeply touching even to someone like me who has long renounced secular life. He had no visitors in Noto because he did not tell any of his disciples about his cave. While I was staying in Matsushima, Kenbutsu disappeared for ten days at the beginning of each month. As I think of him sequestered at Noto during that time, I am often moved. His first disciple took care of the temple during his absence. None of his disciples seemed surprised by his monthly disappearance for his ascetic practice.

3-2 Gubu Jōen

Some time ago, Sumiyoshi Shrine in Settsu province[6] held a service at the abbot's residence. Wishing to form a relationship with the officiating priest,[7] I attended the ceremony and wondered who he was, for he seemed to lack knowledge and faith in the Way.

The congregation at the ceremony was full of beggars and lame people. Among them was a mute monk carrying a small bell and wearing a tattered straw mat around his waist. I thought at first I was mistaken, but he really was Gubu Jōen[8] of Mount Hiei.[9] Making my way through the crowd, I walked over to him, but on seeing me, he calmly left through the gateway. I followed him to a quiet place to talk with him.

---

6. The Sumiyoshi Shrine 住吉神社 is in the city of Osaka (Sumiyoshi-ku). The holding of a Buddhist service in the compound of a Shinto shrine is another example of Shinto-Buddhism syncretism.

7. Attending Buddhist services and lectures gave the audience a chance to become acquainted and form a relationship (*kechien* 結縁) with leading monks. This was important because attaining buddhahood was easier if people had teachers (*zenchishiki* 善智識, "good knowledge") who could lead and guide them on the Way. This is a typical example of *tariki hongan* 他力本願 salvation, that is, relying on the power of others, including Amida Buddha and Bodhisattva Kannon, as opposed to *jiriki hongan* 自力本願 salvation, or self-reliance, practiced in the Zen Sect.

8. Jōen 静円 was a son of Fujiwara Norimichi 藤原教通 and Koshikibu no Naishi 小式部内侍, a daughter of Izumi Shikibu 和泉式部. He died in 1074 at the age of fifty-nine. *Gubu* 供奉 was a title of monks serving at the imperial palace.

9. Here Mount Hiei refers to Enryakuji Temple 延暦寺, the headquarters of the Tendai School in Japan.

As we sat beneath a pine tree, Jōen began, "I wondered how long I should stay at the temple on Mount Hiei, and so I began to wander about. After a while, my desire for the Way was weakened, and I thought of returning to the mountain. But I am still wandering like this because I am disturbed by people's gossip and rumors. I wonder how my father is—the Minister of Ōmiya.[10] I worry about him. Since I don't want to see people, leave me now. But please return tonight as I want to hear about my father." Jōen told me where he was staying and repeated, "Please come back to see me." So I left him and looked forward to our meeting after sunset.

As soon as the sun disappeared behind the mountain, I hurried to the place agreed upon, but he was not there. Disappointed, I waited, hoping that he might come later, but I spent the whole night sitting there in vain.

Jōen was a disciple of Abbot Son'e[11] and the youngest son of Minister Koremichi of Ōmiya. Since his youth, he had aspired to the

---

10. *Ōmiya no Daishōkoku* 大相国 (grand prime minister) was a title usually used to refer to Fujiwara Munemichi, who died in 1165 at the age of seventy-three. He had no son called Jōen.

11. Son'e 尊恵 could be Jishinbō Son'e 慈心房尊恵, who was a son of Emperor Nijō (r. 1158–1165). For his identity, see *Senjūshō zenchūshaku* I, p. 243.

Way and always retired to quiet places. It was noble of him to renounce the secular world at such a young age. Whenever I think of him, I lament that I myself cannot completely abandon the world. It is most extraordinary that, although having left secular life, he is still troubled by people and pretends to be a mute.

There are many ways of hiding virtue. Monk Eei[12] of China went eight thousand *ri* from home, changed his appearance, and became a shepherd tending sheep. Monk Shinpan[13] of our country also became a poor man and pretended to be dumb. All these examples show that holy men of old had difficulty in hiding their virtue and so had these extraordinary experiences. It is unfortunate that Jōen's experience was so difficult to bear that he had to pretend to be dumb. Why did he leave Mount Hiei? I am concerned about him for he became so distressed that he eventually detested this life, just like we detest the autumn wind when it begins to blow.

If we think deeply about this, we realize that our life is like rootless grass distant from the shore or a boat drifting on the water. Before the grass and the boat are blown away by the wind and disappear, we should prepare ourselves as we calmly reflect on Jōen's deeds and his way of life.

3-3 How a Courtesan of Muro Abandoned the Secular World

Long ago, there was a nun who lived in a hut and practiced the Way in Takenooka in Harima province. A good-looking courtesan of Muro,[14] she was once favored by Middle Councilor Akimoto of Daigo,[15] and she

---

12. Monk Hui Rui 恵叡, who lived during the Song dynasty, took the tonsure when young and tended sheep; he died before 453 at the age of eighty-five.
13. Shinpan 真範 (d. 1054), a son of Taira Shōshō, became the administrator of the Gangōji 元興寺, Kōfukuji, and Hasedera temples. Strongly desiring to renounce the world, he wandered around as a beggar and, when seeing someone he knew, feigned ignorance.
14. Muro 室, or Murotsu 室津, in Harima province, was a port on the Seto Inland Sea and had pleasure quarters with many courtesans.
15. Akimoto 顕基 (1000–1047), an adopted son of Regent Fujiwara Yorimichi and a younger brother of Takakuni 隆国, Grand Councilor of Uji, received the tonsure at the age of thirty-seven. His association with the courtesan in Muro was possible while he was an assistant to the governor of Harima from 1020. A similar story appears in the *Kankyonotomo* (II:3).

lived in the capital for a year. But for some reason she was treated coldly by her lord. She returned to Muro, but never lived as a courtesan again.

When she learned that the middle councilor's attendant was traveling by boat to the capital from a western province, she cut her hair, wrapped it in a sheet of fine paper, and wrote a poem:

Tsuki mo sezu
Uki o miru me no
Kanashisa ni
Ama to narite mo
Sode zo kawakanu

Seeing the futility
Of my sequence of sadness,
I have become a nun,
But the tears on my sleeves,
Alas, never dry.

When she finished her poem, she cast it with her hair into the boat. She then moved to a hut where she could keep her heart and mind pure.

After reading her poem, the middle councilor missed the woman so much that he shed tears like rain. The nun recited only the Buddha's name from morning to night until she finally attained birth in the paradise of the Pure Land just as she had aspired to. Many worshippers came to establish a relationship with the enlightened nun.

A piece of decaying wood remained at the site of her grass hut [when I visited it]. It could have been the pole of the hut. When I glanced at the straight pole with a knot in it, I was overcome with tears as I recalled her life. Far from the village, the nun was reduced to poverty and must have had difficulty living in the hut. What was her life like? How did she manage to obtain food?

Other abandoned courtesans would not have made such a firm decision, but this nun completely renounced secular life. Her strong resolution was most remarkable. Likewise, the middle councilor himself must have been a fine, enlightened man, as recorded in the *Ōjōden*.[16]

---

16. The *Ōjōden* 往生伝, biographical records of the enlightened ones, may refer to *Zoku honchō ōjōden* 続本朝往生伝 (IV) by Ōe Masafusa 大江匡房, although it lacks this story.

Thus, coldly treated, and aware of the futility of this life, an ignorant courtesan finally abandoned her secular life like the autumn wind [anticipating a cold winter]. This friendly pair of newly born bodhisattvas [i.e., the nun and the middle councilor] certainly gives a very noble impression.

3-4 Holy Man Kanjaku

Long ago Holy Man Kanjaku[17] renounced secular life. When he was young and a nobleman, he associated with many courtiers and finally became governor of Tōtomi province. But for some reason, he left home one day, received the tonsure, and became a beggar wandering and seeking the Way. Since he had no son, he gave all his land to his wife and never returned home.

Without performing any ascetic practices, he spent his days doing nothing but visiting people and telling them stories of the past and present. Since his tales were interesting, he was often invited by ministers. He paid no attention to his clothes and rarely washed his hands and feet.

Once when Lord Fuke[18] was still a lieutenant general and living in Nijō, Kanjaku went to him and said, "I will probably die today. I thought of secluding myself in a remote place on the mountain, but I want to pass away near your mansion. I am determined to attain enlightenment at my last moment, so I wish to form a relationship with other Buddhists.[19] I hope I am not being intrusive."

Moved by his words, the lord replied, "No, no. You are not a nuisance at all."

"I am very pleased," Kanjaku said and went to the waterfall on the mountain to the east of the mansion. He sat on a rock, faced west and

---

17. Unidentified.
18. Fujiwara Tadazane 藤原忠実 (1078–1162), the first son of Regent Moromichi and the daughter of Toshiie, the Minister of the Right. He became a regent in 1105 and prime minister in 1112, and received the tonsure in 1140. His conversation appears in the *Chūgaishō* 中外抄 and the *Fukego* 富家語. For another story about him, see *Senjūshō* 6-6.
19. In their final hours, Buddhists traditionally wish to establish a relationship with those who have attained buddhahood; this is called *kechien* 結縁, or "forming a relationship." A similar belief was common among poets who traveled to places that had inspired famous writers in the past in an attempt to share their poetic experience. Such places were called *utamakura* 歌枕, or "poem pillows."

joined his hands in prayer, and soon passed away in that posture. A purple cloud appeared and a pleasant fragrance filled the mansion. Many people came to pay their respects to him. Someone made a sketch of him and left it by the rock, and there it still remains. It shows Kanjaku wearing a robe that has a tear at the shoulder and a straw mat on his back. He died on the third day of the twelfth month. This was most remarkable.

Kanjaku abandoned all his riches and land, became a poor man, and visited strangers as well as people he knew, begging for food. Unlike heartless rocks and trees, the people were tearfully touched by him and his way of life. It is indeed commendable that he never returned home. It must have been difficult for him to beg from people he knew, living in familiar places. He spent his days only telling stories and doing nothing in particular. Although he appeared common, he must have had a pure and serene heart. He is truly a good example of the old saying "A true ascetic is one found in a secular town."[20]

---

20. 大隠は朝市にあり, that is, a person who has truly transcended secular matters can live in a town rather than in a secluded place in the mountains.

3-5 A Retired Monk of Miidera Temple

Once when I passed through Ikuno village near Mount Ōe,[21] I saw a monk in his sixties, living in a hut built in a remote place on the mountain at some distance from the village road. The hut looked very clean and neat, and all I heard was the sound of water flowing through a bamboo pipe. Dressed in only a hemp robe, the monk appeared very noble and I asked him some questions.

He replied, "Once I was a scholarly monk at Miidera Temple, but the Miidera and Enryakuji temples did not get along well.[22] After the Enryakuji monks burnt down Miidera, I felt most disillusioned and frustrated, and so I finally left the temple. Since then, I wandered in various places until I came to live here in my old age. In the beginning, I went to the village to beg for food, but now as I am no longer attached to life, I live on what I can find here; some villagers occasionally visit and bring me food. So in this way I manage to survive." I noticed that the monk was blessed with a truly pure heart.

Buddhist teachings have long flourished at Enryakuji and Miidera on Mount Hiei. Monk Kyōtai[23] of Miidera wisely entrusted the temple to Great Master Chishō,[24] declaring that the temple would last until Miroku Buddha appeared.[25] Seeing the temple's buildings and its many sutras and writings destroyed by fire must have caused him great anguish.

It is most noble to observe the teachings in this degenerate age. It is regrettable that some people, ignorant of the futility of life, were

---

21. Mount Ōe 大江山 is located northwest of Kyoto. Ikuno village is present-day Fukuchiyama-shi, Kyoto-fu.
22. Miidera Temple 三井寺, also called Onjōji Temple 園城寺, is in the city of Ōtsu and was established by Master Chishō in 858 as a branch temple of the Enryakuji Temple of the Tendai School. Eventually the two temples became engaged in constant conflicts, and Miidera was burned down by Enryakuji's monk-soldiers several times in the Heian and Kamakura periods.
23. Monk Kyōtai 教待 lived in Miidera Temple for a long time until Master Chishō succeeded as abbot of the temple. He was said to have died at the age of 162.
24. Master Chishō 智証, or Enchin 円珍 (814–892), went to China to study in 853 and became administrator of Miidera Temple after returning to Japan. In 868, he became the fifth Tendai *zasu* 天台座主, or abbot of Enryakuji.
25. Miroku Buddha 弥勒仏, the future Buddha, will appear to those who fail to hear Shaka Buddha's preaching. His appearance is usually referred to as the Dawn of the Three Meetings (*san-e no akatsuki* 三会の暁), meaning that he will break through the darkness and offer three meetings, or services, to deliver sentient beings.

attached to self-indulgence and ultimately destroyed their temples. Even those who dress like scholarly monks and talk as if they were the Shaka Buddha's disciples often conspire to fight. So it is quite natural that people ignorant of the correct teachings act unreasonably in accordance with their desires. I am strongly convinced that they will never be free of worldly suffering unless they completely abandon secular affairs.

Man's great suffering is hatred. What causes this? Life itself creates hatred and this eventually produces anger. Conflicts and fighting naturally arise from hatred and anger. People suffer and create their own illness. But this is the way of our life.

3-6 Monk Hōnichi and a Poem

Long ago Hōin Kōmyō,[26] a noble and learned monk of Mimuroto Temple, wanted to go to China. He went to a province to the west [of Kyoto] and stayed at a place called Akashi in Harima.[27] One day, a poor monk came to beg for food. He was almost naked and he carried with him a puppy, and so people laughed at him. Thinking this strange, Kōmyō looked at the monk closely and realized that he was Monk Hōnichi[28] of Kiyomizu Temple in Kyoto. He looked at him still more carefully; there was no mistake. Overwhelmed, Kōmyō ran to the monk, exclaiming, "You look so strange!" The monk smiled and replied, "I am truly crazy." He started to run away and the people tried to stop him, but he quickly entered a dark grove, so they gave up chasing after him.

Feeling unbearably sad, Kōmyō remained in the village and sought the monk everywhere, but all in vain. Finally, he asked the villagers about him, and they said, "We didn't know where he came from, but he stayed here about twenty days." Kōmyō thought this was so sad.

---

26. Hōin 法印 is a title equivalent to *sōjō* 僧正, abbot. Kōmyō 隆明 (1019–1044), a high-ranking monk of the Tendai Sect, was a son of Fujiwara Takaie 藤原隆家 (979–1140) and has a poem included in the *Zoku gosen wakashū* 続後撰和歌集. He was also called Mimuroto Sōjō 三室戸僧正, Abbot of Mimuroto, since he added many buildings to Mimuroto Temple in Uji, Kyoto. The temple was originally a *mimuro*, or honorable chamber, belonging to Emperor Kōnin (r. 770–781) and was used as a detached palace for the three emperors Kōnin, Hanayama, and Shirakawa.

27. Present-day Hyōgo prefecture (Nanbuakashi-shi).

28. Unidentified. Monk Hōnichi's poems appear in the *Hosshinshū* (6-9) and the *Jukkinshō* (10-53).

When people abandon secular life, they usually do not give up all their clothes, so it was most noble and impressive that the monk had given up everything he owned in this world.

This holy man, Hōnichi, always behaved strangely. At one time, he stood under the Kiyomizu waterfall and washed his private parts, catching water in a *gōshi* container. At another time, he was very quiet while he pondered deep thoughts and appeared quite different and distinguished. His inner life must have been clear and purified, but he deliberately made his outward appearance strange and his conduct odd. Was it because he did not want people to discern his inner life?

When the Regent[29] passed away, the holy man confined himself to Hōkōin Temple[30] and composed a poem when he heard plovers crying at dawn:

Akenu nari
Kamo no kawarani
Chidori naku
Kyō mo hakanaku
Kuremu tozo suru

At dawn
Plovers are crying
On the Kamo River's banks,
And this day as well
Is passing in vain.

The poem is included in the *Shūishū* collection.[31] The holy man must have assumed that from the very moment of dawn the day would pass in vain. The poem is listed under the name of Hōin Enshō in the anthology, but it must have been composed by Monk Hōnichi.

---

29. Fujiwara Michitaka 藤原道隆 (953–995), a grandfather of Kōmyō, became a regent after his father, Kaneie 兼家, died.
30. Hōkōin 法興院 was a villa belonging to Kaneie and was located to the east of Kyōgoku Avenue.
31. See the *Goshūishū* (*Goshūi wakashū*) 後拾遺和歌集 (17, Miscellaneous 3) and the *Hosshinshū* (6-9).

3-7 Holy Man Sensai Gives Robes to a Woman

Holy Man Sensai[32] lived in Ungoji Temple in the eastern part of the capital. Greatly learned and devoted to the Way, he had renounced secular life and earnestly engaged in ascetic practices for his future salvation. In the winter, when Sensai was living at Lord Kyōgoku's palace[33] at Awataguchi in the capital, a strange woman came and said to him, "It's very cold. Please give me something to wear." Feeling sorry for her, Sensai took off his robe and gave it to her. The following day, the woman came again, saying, "I lost the robe you gave me yesterday. I would like to have another." Sensai immediately gave her another one. On the third day, the woman, wearing only a straw sheet, appeared again and asked him again for a robe.

Puzzled, Sensai said to her, "I've given you two robes, but no more. I can't help you any longer." The woman became angry and retorted, "You are very narrow-minded. I will not accept any alms from a narrow-minded man!" She then threw the two robes back at him and disappeared. Believing she was an incarnation of a buddha or a bodhisattva who had come to test his heart, Sensai repented and lamented his narrow-mindedness. This is an extraordinary story that will surely touch people's hearts.

Many stories of incarnated buddhas and bodhisattvas appeared in olden times, but there are hardly any in these degenerate days. We are curious to know which buddha or bodhisattva appeared as a woman to Sensai. He himself said that the woman was Bodhisattva Monju,[34] and I wonder whether he observed any signs that led him to this conclusion. It is moving that he felt his pure and clear heart becoming obscured like a clear moon clouding over.

We humans are truly saddened by our unsettled minds and

---

32. Sensai (1062–1127) practiced the Law on Mount Hiei. Excelling in preaching, he contributed to the building of many halls at the Ungoji Temple 雲居寺 while living there.

33. Lord Kyōgoku 京極殿 refers to Fujiwara Morozane 藤原師実 (1042–1101), a grandson of Michinaga. He became prime minister in 1088 and received the tonsure in 1101. Having mansions in the Kyōgoku and Sanjō areas, he was called Lord Kyōgoku and Lord Sanjō. Sensai was possibly practicing the Law with Morozane's help since he lived at one of his mansions.

34. Monju Shiri 文殊師利, a bodhisattva representing wisdom. The *Ujishūi monogatari* (14-1) narrates how Monju appears as a woman.

hearts. Instead of retiring to grass huts deep in the mountains, we pass our days and months like playful children in small boats, sailing in the waves until old age and death: We are eventually crushed against rocks near the shore only to return to the sea of suffering in life and death. Ignoring the teachings and forgetting to clear the moon in our hearts, we fall into the darkness of delusions. Our sadness is truly indescribable.

3-8 Monk Shōjiki Served Others

Did I hear correctly that this happened in Mino province?[35] There was a strange monk who went around a village in that province, employed as a servant. As he was honest and sincere, many villagers competed for his services. But the monk would stay in one place for only a few days and never any longer. Some villagers called him Shōjikibō (Honest Monk), while others called him Jikishinbō (Sincere Monk). He stayed in the village for about five years and then suddenly disappeared.

The villagers thought this was strange and searched for him everywhere, and finally they found him dead at the foot of a mountain. He was sitting upright facing west with his hands joined together as if in prayer. There was a tree nearby bearing an inscription written on its trunk in beautiful calligraphy: "I attained enlightenment on the fifteenth day of the second month of Hōen 2 (1136) in spite of my mind being impure in every respect."[36]

Feeling very sad and moved, the villagers faithfully commissioned the monk's portrait, showing him with long hair and wearing an unlined kimono and a *hinoki* woven hat. When I heard of this portrait, I could not suppress my tears.

What kind of noble monk was he, serving others to hide his virtue as he practiced the Way? I truly miss the old days of Hōen [when the monk was alive]. It was truly noble of him to deliberately limit his stay in any one place to a short time. I wonder if he stayed only in Mino. He must have traveled to other provinces where he also worked as a servant. I am deeply moved when I think that he passed away when his

---

35. South of Gifu prefecture.
36. The inscription suggests the monk's modesty as he implies that he was not as virtuous as people thought.

karmic ties to this world were exhausted. I feel sorry for him, trying so hard to hide his virtue and eventually having it discovered. His heart and mind must have been extremely pure. He also must have been very humble because he described himself in the inscription as having an impure mind. I find this very interesting.

When I heard the honest monk's story, I was so moved that I immediately left for Mino to see his portrait. But unfortunately I fell ill when I reached Hosokawa in Bizen province and returned to Kibitsumiya,[37] too unwell to continue traveling. Since then, my interest has decreased and I haven't visited him yet, for I thought that the portrait would remain there for a while. But sometimes I feel regretful that my karmic relationship with the monk is not as strong as I had thought.

On hearing an evening bell ringing out from a mountain temple, my heart becomes pure and my eyes tearful. I hope that my weak dedication to the Way will not decrease when I hear the bell tolling daybreak. I still envy those who have left secular life as the autumn wind blows, and I still believe that the virtue of karmic relations is not futile after all.[38] With a completely pure heart, how can anyone be disturbed on seeing old friends? The honest monk's heart would have become even more purified.

Although a humble servant in this life, the monk of Mino may be now associating with holy people in Paradise.[39] Or I wonder if he was reborn in Tosotsu Heaven,[40] above the clouds in a distant sky. Or is he among those who are listening to the holy scriptures of great mercy on the south shore of Fudaraku?[41]

That only his portrait remains in this life, an expression of those past times, is particularly moving.

---

37. Kibitsumiya could have been the Kibitsu Shrine 吉備津神社 in the present-day city of Okayama. Bizen province was located southeast of Okayama prefecture.

38. The karmic relation here has an unexpected power as the author's knowing the monk's story and wishing to see his portrait would deepen his dedication to the Way.

39. An'yōkai 安養界, Gokurakujōdo 極楽浄土, Amida Buddha's Pure Land.

40. Bodhisattva Miroku 弥勒 resides in the Inner Palace (*naiin* 内院) of Tosotsu Heaven 都卒天 while other heavenly beings exist in the Outer Palace (*ge'in* 外院).

41. Kannon 観音, the most merciful bodhisattva, lives in Fudaraku 補陀落, located south of the Indian Ocean.

3-9 A Poor Man Renounces Secular Life

Some time ago while on my way to Kii province,[42] I came to a shabby hut at the foot of Mount Kazuraki.[43] It was so small that even one person could barely live in it; the hut had been built in a place to avoid strong winds and had a commanding view. I saw no one inside it. I was deeply moved by the thought that the person who had lived there had left and was no longer attached to the place. But while I rested by the hut, I saw a man of fifty or sixty years of age. On that cold day he was wearing a sleeveless one-layer kimono as he climbed up and down the mountain collecting something. Soon he entered the hut and fell asleep.

After a while, I asked him many questions. He replied, "While living in the secular world, I was very poor. When I had a job, I was deeply attached to greed and spent days thinking only of success in my work, but eventually I failed. When some people insulted me, I thought of killing them then myself. But then I became sad as I reflected that being attached to fame [and wealth] in this temporary life is not worth the cost of losing my future life. So I compensated for my loss with my house, left my wife and children, and here I am. I abandoned my former life because of hardship. But I am happy now because my failure led me to the Way. I have wanted to cut my hair, but with no one to help me, I think that my appearance doesn't matter as long as my inner life is pure. Thus I have spent seven years at this place." I was so moved by his story that tearfully I almost fell at his feet, saying, "I would like to help you cut your hair."

"That would be fine," he said, and so I cut his hair.

His is a most extraordinary story. People are usually unaware of their faults and become so angry at other people's criticism that they eventually hurt or destroy them. But this man realized the futility of seeking fame in this temporary life. He compensated for his loss, left his loving wife and children, lived in a remote place with no visitors, and slept under the white clouds while reciting only Amida's name in the morning and evening. Truly the Buddha must have admired him!

....

42. Present-day Wakayama prefecture.

43. A 960-meter-high mountain located between Nara prefecture and Osaka. Another Mount Kazuraki is on the border between Izumi (Osaka) and Wakayama. These two mountains were regarded as connected to each other and often appear in anthologies.

The place where this recluse was living appeared most serene and peaceful. It was around the tenth day of the tenth month when I visited him. The hut had no trees around it, and so whether it was a cloudy or bright night, the moonlight shone most beautifully with nothing to obstruct it. Wind blowing through the trees on the mountain weakened by the time it reached the pampas grass in the withered field, turning into a soft breeze. As if tiring of this mundane world, it blew to scatter the red leaves, which looked as if they had been dyed in a dew of crimson tears. Such a sight was most appealing as it reminded me of the futility of this life.

When I recall the wise men of the past like Gijōsanzō,[44] who once said, "Choose a place to purify your mind," and Zen Master Chirō,[45] who taught, "Your heart will be purified by a place," I become deeply moved.

---

44. Yi-jing 義浄 (637–713) was a Tang monk who went to India and brought back and translated many Buddhist sutras, including the *Kegonkyō*.

45. Gijōsanzō 知朗禅師 was a descendant of Emperor Montoku (r. 850–858). He received the tonsure and held a sutra recital in 954.

4-1 Sanechika Abandons Secular Life after His Mother's Death

Some time ago, there was a skillful archer in Sagami province named Taira Saburō Sanechika of Toi.[1] After his father died, his mother raised him. Strong and brave by nature, he was always traveling around and earning merit on the battlefield.

But when he was thirty-three years old, his mother passed away. As he had no siblings, he inherited everything from his parents. Left alone, Sanechika greatly lamented his mother's passing. Finally, he received the tonsure and faithfully attended Buddhist services every seven days after his mother's death.

Fifty days passed and his grief increased. He built a five-span square worship hall with the wood of the evergreen cypress, and there he respectfully placed the three Buddhist statues.[2] He also gave up all the land he had inherited to pay for the expense of offering the *Hokke sanmai* service.[3] Finally, wearing a black hemp robe, he began to wander here and there and no one knew his whereabouts. When I heard his story, I was very moved.

Affection between parents and children is often so deep that they lament their departure from this transient life. Some people eventually manage to overcome their grief after some time, while others faithfully hold services for the deceased and continue to grieve. It was very noble of Sanechika to honor his parents so deeply, to build a worship hall with Buddhist images, and to dedicate all his inheritance to pay for the *Hokke sanmai* service. He finally abandoned this life and disappeared.

A mother's affection is so profound that even a buddha cannot explain it, even though it endures for as long as one *kalpa*.[4] How can an ignorant person fathom the depth of his mother's merciful affection? Conceived in her body, he burdens her for ten [nine] months, drinks 180 *koku*[5] of her milk, all the while poking her breasts morning and night

---

1. Toi is in present-day Kanagawa prefecture (Ashigarashimo-gun, Yugawara-chō).
2. The three Buddhist images 三尊 are Amida Buddha 阿弥陀仏 flanked by the bodhisattvas Kannon and Seishi 勢至.
3. *Hokke sanmai* 法華三昧 is the service to help acquire enlightenment of the Middle Way by reciting the Lotus and *Kanfugenkyō* sutras.
4. *Kalpa*, or *kō* 劫, is a long period of time in Buddhist cosmology.
5. One *koku* 石 equals 180 liters.

and playing on her lap as he enjoys her perpetual smile. Thus, whether or not in hardship, he will be raised amid her deep affection. How can he understand and measure the obligation he owes to his mother?

We may try to reward our parents by being filial to them, but often we spend time only thinking about this, not practicing it. We even neglect our parents while they are alive and grieve for them only during the short mourning period. Sanechika, however, understood everything, abandoned secular life, left his native place, and wandered away. That was indeed noble. If intelligent and reasonable people have difficulty practicing filial piety, how could a crude man of the eastern provinces cultivate such a gentle heart? Perhaps his filial feelings were deeper and stronger than usual. I really wonder into which Pure Land Sanechika was reborn.

4-2 Sōjō Ryōen

Chūjō Yorizane of Shiga received the tonsure and was called Sōjō Ryōen[6] of Imahashi.

One day in the ninth month when Lord Fuke[7] was living at Hosshōji Temple,[8] someone found in front of the temple a dear little baby wrapped in a reddish pink robe on which was written:

Mini masaru
Mono nakarikeri
Midoriko ha
Yaran katanaku
Kanashi keredomo

Nothing counts
More than self[9]
But alas,

---

6. Yorizane 頼実 and Ryōen 良縁 are unidentified.
7. Fujiwara Tadazane (1078–1162), a son of Moromichi, was a regent and also called Lord Fuke 富家殿 and Chisokuin; see *Senjūshō* 6-6.
8. Hosshōji 法性寺 Temple was on the site of the present Tōfukuji Temple in eastern Kyoto. There is no evidence that Lord Fuke lived in the temple, but both his father and his son, Tadamichi, lived there.
9. The poem appears in the *Kin'yō wakashū* (10, *Zatsu* 2, 622) by an unknown poet.

Leaving a baby is
Helplessly sad.

    Hearing this, the lord was deeply touched and declared, "Whoever it is, the parent must return here someday. Then I will take care of him as well as this baby." So he raised the baby, who [was called Yorizane and] eventually became a lieutenant general.

    Yorizane lived in a mountain village in Shiga. One evening, he had a visitor, a very poor and shabby monk who appeared to have recently taken the tonsure: His head looked freshly shaven. Yorizane asked him, "Who are you and why have you received the tonsure?"

    The monk replied, "I have something to tell you, but the details are in this letter." With this, he gave him the letter and left.

    Yorizane thought this was strange and opened the letter. It read: "Please excuse my telling you that I am your father. You were born healthy, but I was too poor to raise you. Hoping that someone would look after you, I left you [by the temple gate]. Now I am most pleased to see you have grown up to be a fine man. If I had kept you for sentimental reasons, you would not be as fortunate as you are now. My wife and I survived those difficult times, but she sadly passed away twenty days ago. Since then, I have abandoned secular life and have been wandering and praying for her afterlife. I have come to tell you to pray for your mother's repose."

    After reading the letter, Yorizane was greatly surprised and saddened as he thought of his father wandering as an ascetic while praying for his mother's afterlife. Without telling his wife and children, Yorizane himself immediately began a journey, wandering until daybreak before finally arriving north of Senkawa[10] on the border between Yamashiro and Yamato provinces. Someone composed a poem [about the place]: "Mount Kase, please lend me a robe as the wind over the river is so cold." On the river banks, he cut his hair and threw it into

---

10. Senkawa 泉川, the Kizu River 木津川, runs through the southern part of Kyoto prefecture. Mount Kase, a hill located between Kamo-chō and Kitsu-chō in Sagara-gun, Kyoto-fu, is a homonym of *kasu*, "to lend." The poem appears in the *Kokin wakashū* (9, *tabiuta*, 408) by an unknown poet.

the water. He went to visit Vinaya Master Senkaku[11] in Tōhokuin Hall of Kōfukuji Temple and received the tonsure with a Buddhist name [Ryōen]. He traveled to various places, praying for his parents in the afterlife and preaching many miraculous revelations of the Law. He finally became an abbot on account of his merit.

Such events touch the heart of even an ignorant man like myself. Usually a person remains in secular life and tries to pray for his parents' souls, but Ryōen abandoned his future, which had been as flourishing as wisteria.[12] With no hesitation, he put on a monk's black robe and traveled as an ascetic while his sleeves brushed off the dew on the narrow paths. How could the buddhas of the three generations of past, present, and future ignore such a noble heart?

Moreover, Yorizane's father's gentle and deep feelings toward his son are unheard of. Some other father in the same situation might have come [often] and told him, "I am your father" or boastfully told others about his successful son. But his father would not see his son for many years until after his mother's death, and then left a letter for him to pray for her. When I think of the father's feelings, I am doubly touched. He could not have been a lowly man. His poem appears in the *Shika wakashū*, which lists its composer as unknown.[13] Whenever I open this poetry collection and read the poem, I am overwhelmed with tears for no reason.

This life is truly sad. To what can we compare it? According to some poems, "Life is like the white wake of a rowing boat"[14] or "Life is like lightning illuminating for a second an autumn rice field."[15] Everything in this life is transient and futile.

Writing the poem "Nothing counts more than self" and abandoning a child may sound [selfish] and foolish, but after I quietly reflect, I

---

11. Senkaku 千覚 (1101–?), a son of Fujiwara Morizane 藤原盛実, was a monk of the Kōfukuji Temple (in Nara, closely related to the Fujiwara clan) and became *gon-no-risshi*, assistant vinaya master, in 1153.

12. He was related to the highly prosperous Fujiwara 藤原 (wisteria field) clan.

13. The poem does not appear in the *Shika wakashū* 白河集 but in the *Kin'yō wakashū* 金葉和歌集.

14. This well-known poem is in the *Man'yōshū* (3, 354) and appears in the *Shūi wakashū* (20, *Aishō*, 1327) and the *Wakan rōeishū* 和漢朗詠集 (*Maki* 2, 795).

15. The poem appears in the *Goshūi wakashū* (17, *Zatsu*, 1013). A similar expression appears in *Senjūshō* 1-6.

must conclude that Ryōen's father had a clear mind because he did not visit his successful son [until after the death of his wife].[16]

4-3 How Saidō Received the Tonsure

Some time ago I passed by Cape Yura in Kii province[17] and saw a man of forty or fifty years of age bitterly crying in a fishing boat near the beach. Wondering why he was weeping so sadly, I waded to the boat and asked him, "What happened and why are you so sad?"

The man tearfully explained, "I am a fisherman and have just caught a large turtle here. When I tried to kill it, the turtle appeared so sad that it shed tears of blood from its eyes. I felt so sorry for it that I decided to release it back into the water. But then my companion pierced its eyes with a hook, and the poor turtle writhed around and around in its suffering. The sight made me unbearably sad."

As soon as the fisherman finished speaking, he jumped out of the boat, ran up to the beach, and then asked me, "Please help me to receive the tonsure." I hesitated for a moment, but he was so determined that I finally cut his hair.

After that, I took him to Mount Kōya, [then] to Kokawa Temple,[18] and finally to the capital where we visited Holy Man Saisen.[19] After I explained how the fisherman received the tonsure, he was very impressed and told me, "That was truly a moving story. I also was once a fisherman and we have shared the same experiences in different places in the south and the west. So it's all right. Please have him stay here." So the fisherman stayed with the holy man. He earnestly practiced the Way and has now become a fervent Buddhist called Saidō.

Saidō must have engaged in fishing until his old age without feeling any pity or guilt when killing or taking life. I wonder what kind of turtle came to help him so that he would turn to the Way. It must have been truly an unbearable experience for him to see the turtle shedding tears of blood. How many people would renounce secular

---

16. This last passage reflects the Buddhist idea of non-attachment.
17. Cape Yura is west of present-day Wakayama prefecture.
18. Mount Kōya 高野山 refers to Kongōbuji 金剛峰寺, the headquarters of the Shingon Sect to the east of present-day Wakayama prefecture. Kokawadera Temple 粉川寺 is in the central northern part of the prefecture.
19. Unidentified.

life on account of such a sad experience? This was a most extraordinary case. Hoping that the fisherman might perhaps renounce the world, a buddha or a bodhisattva may have changed himself into the turtle. When I think of that, tears overwhelm me for no particular reason.

The proverb "Those who fall on account of earth will rise because of earth"[20] is indeed true. It is remarkable that this man, who had fallen into the suffering cycle of life and death because of his being a fisherman, successfully delivered himself from the suffering of life and death precisely because he was a fisherman. So what makes us fall and what makes us rise? Alas, I wish I knew.

All living beings naturally cherish life. Unfortunately, owing to their bad karma, some are born as birds and animals. And since they do not speak human language, we are ignorant of their thoughts and kill them so that we may survive. This is truly foolish and pitiful. Killing for food is sinful since birds and animals are truly as alive as we are.

It is sad to spend our fleeting time accumulating sinful deeds by

---

20. That is, a bad karma becomes a good one; this story provides an excellent example of this. The expression popularly appears in various Buddhist writings; see *Hokke monguki* 法華文句記 10 (*Daizōkyō*, 34, p. 349).

killing and eating animals. It is also futile to consume so much food. Sharihotsu[21] said, "You should take only one or two mouthfuls of food," while Bodhisattva Nāgārjuna[22] carefully warned us, "Eat little and perspire more [because of work]." The Buddha also instructed us, "Think of the hundred hard labors undertaken to produce just one grain." How much rice produced by such strenuous work do we eat every day? And even if we prolong our life by eating such precious rice, how many more of the sacred teachings can we read throughout our lives? As I reflect on these things, I feel very regretful.

4-4 How Han'en Was Separated from His Wife

Some time ago, Holy Man Han'en lived at Yokotake in Tsukushi.[23] Blessed with intelligence and experience, he was benevolent to all living beings and devoted to the merciful teachings of Bodhisattva Kannon. Before receiving the tonsure, he was called Middle Councilor Yoshida Tsunemitsu.[24]

When he was appointed director of the Dazaifu Police Headquarters in Tsukushi province in the south, he took with him his loving wife from the capital. But for some reason or other, he became attracted to another woman and began to neglect his wife; the feeling reminded her of a cool autumn wind passing through thin sleeves. Finally, Tsunemitsu's coldness toward her caused her to fall ill. She wanted to return to the capital but had no way to cross the sea and mountains. In time, her illness grew worse and she finally sent her husband this poem:

---

21. Sharihotsu 舎利仏, or Śariputra, one of the ten disciples of the Shakamuni Buddha (see *Konjaku monogatari*, 1-9).

22. Ryōjubosatsu 龍樹菩薩 Nāgārjuna (150–250?), a Brahman of south India, was a scholar of Mahāyāna Buddhism. For the quotation, see *Daichidoron* 大知度論 68 (*Daizōkyō* 大蔵経, 25, p. 538); for his deep knowledge, see *Konjaku monogatari*, 4-25, and *Ujishūi monogatari*, no. 138.

23. Han'en 範円, a seventh grandson of Fujiwara Michitaka 藤原道隆 (1155–?), a high-ranking monk of Kōfukuji Temple, is not identified with the protagonist of this story, Yoshida Tsunemitsu. He could be Fujiwara Tsunemitsu (1241–1274) or Fujiwara Sadataka, also called Tsunemitsu, who became middle councilor in 1220 and died in 1238 at the age of forty-eight or forty-nine. Yokotake is in Fukuoka prefecture (Tsukushi-gun).

24. Unidentified.

Toe kashina
Okidokoro naki
Tsuyuno mi ha
Shibashi mo koto no
Ha ni ya kakuru to[25]

Oh, visit me once more,
The fragile dew
Finds no place to hide
Even for a while
But on the leaf of your words.

After reading the poem, Tsunemitsu felt great pity as he remembered their early life together. A messenger then brought him some news: His wife had passed away. As if dreaming, he immediately cut his hair, left his life, and began to practice the Way at Yokotake with a pure heart.

He heard the chirping insects in the roots of the thick grass blown by the wild wind in the field in front of his place. Strong gusts passing through pine branches from the mountain behind sounded like loud *koto* music. He saw the expanse of the sea on his right while faintly hearing the waves pounding against the soaring cliff on his left. This was the place where he built a small hut with a *tsuki-no-wa*, a moon-viewing hole, carved out of the left side of the plank wall. Thin smoke [from incense] wafted out of the hole and created a purple cloud in the sky.[26] Wishing and waiting for Amida Buddha and his attendants to come and receive him in his last moments, he quietly chanted Amida's name. Finally, some time in the Tenshō era (1131–1132), he passed away [as he had wished]. This is indeed impressive and noble.

His wife had been the daughter of a certain prince. Owing to a karmic relationship, she [married Tsunemitsu and] was taken to Tsukushi. Her husband dearly loved her, so how could he have deserted her? Was it due to a deeply hidden karma that eventually caused him to renounce

---

25. *Kotonoha* ことの葉, "language" or "words," includes *ha* 葉 (leaf) on which dew rests; the fragile dew refers to the weak protagonist herself. The poem appears in the *Goshūi wakashū* (17, no. 1006).

26. In the last moments of a devotee, Amida Buddha and attendants come riding in on a purple cloud from the west to receive the dying person.

secular life? If so, it touches my heart so much more. Her poem must have been included anonymously in the *Shikashū*[27] to avoid embarrassing her.

Thinking about her reminds me of the futility of life. Born as noble and as pure as the clear upper stream of the Isuzu River,[28] the princess, with a beautiful crown on her lustrous black hair, could have been admired as an imperial consort at court. Instead, she followed the middle councilor and went to a distant, rural place. After leaving the brilliant capital, she must have wet her sleeves with tears as she spent days traveling on a boat. In spite of deep feelings for her husband, he eventually deserted her and she was treated coldly, pierced as if by an autumn wind. While constantly shedding tears and feeling as fragile as the dew, she sent her husband a poem begging him to visit her, as she had no place to stay, and she finally passed away. How sad and pitiful her life was.

I wonder if the wife was fated to lead a short life. How could she foresee that, despite her noble birth, she would marry a middle councilor? Did she ever imagine herself eventually perishing among the wild grasses in a distant countryside? Rise and fall are constantly repeated in this transient life, and living in a palace or a straw hut will not last forever, but her life was truly pathetic. When she composed the lines "Finds no place to hide," did she know that she would soon perish? Although we know our breathing can stop at any moment, how can we explain her sudden departure? Everything in this life is truly futile.

Oh, how I wish I could have a detached mind with no thought of myself—only the feeling of mutability deeply imbedded in my heart! Then I would feel the transience of life in the four seasons—in the blowing wind, in the blooming and scattering of plum blossoms in the south and north branches [of a river],[29] in the short reed sprouts bursting forth in the fields after the ice melts, in the new willow leaves swaying in the breeze and caressing my hair, and in the old moss cleansed

---

27. See note 3.

28. The Isuzu River in its lower reaches runs through the compound of the Ise Shrine, which enshrines Tenshō Daijin 天昭大神, the Great Heavenly Illustrious Deity, the ancestral deity of the imperial family.

29. A similar expression, the antithesis of the willows of the east and west banks, appears in *Wakan rōeishō* 1:11.

by waves and looking like a damp beard.[30] Thus at the change of every season, I would be deeply moved by the transience of life.

Now the Hour of the Sheep has already passed and the Hour of the Monkey[31] has begun. How foolish am I, ignorant of death as it approaches moment by moment!

4-5 Lord Akimoto

Middle Councilor Akimoto[32] once served Emperor Go-Reizei. Greatly favored by the emperor, Akimoto was promoted over many other officials and advanced to Second Rank. In spite of this, he always aspired to retire to a forest and renounce the secular world, but he did not have a chance to do so. Finally, after the emperor passed away, Akimoto went to Mount Hiei, shaved his head, received the tonsure, and began to practice the Way in Ōhara.[33]

While serving at court, he used to say tearfully, "Oh, how I wish I could be a sinless man and gaze at the moon in a remote place."[34] Or he would ask himself, "Whose grave is this? I see no name on it but only the spring grass profusely growing around it."

While successfully practicing the Way, Akimoto became known for his learning and virtues. One day, Lord Uji[35] wanted to form a relationship with him, and so he went to Akimoto's hut in Ōhara and spent the night with him. During the visit, Akimoto spoke only about the future and ignored present affairs. When the lord was about to

---

30. This expression also appears in *Wakan rōeishū* 13 and *Jukkinshō* 10-6.
31. The Hour of the Sheep is 2 p.m.; the Hour of the Monkey, 4 p.m.
32. Akimoto 顕基 (1000–1047) was an adopted son of Regent Fujiwara Yorimichi and served Emperor Go-Ichijō; he received the tonsure in 1036 after the emperor died. His Buddhist name was Enshō. For a biographical study, see Fujiwara Hidetaka, "Akimoto chūnagon shukke setsuwa o megutte," in *Setsuwa bungaku kenkyū*, no. 8.
33. Many ascetics built their huts in Ōhara in Kyoto, in present-day Sakyo-ku. Akimoto's retiring to Ōhara is mentioned in the *Kojidan* (1-47), the *Hosshinshū* (5-8), and the *Jukkinshō* (6-11).
34. *Haisho* 配所, or officially designated remote places, were distant locations far from the capital; exiles were sent there on account of their crimes or offenses.
35. Fujiwara Yorimichi (992–1074) served the emperors Go-Ichijō, Go-Suzaku, and Go-Reizei as regent. He was called Lord Uji 宇治殿 since he lived in a villa in Uji, which he inherited from his father, Michinaga 道長; later he built Byōdōin 平等院 Temple on the site of the villa. Lord Uji appears in other *Senjūshō* tales (6-2, 8-34).

leave at dawn, Akimoto came out of his hut to see him off and said to him alone, "My son, Toshizane,[36] is still immature." He must have meant to ask the lord to look after him, for even after renouncing the world, Akimoto could not abandon his concern for his son. It is said that Lord Uji looked after Toshizane, and he advanced to the rank of grand councilor with an *azechi* position.[37]

Meanwhile, Akimoto continued to enjoy a quiet life in his grass hut and successfully attained the Way. When reading his story in *Yūshinshū*,[38] I could not suppress my tears as I thought of his pure heart when he received the tonsure. It was most noble of him to retire to Ōhara to practice the Way in accordance with the worldly saying, "A faithful retainer will not serve two lords."

Ōhara was a serene place. The faint sound of firewood being cut

---

36. Although similar tales in the *Kojidan*, the *Kokochomonjū*, and the *Jukkinshō* mention Toshizane as Akimoto's son, the *Sonpibunmyaku* 尊卑分脈 lists him as a grandson of Akimoto's younger brother, Takakuni. Toshizane 俊実 died in 1119 at the age of seventy-four; his poems appear in imperial anthologies such as the *Kin'yō wakashū*.

37. This is a supervisor of local officials. Toshizane appears in the *Sonpibunmyaku* as Grand Councilor of the Second Rank with the title *azechi* 按察; see Totani Mizue, "Akimoto no setsuwa no *Tsurezuregusa*," in *Gakuen* (Shōwa Joshidaigaku, February 1974).

38. *Yūshinshū* 遊心集 is unidentified. The title of this work appears in other *Senjūshō* tales (1-8, 2-1, 9-6) and also in the *Kankyonotomo* (1-10).

echoed through the surrounding mountains, and the cries of the cuckoos on the summits were heard all day long. Among the autumn grasses and vines grown so high that they hid the gateway to his hut, Akimoto must have heard the insects chirping near his pillow. It was in a place such as this that he purified his mind and heart.

By all means, a man should seek a place he likes. Isn't it true that his heart depends entirely on the place in which he settles? When I hear of holy Indian places, such as Chikurin Shōja, Bardaiji Temple, and the rivers Batsudai and Niren,[39] I wish I could live in such purified surroundings. As I learn more about peaceful places such as Eonji Temple of Rozan and Mount Shūnan in Kōshu province[40] in China, I regret that I do not live in such places. Ōhara, Ono village, and the deep mountains of Yoshino[41] are the ideal locations in which to live [in Japan].

It was most noble of Akimoto to wish to be free of sin and watch the moon in a remote place. As he recalled the fifteenth year of Genwa[42] in olden times [when Bó Jū-i was exiled], he must have been greatly moved. When he saw old graves without any names, only grass growing around them and wooden stupa markers decaying and leaning over, he must have felt most sad. The names on the graves and their markers must have remained for a while, but eventually the markers would have burned down, disappearing into the sky as smoke, then reduced to earth as they lay buried. Akimoto must have felt wretched when he saw all of these things, and I also shed tears as I think of him.

The pampas grasses growing in inner Ōhara are as thin as threads. The autumn dew clinging to their tips appears most fragile as the grasses sway and bend.

....

39. Shaka Buddha is associated with these Indian places, including the Nairañjanā River (a tributary of the Ganges), where he cleansed his body and was enlightened under the bodhi tree by the river bank, and the Kakuṭṭa River, where he took his last bath. The Chikurin Temple, Bamboo Grove Monastery, located to the north of Rājagṛha, the capital of Magadha, was the first Buddhist temple built by King Bimbisāra.

40. Lu-shan 廬山 in Jian-xi province is famous for its scenic beauty and its Buddhist activities since the Eastern Jin period (317–420). The Hui-yuan Temple 惠遠寺, the first temple of the Chinese Pure Land Sect, was built in 384 by Master Hui-yuan. Mount Zhong-nan 終南山 in Xia-xi sheng is as renowned for its scenery as Mount Lu-shan.

41. Ono village is present-day Yase in the north of Kyoto; Ōhara is located to the north of the village. Mount Yoshino refers to the mountains in Nara prefecture.

42. The year (820) suggests the time soon after the exile in 815 of the Chinese poet Bó Jū-i (Hakkyoi 白居居 or Hakurakuten 白楽天) to Jian province. *Haisho*, "an isolated place," suggests the remote place where the Chinese poet was exiled.

4-6 Monk Kyōen

I once traveled to the Koshikata region[43] in the north. While I was crossing the Funasaka River[44] by boat, I saw on board an elegant-looking monk, younger than twenty years old. Under the cold sky, he was wearing only a thin robe over a white *katabira* kimono.[45] He appeared very quiet and reticent as if wishing to avoid any attention. I felt both pity and curiosity toward him, but hesitated to ask him any questions.

The boatman had stopped using his oars and began to let the boat float down the river. I casually recited the opening of a poem:[46]

Minarezao
Toradezo kudasu
Takasegawa[47]

Using no oars
He let the boat float down
The Takase River

The young monk finished the poem with:

Tsuki no hikari no
Sasuni makasete

Under the shining
Light of the moon.

I was most moved and asked him, "You look so young. Where are you traveling all by yourself and why?"

The monk replied, "I have no particular destination. I am Minister

---

43. The region included present-day Ishikawa, Fukui, Toyama, and Niigata prefectures.
44. Unidentified.
45. 帷; cotton or hemp one-layered kimonos were worn in summer.
46. The poem appears in the *Goshūi wakashū* (book 15, no. 835).
47. The word is *Takasebune*, or "Takase boat," in the original poem.

Tokugyō Kyōen[48] and live at Tōdaiji Temple in the capital, Nara." After that, he did not speak a word. He got out of the boat and began walking north. Wondering why such a young monk had left Tōdaiji, I became curious and visited the temple the following year.

I asked Hōkyō Shun'e[49] about the young monk, telling him, "I met him and have been wondering what has happened to him."

"Yes, he lived here. So, you met him," replied Shun'e, lowering his head in tears. After a while, he wiped them away and continued, "He was called Minister Tokugyō Kyōen and was a son of Minister Kuga. He was a disciple of the director of Tōnan'in, the living quarters.[50] Although young, he was blessed with talent and had a bright future, as he excelled in both Buddhist and non-Buddhist writings. But three years ago at dawn in the tenth month, he suddenly disappeared, leaving behind a poem:

Kono yo o ba
Omoi hanaren to
Bakari ni
Omoeba kane no
Uchi sasofu nari

As I am thinking
Of renouncing the world,
I hear the bell
Tolling and calling me
To abandon this life.

"The poem was written on the paper door of his room. Since then, we have not seen him. We miss him, saying to each other, 'So he has left us, called by the tolling bell.'" As Shun'e finished his story, I felt unbearably sad.

---

48. *Tokugyō* 得業 is a priestly rank. Minister Kyōen 慶円 may refer to someone related to a certain minister, but Kyōen is unidentified.
49. *Hōkyō*, or *hokkyō* 法橋, is a high priestly rank next to *hōgan* 法眼. Shun'e 俊恵 (1113-1192), a son of poet Minamoto Toshiyori 源俊頼, taught poetry to Kamo Chōmei 鴨長明. He also appears in another *Senjūshō* tale (5-14).
50. Tōnan'in 東南院 was located east of the Nandaimon 南大門, South Great Gate, of Tōdaiji Temple.

I feel so moved when I think of Kyōen, who left the temple with such firm conviction. He was as young as a *kuretake* bamboo with leaves still growing at the second joint.[51] Even some of us who are old enough to consider various matters find it difficult to renounce the world, although we may wish to do so. People feel uneasy about their future if they abandon their accustomed lifestyle. Thus they vainly spend months and years without coming to any decision. This is the usual way with people.

Called by the tolling bell, Kyōen felt a strong desire to renounce the world, and so he left the temple to seek the Way in the Godless Month[52] during a violent storm with rainy winds and threatening clouds. He did not rest at any travelers' huts and headed directly north. He lay down with grass as his pillow in withered fields. Although he had abandoned the world, I was overwhelmed by compassion for him when I thought of his hard life. He surely must have had an extraordinarily strong conviction in the Way. Thanks to the Five Commandments and the Ten Good Deeds,[53] which he had observed during his secular life, he must have been unaffected by the cold autumn[54] wind, frost, snow, and storms.

As I quietly ponder this, I see how futile it is to cling to life. After my life ends, my body will decay or change into smoke ascending to the sky from the graveyard at Toribe or Funaoka. If my body lies buried in a field, it will turn into a handful of clay or be eaten by beasts like wolves while my heart and mind will be overcome by the demon called transience.

Our bodies are merely places or containers in which we rest our hearts for only a short while. Why should we care for such containers? Our minds and hearts will transmigrate from one form to another in the Six Realms. If born as birds, we cherish our appearance as birds.

---

51. The *kuretake* 呉竹 bamboo has many joints. Hence, the leaves growing here on only "the second joint" suggest youth.
52. *Kannazuki*, or "godless moon," refers to the tenth month.
53. A Buddhist avoids the five deeds of killing, stealing, lewdness, false words, and drinking. The ten good deeds are not to kill, not to steal, not to practice lewdness, not to speak falsely or exaggerated words or ill of others, not to be talkative, and not to have avarice, anger, or evil views.
54. Here *aki*, "autumn," suggests *aki*, or *akiru*, "boredom" or "to become tired of," suggesting that the young monk became tired of the secular world.

But if born as human beings, we admire our reflections in mirrors; this is due only to our false thinking. After we die, we suffer in the morning and in the evening as we endlessly repeat the cycle of birth and death in the Evil Realms.

I have often wanted to abandon this life, but, alas, the clouds of my delusion are so thick that they overcome my desire for the Way. My conviction used to be as clear as the bright moon, but these clouds make it most difficult for me to leave this world.

How could Kyōen, born with a bright future and admired by many disciples since youth, abandon his life and disappear at such a young age? And why do I, an old monk, still vainly remain in this life? This indeed is most regrettable.

4-7 Abbot Myōun's Hut in Awaji Province

Long ago when I was traveling through Awaji province, I heard of Fujino Beach, which faces a long expanse of sea in the south and a steep mountain in the north. It is a difficult place to reach, and hardly any travelers go there as they must row close to shore, paying careful attention to the tides.

But I was drawn by the name Fujino (wisteria field) and sought it out until I finally came to a dilapidated hut on the beach. Being curious, I looked inside and found a black robe and an inkstone. I also saw some writing on a board: "This is the hut of Senior Abbot Myōun[55] of Enryakuji Temple on Mount Hiei." I was deeply moved as I thought of Myōun living in that hut and I could not suppress my tears.

Because he had left his robe and inkstone, I thought the abbot might return, so I decided to remain for a while. Toward evening, I saw the abbot coming down the mountain holding a branch of cherry blossoms in his hand. He was surprised to see me and asked, "What is the matter? Why are you here? Is there any message from the capital? I left Mount Hiei and have decided to live here like this." I could not answer him but only shed happy tears to see him. We spent the night talking about various matters, confiding in each other, and wringing

---

55. Myōun 明雲 (1115–1183), a grandson of Prime Minister Kuga Masami and the second son of Grand Councilor Minamoto Akimichi, was the fifty-fifth and the fifty-seventh Tendai *zasu*, the senior abbot of the Tendai Sect.

out our tear-soaked sleeves. But I could not stay any longer and tearfully left him in the morning.

It is a great and shameful mistake to assume that a talented man such as Myōun, with important roles both at court and at a temple, did not seriously think of his future until he felt the futility of his present life. In spite of his high-ranking positions, Myōun was full of compassion and devoted to the Way. A gifted person like him thinks of his future as he realizes the transience of life at a lonely beach, in the rising waves and blowing wind. A fool vainly spends his time in false ways, constantly thinking of delusions, which will attach him to the cycle of life and death. It is indeed extremely shameful and foolish.

So quietly consider this. After prosperous people reject this life, their appearance turns shabby. Asuka River, once deep, has become shallow, but it will become deep again.[56] Likewise trees and grass eventually turn into withered fields, mountains crumble, and deep seas grow shallow. In such a changeable world, how can a person with a weak body dare to regard this world as a good place to live?

Your dear wife and children cannot accompany you always and will leave you one day. Even if you live for tens of thousands of years,

---

56. A reference to the constant changes in life.

separation is sad for everyone and we all yearn for life. Why don't we leave the world, which is so full of sadness and suffering? Instead, we just let yesterday and today pass. Why do you think this life will last forever and never wonder whether you may perish in the morning or live only until the evening? We ignore the practice of the Way to obtain our future life; morning and evening we think only of how to survive, busily running hither and thither. Isn't it truly pathetic to see ourselves in such a state?

4-8 Kyōso of Miidera Temple

Great Ajari Kyōso, a Zen monk of Miidera Temple,[57] was unmatched in practice and intelligence. He appreciated the clear bright moon that appeared over the pine trees above his private hut when he concentrated on the *getsurinkan* practice.[58]

Devoted to the Way, Kyōso wanted to visit Mount Jubu and Gionshōja,[59] where Shaka Buddha had once preached. As he began to prepare for the long journey, more than fifty people vowed to join him. By the time he and his party reached Akashi Beach in Harima province, only thirty remained. On his arrival at Tsukushi in Kyushu, everyone had left him except Shinjakukō.[60]

When the two men visited Usa Shrine[61] to pray for their safe journey, they received an oracle: "The Law in central India has died out, and tigers and wolves live in Gionshōja; only wild grass grows in the

---

57. For Miidera Temple, see note 2 of story 3-5. Kyōso 慶祖 (955–1019), a Tendai monk, was involved in the strife between the Jikaku and Chishō factions: he left Mount Hiei and moved to Miidera Temple, where he died at the age of sixty-seven. *Ajari*, or *azari*, is a high-ranking priestly title of the Tendai School and was granted by the imperial court.

58. In the cult of *getsurinkan* 月輪観 (gazing at the moon ring), the observer feels his heart is as pure and clear as the full moon and will be able to obtain enlightenment by getting rid of delusions. Sometimes the cult is practiced before an illustration of a *getsurin* moon ring with a white lotus flower of eight petals and the golden character 阿 in the center.

59. A reference to Ryōjusen 霊鷲山 (Gṛdhrakūta, Numinous Eagle Mountain). Gionshōja 祇園精舎 (Jetavanavihāra) was built near Śrāvastī in central India by a wealthy man, Shudatsu, for Shaka and his disciples. It was reduced to ruins by the seventh century when Genjō Sanjō visited.

60. Unidentified.

61. Usa Hachimangū 宇佐八幡宮 is in present-day Ōita prefecture.

White Heron Pond, and Ryūsa and Sōrei[62] have changed so much that no trace of Buddhist influence remains. Do not go there." Both Kyōso and Shinjakukō grieved greatly when they heard about the deterioration of the Law in these places and returned home. Had they heard that the Law was still prospering, they would have rejoiced but still they would not have gone. Learning that places had deteriorated where the Law had once been preached was most disheartening.

Long ago Master Genjō Sanzō[63] of China went to India and traveled widely. He discovered that the teachings of the Great Vehicle[64] prospered in only 15 of 130 countries[65] he visited. Hearing about the Law dying out even in those fifteen countries was extremely discouraging. There is a poem: "Shaka Buddha is omnipotent on Mount Ryōju, but he hides himself behind clouds when the people's minds are clouded by their delusions."[66] I wonder if the Buddha has completely hidden himself? As time passes, his teachings may disappear. If that is so, when the faint light of the Law appears bright for a short while like the flame of a candle fluttering in a breeze, shouldn't we try our best to escape the suffering sea of life and death?

---

62. The White Heron Pond 白鷺池 was in Bamboo Grove Temple in the north of Rājagṛha of Magadha in central India. Ryūsa 流砂 refers to the Taklamakan Desert and Sōrei to present-day Pamir.
63. See note 9 of story 1-8.
64. Mahāyāna Buddhism.
65. The Hōonjurin 法苑珠林 states "more than 150 countries" (Daizōkyō vol. 53, p. 496); "110 countries" is recorded in the Daitōseiiki 大唐西域記 (Daizōkyō vol. 51, p. 867).
66. A reference to the Shika wakashū 詞花和歌集 (maki 10, Miscellany II, no. 415).

5-1 Sōzu Eishō

The noble and learned Great Sōzu Eishō of Yamashina Temple[1] excelled in the teachings of *yuishiki* (consciousness only) and *inmyō*.[2] He greatly desired to leave the secular world because he felt socializing and attending to temple affairs were impediments. After he was promoted to abbot, he disappeared without telling anyone, not even his disciples. They were surprised and searched for him everywhere; after many days they lost hope and dispersed.

Meanwhile, Eishō reached Kiso in Shinano province[3] and settled there. When he went deep into the mountains, he felt the futility of life in the blowing wind. At other times, he went down to the village to help the poor by fetching water and cutting firewood for them. The villagers might well have wondered if Eishō was a man of some status, but he always pretended to know little about the Law, just as Genpin[4] had done in olden times.

I often asked myself how the noble Eishō was able to work in rice fields. While working for the villagers as a lowly laborer, no task seemed unfamiliar to him, such as rowing a boat to cross a river. Whatever Eisho had done [previously], he must have had a pure heart indeed. Although he felt that associating with people was a great burden, he freely took on various jobs. It was truly extraordinary of him to show mercy to all living beings and help them attain salvation.

Eishō avoided socializing but did not seem affected by noisy secular affairs. Such a man could not have been regarded as a lowly commoner, and living deep in the mountains was the best practice for him. His heart, completely purified, would not in the least have been spoiled by mingling with others. He had grieved with the poor and rejoiced

---

1. Eishō 永昭 (989–1030), a son of Fujiwara Motowaza, became *bettō* 別当, or supervisor, of Kōfukuji Temple in 1025. *Bettō* controlled the administrative affairs of large temples such as Tōdaiji and Kōfukuji; for Yamashina or Kōfukuji temples, see *Senjūshō* 1-8, 2-1, and 2-4. *Shōyūki* 小右記 mentions that Eishō lectured on a sutra at Fujiwara Michinaga's mansion in 1019 (*Dainihon kokiroku*, p. 197).

2. *Inmyō* 因明 (*hetu-vidyā*) teaching emphasizes the study of the true-false nature of phenomena based upon reason, while the *yuishiki* theory is based upon consciousness only and teaches that all phenomena depend on a person's consciousness.

3. The region to the southwest of present-day Nagano.

4. Genpin died in 818 at the age of eighty-five (*Dainihon bukkyō zensho*, vol. 65, p. 8); for more about him in the *Senjūshō*, see 2-4 and 2-8.

with the rich. Once he had abandoned such feelings of grief and joy, what else in this life could have affected him?

I wondered about Eishō's last moments. I wanted to find out what they were, but I did not know where he had died. Into which Pure Land was he reborn? I am much concerned about him.

5-2 Chikamune Receives the Tonsure because of His Angry Wife

Long ago, there was a strong and steadfast samurai named Saburō Chikamune of Ōse, a retainer of Yoriyoshi.[5] When his master attacked Sadatō, Chikamune killed and wounded many people. Later, repenting his sins, Chikamune recited the Buddha's name with a pure heart. As time went on, he had cause[6] to leave his wife after seeing her lose her temper for no particular reason. Soon after he cut his hair and wandered about, reciting the Buddha's name. Steadfast by nature, his devotion to the Way was very firm.

Chikamune arrived in the Ochi area,[7] built a small hut in a remote place on a mountain, and remained there. He possessed nothing but a coarse hemp robe, but he managed to survive with the little food brought to him by the villagers nearby.

One day, he told a villager who had brought him some food, "I am going to observe abstinence, so please do not come here for the next five days." The villager agreed and no one saw Chikamune for five days. When the people came to see him on the morning of the sixth day, they found he had passed away while sitting erect and facing west, seemingly still alive.

Wasn't this indeed noble? Other people with greater understanding have difficulty leaving the secular world and entering the Way, but Chikamune, a samurai and far from the Way, was able to leave his old

---

5. Minamoto Yoriyoshi 源頼義 (988–1075), a son of Yorinobu, destroyed Abe Sadatō 安部貞任 (1019–1062) and his father, Yoritoki 頼時 (d. 1057), during what is known in English as the Early Nine-Years War in Mutsu province. Chikamune 近宗 is unidentified. A story in the Konjaku monogatari (25:13) narrates the rebellion based upon the Mutsuwaki 陸奥話記 (Senjūshō zenchūshaku, I, p. 448).

6. The term zenchishiki 善智識 is used. This usually refers to good friends and teachers, but here it refers to good causes.

7. The northwestern area included Echizen, Etchū, and Echigo provinces.

life because of his angry wife and live deep in the mountains. This was quite remarkable.

It is said that "The Pure Land of the Buddha is wherever you have a pure heart."[8] This may be true, but we are easily confused and have difficulty in keeping our hearts and minds pure. When we live with a bad spouse, how can we not become upset? Although we try not to grow angry, if someone near us is angry for no reason, we will lose our temper. In such cases, we ought to leave and go elsewhere. But being weak-minded, we cannot leave the familiar and a lifestyle to which we are accustomed so easily.

Given his firm conviction, Chikamune would never have gone against the Buddha's Way. I shed many tears when I remember his story and pray for a strong devotion to the Way like his. It is most noble that everything depends having on a deep karmic relationship with the Buddha's Way.

---

8. 随心浄処即浄土摂; a similar sentence appears in the *Yuimakyō* 維摩経 (*Daizōkyō*, 14, p. 538).

5-3 Naiki Nyūdō

Some time ago, Yasutane[9] served as a *naiki* (imperial secretary). He was very compassionate toward all living beings. Once, while feeding his dog, a neighbor's dog was watching nearby and, feeling sorry for it, Yasutane gave it some food. Then the two dogs began to fight over the last grain of rice. Surprised, Yasutane tearfully said to them, "How mean and debased you are! Quickly, abandon your lowly minds!" Seeing Yasutane do this, Master Jie[10] said to himself, "He is certainly not an ordinary man." Yasutane eventually received the tonsure and attained enlightenment, something he had long desired.

This was truly noble. How did Yasutane obtain such a sympathetic heart? His compassion was different from the love a man usually has for his wife and children; it was more like that of buddhas and bodhisattvas, who are merciful to every sentient being in this world. Such compassion arises from a pure heart.

In general, love for wives and children is based on personal delusions and attachments. So we are often upset and distracted [because of our love] and experience the Three Sufferings.[11] What a pity to see anyone love and be attached to someone or to something. If we practice the Law, we cast away feelings of love and hatred that arise from our desires and delusions.

What and why do we love and hate? According to the Law, since there is nothing to love or hate in the beginning, neither love nor hatred should ever arise. We all want to discard attachments [to free ourselves from suffering], but we always have difficulty abandoning the wrong attitudes and cultivating the right mind. Although we may wish to acquire the pure mind of a buddha, we often fail to attain our goal before our last moments.

I have more admiration for those who have compassion for others than those who retire deep into the mountains to purify their mind.

---

9. Naiki Nyūdō 内記入道, or Yoshishige Yasutane 慶滋保胤 (934–1002), was the second son of Kamo Tadayuki and a Yin-Yang master. He was famous for such texts as the *Nihon ōjō gokurakuki* 日本往生極楽記 and the *Chiteiki* 池亭記. *Naiki* is "imperial secretary," and *nyūdō* a priestly title.

10. Master Jie 慈恵, or Ryōgen 良源, (912–985) was the eighteenth Tendai *zasu*. Yasutane was a close friend of Genshin 源信, a disciple of Master Jie.

11. The sufferings *sanzu no kuka* 三途の苦果 are fire, the sword, and blood after death.

5-4 Sōjō Yōen

Yōen[12] was an administrator of Yamashina Temple.[13] Talented and profoundly learned, he excelled especially in the Way of Poetry.[14] Sometimes he sequestered himself in the Buddhist world, purifying his mind in the way of the dharma, and at other times he composed poems under the moon and among the flowers.

When the *unohana*[15] begins to bloom on the hedges around the villagers' houses and the cuckoos come down from the mountains, our minds become unsettled. One day, a monk acquainted with Yōen visited him and asked, "I wonder if composing poems will hinder your practice of the Way?"

Yōen replied, "How can you say such a thing? When composing poems, my sadness and yearnings for love are controlled as I concentrate my mind on a single thing—that is, composing poems. And this is nothing but the practice of *yuishiki*, consciousness only.[16] There is no dharma except in one's mind, which should constantly seek it. If your mind is not settled, you will not be able to attain enlightenment. People agitate their own minds when they say things like 'Composing poems is a hindrance to learning.' What can I say to this?" And so Yōen tearfully left him.

Even if ignorant in the Way, those who engage in the Way of Poetry have elegant and pure hearts because they easily forget hatred and grudges [while composing poems]. Yōen, a devout Buddhist, must have composed poems with deep feelings toward the Way. I feel most envious of him.

....

12. Yōen 永縁 (1048–1125), a poet monk and a son of Fujiwara Eisō, became a *bettō* administrator of Yamashina Temple. He was also known as Sōjō Hatsune. *Sōjō* 僧正 is a title of a high-ranking monk, similar to abbot. Yōen's poems appear in imperial anthologies such as the *Kin'yō wakashū*, and his stories in other collections such as the *Ujishūi monogatari* (3:10).

13. The temple in Nara was supported by the Fujiwara clan; it is now called Kōfukuji. The Karin-in Hall in the compound is famous for its poetry meetings.

14. The expression *rikugi no fūzoku* 六義の風俗, the six kinds or styles of the poems mentioned in the Japanese preface of the *Kokin wakashū* (or *Kokinshū*), generally refers to the poetic styles of the *waka* poems. The expression appears in other *Senjūshō* tales (5-10, 6-1).

15. The tiny white deutzia flowers are popularly called *unohana* 卯の花, "flower of the month of U," the fourth month, since they bloom during the time of rice planting.

16. See note 7 of story 1-1.

The way to attain enlightenment is found only in our minds, but alas, when can we clear our hearts and hold the pure moon there? I always feel vexed, lamenting my ignorance. Whenever I hear "The Thirty-Seven Noble Steps to enlightenment are all in the mind,"[17] I feel like worshipping them as I open my heart, but I soon grow despondent and wonder, "Being ignorant, how can I see the noble appearance of a buddha?" Thus, I foolishly spend my days despising my ignorant heart and mind.

5-5   Kakuson and the Monk with a Poem about Rattles

Some time ago, a poor monk was wandering in Suruga province[18] and living in a crude hut on Mount Fuji. Wearing straw mats and eating fish and birds, he seemed like a crazy person, mumbling often and incoherently. But at times he appeared to have a good mind and said things that were intelligible.

---

17. A reference to the thirty-seven steps of enlightenment in the Diamond Mandala, *Kongō mandara* 金剛曼荼羅.
18. Present-day Shizuoka prefecture.

Once, when Hijiri Kakuson passed through Narumikata[19] on his way to the eastern provinces, the monk came to him and begged for alms. Impressed by his extraordinary appearance, Kakuson asked the monk to sit with him, and with no hesitation the monk sat and talked with him. Kakuson's attendants and the villagers were also impressed by his unusual appearance. After a while, Kakuson asked the monk, "Will you tell me a verse from a dharma text?"

Smiling slightly, the monk recited,

Naruko o ba,
Onoga hakaze ni
Yurugashite
Kokoro toki hagu
Murasuzume kana

Disturbed by the sound
Of rattles[20]

---

19. Narumikata was to the east of the present-day port of Nagoya.
20. A reference to *naruko* 鳴子, a rattle or clapper made with bells set up to scare birds from rice paddies.

Caused by the wind,
And blown by flapping their wings
The common sparrows!

After reciting the poem, the monk left. Disappointed [by his departure], Kakuson sent people to look for him but they were unsuccessful.

Indeed, just as ignorant sparrows are disturbed by the sound of rattles, people are attached to this and that, believing that their minds and objects are separate, and because of these objects [to which they are attached] their minds are greatly disturbed. The monk's poem is based upon *yuishiki* (consciousness only) and is very noble.

No one knows anything about the monk's last moments. I wonder how well he observed the ideal of *yuishiki* since having such a strong faith and living deep in the mountains merit a reward. Unable to hide his virtues, he might well have appeared in other remote areas. He was truly an interesting person.

5-6 The Lady of the Middle Councilor

A woman called the Lady of the Middle Councilor[21] served Lady Taikenmon'in.[22] She cut her hair and received the tonsure after the death of her lady. She moved to the foot of Ogura Hill[23] and practiced the Way with a pure heart. Hearing about her, I began to search for her at the beginning of the ninth month.

After walking along a path hidden by the tall grass, I finally reached her dwelling. In the bright moonlight, I clearly saw the eaves of the house, the hedge, and the dew on the flowers among the vines and pampas grass. With an untended field in front and a mountain path on the side, the house appeared very lonely amidst the insects' chirping and the monkeys' cries from the mountain. An autumn breeze blowing through

---

21. This woman, who received the tonsure after the death of the lady she served, was the daughter of Fujiwara Sadazane 藤原定実. She excelled in poetry and one of her poems is included in the *Kin'yō wakashū* (Spring Section).
22. Taikenmon'in 待賢門院 (1101–1145), a daughter of Fujiwara Kimizane 藤原公実, was the empress of Emperor Toba 鳥羽 and the mother of the emperors Sutoku and Go-Shirakawa. Her attendants included many talented poets.
23. Ogurayama, a small hill, is in the present-day Ukyo district to the west of the capital. Later she moved to Amanobessho at the foot of Mount Kōya.

the pine trees and over the *hagi* leaves softly whispered by the woman's pillow and made the place seem even more desolate and lonely.

When I met her, she said to me, "After receiving the tonsure, I missed my lady when I sadly recalled her and other people. But now I have completely forgotten them and do not grieve for any of them. Thanks to practicing the Way, I have abandoned the joy and grief of secular life. Even though I am an ignorant woman, I have reached this stage. Someone like you who has practiced the Way for months and years must certainly have a clearer heart." I was deeply impressed by her remarkable words.

A wise man said, "Leaving the joy and grief of the secular life is Zen." We try to forget secular delusions, but this is difficult because many futile ideas arise one after another in our minds. However, this lady completely abandoned her delusions. Probably she was able to do this not only on account of her karma in this life, but also because of the merits she had accumulated by practicing virtue in numerous past lives. Thanks to these merits, she was able to cast off the delusions of this life.

I entered the Way long before she did, and I have devotedly practiced the Way, ignoring fame and profit, yet I remain inferior to her. I felt most ashamed and upset as I left her. On my way back, I suddenly realized that feeling annoyed and vexed was due to my failure to abandon secular delusions. I thought of returning to tell the woman of my feelings, but I did not want to disturb her so there was nothing to do but continue my way down the hill.

Three years later when I heard the lady had fallen seriously ill, I wanted to visit her. But then I learned that she had passed away in the correct manner; sitting upright with her hands joined, facing west. I tearfully returned home thinking that she had truly abandoned all delusions.

5-7   A Monk in Nishiyama

Recently a monk built a flimsy hut at the foot of Mount Nishiyama[24] and lived there. Since he owned nothing but a Buddhist image, a sutra, and a hemp robe to wear, no one knew about him or came to rob or disturb him. And as he did not seem to know the Law, no one came

---

24. The Nishiyama mountain range runs west of Kyoto and includes Arashiyama and Atagoyama, mountains with many shrines and temples.

to question him or talk about such matters with him. How could he maintain a life that appeared so pitiful and as fragile as dew? People [in the capital] heard of the monk and talked about him, and soon the minister of Tokudaiji Temple[25] said to an attendant, "What kind of a monk is he? Bring him here."

But the monk completely ignored the minister's summons. The distressed messenger reported this to the minister, who said, "He must have his reasons. Go to him again and bring him here!" So the messenger returned to the hut only to find that the monk had already left. Feeling curious, the messenger looked inside the hut and found nothing but a poem written on a board:

Sugi yukishi
Kata mo kuyashishi
Shiba no iori
Waga sumika tote
Nani taorikemu

---

25. Fujiwara Sanetaka (1096–1157), the fourth son of Kimizane and an older brother of Taikenmon'in, was called the Minister of Tokudaiji 徳大寺の大臣 and was a poet. Saigyō served as a samurai in Tokudaiji Temple before he received the tonsure; for his relationship to the temple, see *Senjūshō* 5-15 and *Kokon chomonjū* (*maki* 15, no. 494).

> I greatly regret
> In the past
> I built
> A brushwood hut
> As my place to live.

No one knew the monk's whereabouts.

According to the poem, the monk obviously regretted building the hut. Although he wished to own nothing, he built the hut to live in and it proved to be an unexpected nuisance. He must have had an extremely pure heart to regret his past deeds. Living deep in the mountains without any attachment, he surely remained serene. They say if a man has a wife and children and some treasure, he will be disturbed by greed and regret whenever he thinks of his possessions and will never reach true enlightenment. I really envy the monk's pure heart.

I wonder if the monk built another hut somewhere else after he left Nishiyama? He must now be living on another mountain or in a field according to his original wish. I would like to know more about him. Since all of this happened recently, he will have nowhere to live except under the vast sky. I wish I could seek him out and establish a Buddhist relationship with him.

5-8 Abbot Shōen

Ajari Shōen, a disciple of Abbot Shōsan[26] of Shūgakuin, was talented, intelligent, and much devoted to the Law. He lived in a temple and practiced the Way.

On a very cold winter night, he felt the wind piercing through the layers of his robes, and lying on the frost-covered floor was unbearable. Shōen felt most sympathetic toward beggars who had hardly anything to wear on such a cold night. He went out and gave most

---

26. Shōsan 勝算 (939–1011) became the abbot of Miidera Temple 三井寺 in 1002. With his miraculous powers, he caused plum trees in the Shūgakuin detached palace 修学院 to blossom and bear fruit during a cold winter. Tales about him are found in the *Senjūshō* (9-3), the *Shasekishū* (2-5), and the *Genkō shakusho* (11). Shōen is unidentified.

of his clothes to the beggars, including four *kosode* kimono.[27] On his way home, wearing only one kimono under an unlined hemp robe, he heard someone crying out in the valley. Feeling pity, he walked into the valley through the thorns and brambles, which caught his feet. He tearfully felt sympathy as he wondered what kind of a person was in such a place.

There at the bottom of the valley, he found a beggar lying and crying with a broken straw mat covering only his waist. When Shōen took his hands and asked him what had happened, the beggar replied, "While I was sleeping by the living quarters of the temple, I tried to change my position to keep warm and fell into the valley. I hurt myself by falling and because of these cuts I am in pain while suffering from the cold." Overcome by pity, Shōen took off his kimono and put it on the beggar, who then asked, "Will you give me your hemp robe, too?"

"Of course," said Shōen, and he put it on him. The monk, nearly naked on a bitterly cold night, remained with the beggar, holding his hands.

Toward dawn, Shōen said to the beggar, "I think I should go now because I will be embarrassed if I am seen not wearing any clothes. I must return before the doors of the living quarters are opened."

But the beggar insisted, saying, "Please don't think of that. If you leave me here now, I will be lonely and will hold a grudge against you." He appeared so lonely and helpless that Shōen again felt tearful pity for him and remained.

Meanwhile, dawn broke on the mountainside and the morning bell was heard. The beggar then said to Shōen, "Please carry me up." With much effort, Shōen climbed out of the valley with the beggar on his back. As soon as they reached the top, the beggar said to him, "Please put me down here." Shōen put him down on the ground carefully so that he would not further aggravate the beggar's wounds. As he began to walk away, he turned back to look at the beggar, and there he saw the Eleven-Faced Kannon,[28] which was his master Shōsan's principal image, lying on the ground and wearing his *kosode* kimono. Amazed, Shōen walked back and tearfully held up the image. He then realized

---

27. *Kosode* 小袖, a kimono with small openings in the short sleeves, were worn as undergarments by the Heian aristocrats and later used by commoners, including women who donned them without wearing *hakama* skirts over them.

28. For another tale of Kannon, the epitome of mercy, see *Senjūshō* 1-8.

that he was not at the foot of the mountain but actually near his own room. Later he placed the image in Shōsan's living quarters in Miidera Temple.

This man was indeed most noble. Only a person with the heart of a buddha or bodhisattva could be so merciful. Mercy is the basis of all that is good and is the image of all buddhas. Without mercy, merits and virtues cannot be revealed. They say that if a person's devotion to the Way is distorted, then his practice and dedication are wasted. So everyone [devoted to the Way] should have mercy. Yet when a person cannot control his anger, he picks up a stick and clenches his teeth because anger has gotten the better of him, and this is most regrettable.

In contrast, this holy man, Shōen, acted nobly; he showed deep, unconditional mercy to the beggar [who was not related to him]. This is why the Kannon was moved by his buddha nature,[29] appearing first as a lowly beggar and then revealing its own true nature. This was truly an extraordinary happening in this degenerate age.

5-9 Sōjō Shinpan

Abbot Shinpan[30] was the superior of Yamashina Temple for a long time, but at the age of fifty he wanted to renounce the world, and so he left the temple. He went to Shiga district in Ōmi province,[31] built a humble hut in a suitable place, and practiced the Way. Although he could see passersby from his hut, it was located in a most discreet place with a mountain path behind it and in front a field where pure water from a waterfall flowed.

His neighbors got their water at the falls, and one day when some women and children were collecting water there, humming songs and chatting about trifles, a child said to his companions, "A noble holy man lives in the hut."

"Don't say such silly things," they replied, but soon many people came to the hut to pay their respects to Shinpan.

Shinpan thought, "Here I am, having left the temple in the capital

---

29. Here the term *ki* 機, "opportunity," also refers to the talent or buddha nature possessed by those who can understand the teachings and put them into practice.
30. Shinpan 真範 (989–1054), a son of Taira Namamasa, served as the *bettō* director of Gangōji, Yamashinadera, and Hasedera 長谷寺 temples. He became *sōjō* abbot in 1049.
31. Present-day Shiga prefecture.

because I wanted to practice the Way while concealing my virtue, but, alas, people have found me out." So he regretfully left the hut and wandered about in a wretched state before going deep into the mountains in Utsu[32] to practice the Way there. He sometimes went down to the village, opened his sleeves as he begged for alms,[33] and then returned to the mountain.

One day some curious villagers followed Shinpan deep into the mountains and found him sitting, facing south, by a stream of pure water in a valley. He appeared to be sleeping with his hands joined as if in prayer. The people returned home and reported all of this to the other villagers, saying, "He must be a true ascetic of the Law, but how does he shelter from the rain?" So they talked about building a humble hut for the monk and taking him food. After their discussion, they sent a messenger to Shinpan to tell him about their decision, but the monk completely ignored him. When the messenger returned to the village and reported this to the others, they replied, "He must be truly a superior person. But how can he refuse us if we all go together and

32. Located on the boundary of Shita-gun and Shizuoka-shi.
33. That is, spreading his sleeves to accept alms.

speak to him?" So they all went into the mountains only to find that Shinpan had already gone. "What happened?" the villagers wondered as they sought him in vain.

Some time later, one of the villagers went to Echigo province[34] on business, and when he passed through the capital of the province, he saw Shinpan walking alone, dressed shabbily to conceal himself among the passersby. "What happened to you?" asked the villager, but Shinpan merely shook a small bell, pretending to be deaf,[35] and said nothing. While the villager watched, Shinpan wandered out to the sea.

It was indeed most noble that Shinpan, who was once admired by three thousand monks as the abbot of a temple, concealed his prestige and virtues and wandered in remote places, mingling with commoners. Even if people dedicate hundreds or even thousands of Buddhist statues, it will all be quite useless if they do not have pure hearts. Only when his mind is free of dreams and delusions will a man be able to attain enlightenment. He will need to keep a pure heart in the Law instead of building temples and donating images. Because Shinpan's faith was born of his learned mind, how could he ever lose it? When we hear of his single-minded devotion to the Law, we think of him as a most noble and reliable man.

Later, it is recorded[36] that Shinpan, wearing his shabby habit, returned to Yamato province and passed away at the foot of Mount Miwa,[37] facing east as if sleeping and reciting the words "Faith in the great deity of Kasuga." This was certainly a man of deep faith in the Law. As abbot of a temple, he presided over everything there. But he left the temple and retired to remote places because he wished to practice the Way. He spent time on lonely beaches and cleansed his heart in pure mountain water. He wandered through towns, pretending to be deaf. He recommended to others that they recite the Buddha's names,

---

34. Present-day Niigata prefecture.
35. The expression "pretending to be deaf" appears in another *Senjūshō* tale (3-2) and in *Kankyonotomo* 1-8.
36. Unidentified. The article written in 1702 [?] about Shinpan in *Honchō kōsōden* 11 (*Dainihon bukkyōzensho*, vol. 63) is believed to be based upon this tale.
37. The mountain in the present-day city of Sakurai in Nara prefecture is known for a legendary tale about the snake deity, Miwa, which appears in the chapter about Emperor Sujin 宗神 in the *Kojiki*.

and in this way he helped all living beings by practicing the cult of benefiting others as well as oneself.[38] This was indeed most noble.

5-10 A Man of Ōmi Lost His Son and Left Secular Life

Recently there was a wealthy man of Ōmi province who led a life of luxury, enjoying delicacies from the mountains and the sea morning and evening. There was nothing unfulfilled in his life. But one day, his only son fell ill and died despite being given every medicine and Yin-Yang treatment.[39] The grief of his father and mother was indescribable.

Fifty days passed, and the man realized his sadness would never be banished by any of his treasures. He concluded that the only way to free himself from suffering was to enter the Way. He explained this wish to his wife, immediately cut his hair, and began his journey, practicing the Way. As he wandered through the mountains, he deeply felt the transience of life while watching the falling leaves; wandering along the sea shore,[40] he pondered his approaching death. Finally, after arriving at Shido in Sanuki,[41] a province far from his home, he succeeded in delivering himself, passing away with his palms joined, facing west.

Wasn't it most extraordinary for this man to renounce secular life and abandon his wealth? Unlike the profound meaning of the Law, the transience of life is easy for anyone to understand; we have only to note the brief existence of gossamer or the easily broken leaves of the *bashō* plant.[42] Although we should leave this futile life as soon as possible, we are unable to do so because of our many delusions, and we will regret this when we face the judgments of King Enma in hell after our death.

Long ago when I was serving at the imperial court,[43] I recited poems and greatly enjoyed the Way of Poetry. I was moved by the reflection of the autumn moon on Hirosawa Pond and the shadow of

---

38. That is, *jigyōgeta* 自行化他, or "practicing for oneself and benefiting others."
39. *On'yōjutsu* 陰陽術: a reference to the cultic prayers in the Yin-Yang Way.
40. "Seashore" here reflects the idea of the Sea of Life and Death and the deep suffering of repeating life and death in the karmic cycles.
41. Present-day Kagawa prefecture (Ōkawa-gun, Shido-chō).
42. Large, broken *bashō* 芭蕉 leaves often appear in poems about the futility of life.
43. Saigyō once served Former Emperor Toba as a samurai.

the moon on the dew of the bamboo leaves in Ono Field. I spent spring days admiring the mistlike cherry blossoms on Mount Yoshino. I visited many places and wherever I went, I composed poems. When I lived with my loving wife and child, I was ignorant of the futility of life. How could I have dreamed at that time that I would be leading the life of a beggar like this? But now, I am most happy that I can put all the sadness of parting and death into my poems, which are nothing more than a skillful means of following the Way of the Law.

5-11 The Nun of Eguchi[44]

Around the ninth month of Jishō 2 (1178), I was leisurely traveling with a *hijiri* monk through various places. We were not in a hurry even at sunset, when we came to a courtesan's house located between the northern and southern banks of the river in Eguchi-Katsumoto.[45]

While gazing at the [shabby] house, we wondered about the life of a courtesan, who engages in temporary relationships with travelers and passes through life committing sinful deeds. "What sort of existence," we mused, "will she have after her death? Is it due to karma from a previous existence[46] that she lives as a courtesan in this life? Indeed, she is engaged in something against the Buddha's Way, spending her short life, which is futile as dew. Her committing sin is one thing, but involving so many other people in her sinful practices is lamentable. But some courtesans and fishermen, who take lives, attain enlightenment by aspiring for deliverance. What does this mean? If everything is due to the Way followed in previous lives, why are they involved in such lamentable practices? If their enlightenment depends on their conduct in this life, how can they attain deliverance?"

As I quietly pondered these questions, I came to wonder if it all depended on their hearts and minds. In order to prolong her futile life, a courtesan associates with this or that man, but she would never attach her heart and mind to them. Even when she says sinful words and

---

44. A similar story appears in *Senjūshō* 9-8.
45. Present-day Higashi Yodogawa-ku, northeast of the city of Osaka. Since it was an important port located between the capital, Kyoto, and the eastern provinces, many courtesans gathered there.
46. *Shukugō*, or *shukugyō* 宿業.

performs evil deeds, if she constantly aspires to her future deliverance, then her heart and mind remain beautiful and this will eventually lead her to enlightenment.

While we were discussing this, the monk and I were about to leave the village when suddenly a shower, violent like winter rain, caught us and we were obliged to take shelter under the eaves of the courtesan's house. We stealthily peeped inside and saw a nun[47] bustling here and there with a piece of board, trying to patch the leaky roof. Seeing her, I casually recited a *renga* linked verse:[48]

Shizuga fuse ya o
Fukizo wazurau

Troubled in trying
To patch the shabby hut

The nun was busily running about, but as soon as she heard my verse, she threw away the board and added her own lines:

Tsuki wa more
Shigure tamare to
Omou ni wa

Wishing for the moonlight
Through [the crack in the roof]
While the shower leaks floods.

Greatly moved by her elegant verse, we could not leave but stayed at her shack through the night, exchanging linked verses. Toward dawn, my traveling companion recited his verse:

Kokoro sumarenu[49]
Shiba no io kana

----

47. Nuns were often involved in prostitution at the time.
48. In *renga* 連歌 poetry one person composes the first two lines of the verse and another completes the poem by adding the concluding three lines.
49. Here *sumarenu* すまれぬ, "not to clear," also means "cannot live or stay."

Truly, your heart can never rest
In this brushwood hut

Immediately, the nun added in reply:

Miyako nomi
Omou kata towa
Isogare te

My heart hastens
As I yearn
Only for the capital.

Her verse truly touched our hearts.
 During my journey through some sixty provinces, I have met many people but none was so elegant as this courtesan. If she had been a man, we would have persuaded her to join us and enjoyed her companionship. My *hijiri* monk companion greatly missed the nun of Eguchi and [talked about her] even after we had left her place.[50]

---

50. The *Hyakuninshu hitoyogatari* 百人一首一夕話 (8:1) mentions the nun of Eguchi exchanging linked verses with Saigyō.

5-12 Itsukushima

Itsukushima Shrine in Aki[51] has a deep mountain behind it and a field and pine grove to the left and right of it, respectively. The shrine faces the sea. A freshwater river, the Mitarai,[52] flows through the field in the east.

A little ways in front of the shrine's three buildings are two galleries running from south to north for thirty-three *ken* and from east to west for twenty-five *ken*. At high tide, sea water flows below the shrine's wooden floor, while at ebb tide the white sandy beach extends for fifty *chō*. People can reach the galleries by boat at high tide, and the sight is most impressive.

No one knows why, but a mirror representing the deities hangs below the screen instead of above it. This may be because the place enshrines female deities. A shrine is generally built on a mountain, but here the galleries are on level ground.

Visitors to Itsukushima feel especially purified when they see the three open sides of the shrine to the east, west, and south. Since the local people do not hunt the deer, you can hear the animals crying out in the mountains, and insects loudly chirp in the field to the east, where dew rests on the grass. Even people without faith are said to cleanse their hearts at this shrine.

5-13 Usa Shrine and the Concept of Seeing in One's Mind

Like Mount Otoko in Yamashiro province,[53] Usa Shrine in Tsukushi[54] province is surrounded by a long range of mountains and is set in a

---

51. Itsukushima Shrine 厳島神社 in present-day Hiroshima prefecture (Saheki-gun, Miyajima-chō) enshrines three female deities: Ichikishima-hime no mikoto, Tagori-hime no mikoto, and Tagitsu-hime no mikoto. Since 1017, the shrine has been called Ichimiya of Aki province. Saigyō once visited the shrine (*Sankashū*, or *Sangashū*, no. 414).
52. This may refer to the Mitarai, or Mitarashi-gawa 御手洗川, Hand-washing River, which was also called Goryōgawa 御霊川, Honorable Spirit River.
53. Mount Otokoyama 男山 was the Iwashimizu-Hachiman Shrine 岩清水八幡宮 in the present-day city of Yawata 八幡 in Kyoto prefecture. During the Jōgan era (859–877), Priest Gyōkyō of Daianji Temple in Nara moved the Hachiman Deity from the Usa Shrine to Otokoyama, and since then the shrine has been the protector of emperors.
54. Usa, or Usa Hachiman, Shrine 宇佐八幡宮 is in present-day Oita prefecture and enshrines Prince Homutawake (Emperor Ōjin), Great Deity Hime, and Princess Ōtarashihime (Empress Jingō).

lonely place where the wind blows through the pine trees. The cries of the monkeys in the mountains there sound especially pitiful. Visitors might mistake this place for Mount Fudaraku[55] because of the attractive way the trees grow. The fresh water flowing inside [the shrine] is called *mitarai*.[56] Visitors' minds truly can be cleansed at this shrine. I was overwhelmed with tears when I recalled the divine words of the deities who had appeared to Priest Kōya[57] and explained the correct teachings to Great Master Kōbō.[58]

While wandering though the western provinces in my practice of the Way, I went all the way to Kanegamisaki.[59] When I passed through Koya[60] in Settsu province on my return journey, I saw an old monk, aged about sixty, with hair hanging down his neck. Instead of wearing an ordinary robe on his shoulders, he had hung a straw mat on his thin old body, and his face, hands, and feet were covered with mud. Completely ignoring other people and mumbling unintelligibly, he was focused on shaking a *sasara* made of split bamboo[61] to purify his mind.

Impressed by his most unusual appearance, I approached him and asked, "What are you doing?"

"I am sounding a *sasara*," replied the monk.

I replied, "Yes, I know that. But will you tell me something about the Law? I have deep faith in the Law, so will you say something, just a

---

55. Potalaka (Fudarakusan 補陀落山), a mountain in south India, is believed to be Bodhisattva Kannon's paradise, where the illuminating trees release fragrance. In Japan, it has been identified as Mount Nachi in Wakayama prefecture.
56. *Mitarai* 御手洗 refers to the water used to wash a person's hands.
57. Kōya 空也 (903–972) was the founder of the *nenbutsu odori* 念仏踊り, the dancing and chanting of the name of Amida Buddha, and contributed greatly to popularizing the Pure Land faith. He appears in other *Senjūshō* tales (1-6, 7-4, 8-29, 9-5).
58. Kūkai 空海, or Kōbō Daishi 弘法大師 (774–835), was the founder of the Shingon School in Japan. After returning from China, he built Kongōbuji Temple 金剛峰寺 on Mount Kōya 高野山 in 819. He was known for his calligraphy and poems. His writings are found in the *Kōbōdaishi zenshū* 弘法大師全集 (ed. Mikkyō Bunka Kenkyūjo).
59. Perhaps a reference to Kanenomisaki, "Bell Promontory," in present-day Fukuoka prefecture.
60. Koya 昆陽, an *utamakura*, or a scenic place for poetry, is in present-day Itani, Hyōgo prefecture. It is said that when Gyōki 行基 built Koya Temple, the *kane*, or bell, was stolen (*Konjaku monogatarishū*, 19-29). Thus *kane* is punned with Kanegamisaki in the previous sentence.
61. The word *sasara* originates from the sound made when shaking a bunch of split bamboo (*sarasara*). The musical instrument was used in preaching and *dengaku* 田楽 dancing.

118 THE SENJŪSHŌ

word, to clear my mind?"

"Ignore life and death by understanding that everything is only in your mind"[62] was his answer. The monk started to leave without saying more, so I begged him tearfully to continue. "You must understand that all phenomena are in your mind."[63] He then ran off, and I remained helpless, wanting him to stay.

Later I asked the villagers about the monk, and someone told me, "He did not want anything to wear, and somehow he lost whatever he was given. He just chanted something while he sounded the *sasara* and walked around."

With his pure mind and [unkempt] appearance, the monk must have had a deep devotion to the Law. When he understood that everything existed only in his mind, how could he not escape the karmic cycle of life and death? I was deeply impressed to have met a man of such deep devotion to the Law even in this degenerate age.

---

62. The phrase *kakuchi isshin* 覚知一心, "seeing and understanding everything in one's mind," means that everything in this life exists only in our minds, as the title of this story indicates. By understanding the meaning of this concept, we will be able to leave the karmic cycle of life and death according to the *yuishiki* mind, or consciousness-only theory (*Daizōkyō* 大蔵経, vol. 43, p. 243).

63. This also means that we should fully realize that all the phenomena in this life are merely the reflections of our minds. This story and the following one (5-14) are influenced by the *yuishiki* theory.

5-14 Kasuga Shrine and Shun'e Admire [My Poems]

Around the same time,[64] I visited Kasuga Shrine[65] while making a pilgrimage through the old capital of Nara.[66] At Kasuga Field,[67] I enjoyed the sight of the two pagodas.[68] When I walked across Madashi Bridge,[69] my steps sounded like those of a galloping horse. I tried to pick some violets, "young purple" in color,[70] in Ozasa Field; dew was resting on the bamboo leaves. Admiring the green pines of Kataoka, which had increased the vibrancy of their color for the emperors over a thousand generations, I stopped to gather the dew under the pampas grass. I saw it turning crimson with my tears as it fell on my sleeves. Meanwhile, the wind dispersed the dew on the pampas grass as well as on the *kuzu* vines. When I saw the moon rising high over the mountain and illuminating everything for a thousand miles, I recalled Abe Nakamaro's poem "As I turn back,"[71] composed in China, and I was deeply moved.

Meandering under the profusely growing tall cedars, I finally

---

64. In light of story 5-2, the year would have been about 1178 (Senjūshō Kenkyūkai ed., *Senjūshō zenchūshaku* 選集抄全注釈, pp. 562–563).
65. Kasuga Shrine 春日社 in Nara was a tutelary shrine of the Fujiwara clan. The four main halls enshrine three prince deities: Takemikatsuchi, Futsunushi, and Amenokoyane; and a princess deity, Himenokami.
66. Nara was the capital from 710 to 784.
67. The field is at the foot of Mount Kasuga, also in Nara.
68. The pagodas were the Eastern Pagoda, built by Regent Fujiwara Tadazane (1078–1162), and the Western Pagoda, by Emperor Toba (1103–1156); their sites are in present-day Nara Park. An old account of the burning of the pagodas appears in the *Heike monogatari* (vol. 5)
69. The Madashi Bridge 馬出しの橋, located to the east of Torii, was a starting point of the *hashiri-uma* 走馬, "running horse," on ceremonial occasions.
70. "Young purple" 若紫 refers to the light purple or mauve of wisteria, *fuji* 藤, thus creating an association (*yukari* in the text) with the Fujiwara (wisteria field) clan, the patrons of Kasuga Shrine.
71. Abe Nakamaro 安部仲麻呂 (698 or 701–770) was sent to China as a student in 716 and died there before returning to Japan. His poem *Ama no hara, furisake mireba Kasuganaru, Mikasa no yama ni ideshi tsukikamo* あまの原ふりさけ見れば,春日なる三笠の山に出し月かも, "Heavenly field, as I turn back, I see the moon appearing over Mount Mikasa of Kasuga," is famous as it tersely depicts his strong nostalgia for Japan. The opening term, *amanohara* (heavenly field), refers to Japan, and the expression *furisake mireba* (turning back) reflects his memories of the moon over Mount Mikasa as well as his country. The poem appears in the *Kokin wakashū* (vol. 9, Journey, no. 400).

arrived at the point where the path[72] divided into six ways, symbolizing the Six Realms through which we transmigrate. Hoping to choose the right one, I walked across the Zenshu Good Bridge[73] and soon approached the four halls of worship, the three corridors, and two-storied gateway.[74] When I stopped in front of some of the halls, I heard strong voices reciting the *Hannyarishu* sutra.[75] As I wandered around the other halls, I felt indescribably uplifted hearing the voices continuously preaching the Yuga and Yuishiki concepts.[76]

After Kasuga Shrine, I went to the foot of the mountain near Tōdaiji Temple where poet Shun'e[77] was living. While we were talking about poem-tales, he asked me, "What sort of poems have you composed?" I answered, "When I built a shabby hut to live in the Tado district of Sanuki province,[78] I composed this poem:

Yamazato ni
Ukiyo itowan
Tomo mogana
Kuyashiku sugishi
Mukashi kataramu

....

72. The path in the text is *Mutsu no michi* 六の道, the six ways symbolizing the Six Realms (hell, hungry ghosts, animals, *ashura*, humans, and heaven). Pronounced *rokudō* 六道, it shares the sound *roku* (deer) and the character *dō* (path) of Deer Path 鹿道.

73. Visitors are blessed with good results if they visit the main halls of the shrine by going across the Zenshu no hashi 善趣の橋, the stone bridge of the good (*Gunsho ruijū*, vol. 2).

74. The structure, Nanmon, or the South Gate, was built in the second month of 1075, during the reign of Emperor Shirakawa (r. 1072–1086) and was used by all visitors except the Fujiwara (*Gunsho ruijū*, vol. 2. p. 59).

75. *Hannyarishu* 般若理趣分 refers to the Great Wisdom Sutra (大般若波羅密多経), translated by Xuang-zhuang (*Senjūshō* 4-8), and the phrase reflects Shinto-Buddhism syncretism. The *honji suijaku* 本地垂迹 concept that buddhas manifest themselves in the Japanese deities who protect the Law became rapidly popularized at end of the eighth century and various Buddhist sutras were recited in Shinto shrines.

76. Both *yuga* and *yuishiki* 瑜加唯識 (consciousness only) concepts were especially propagated by the Hossō Sect, the headquarters of which was Kōfukuji Temple; the Fujiwara were patrons of the temple.

77. Poet Shun'e 俊恵 (1113–1191), a son of Minamoto Toshiyori (1105–1129), wrote the *Toshiyori zuinō* 俊頼髄脳. Shun'e received the tonsure at Tōdaiji Temple while still young. He studied poetry with his father and taught poetry to Kamo no Chōmei 鴨長明 (1155–1216), who wrote the *Hōjōki* 方丈記. Shun'e appears in another *Senjūshō* tale (4-6).

78. Tado district is in and near the present-day city of Zentsūji in Kagawa prefecture.

If I had a friend
Who had abandoned
This secular life,
I would talk with him
About the times we spent so vainly.[79]

When I passed by Naniwa Bay, I composed another poem:

Tsu no kuni no
Naniwa no haru ha
Yume nareya
Ashi no kareha ni
Kaze no wataru nari

Was the spring in
Naniwa Bay in Settsu
A dream?
Now the wind blows over
The reeds' withered leaves.[80]

Shun'e praised my poems, saying, "Your poems were superior to the verses of other poets, and now they are even better." I am very much afraid of writing something so indiscreet as this, but since I have been practicing the Way, I should be unaffected by other people's remarks, whether praise or scorn. So I have decided to write down exactly what Shun'e told me. While living in the secular world, his words made me feel proud and pleased, but thanks to the power of the Way, I now feel nothing special about them.

5-15 Creating a Human Figure at Mount Kōya

Around this time,[81] I was living deep in Mount Kōya. On every

---

79. The poem also appears in the *Shin kokin wakashū* 新古今和歌集 (no. 1659) and the *Saigyō hōshi kashū* 西行法師家集 (no. 547).
80. The poem also appears in the *Shin kokinwaka* 芦刈 of the Noh text.
81. See the previous tale, 5-14.

moonlit night I went out and met my *hijiri* friend[82] on a bridge and enjoyed the scenery with him. But soon he went off to the capital on an errand. After he had so unfeelingly left me, I somehow missed him for he disliked this transient life and understood the hearts of flowers and the moon. One day I happened to hear someone trustworthy casually talking about creating a man just as a demon would by gathering human bones.

So, just as I had overheard, I went out to a large field, gathered human bones and created a figure that looked human. But its color was bad and it had no heart. It had a voice like a stringed musical instrument. Indeed, a man can only speak when he possesses a heart. I concentrated on producing a voice, but it sounded only like someone playing a flute badly. That was all I could do, but still it was most extraordinary.

I thought, "Now what should I do with this human figure that I have made? If I destroy it, it would indeed be murder. But since it has no heart, it is just like a tree or a plant. Still, it does resemble a human." Hoping to preserve it, I placed it deep in Mount Kōya where no one would find it. If someone saw it, he would surely be frightened by such a demonic sight.

I felt all this to be most unusual, so when I went to the capital, I visited Tokudaiji Temple[83] to see the man who had told me how to create a human figure. But he was away at court, so I left without seeing him. Next I visited Lord Moronaka of Fushimi,[84] the former middle councilor, and asked him about [making a man]. He asked me, "How did you do it?" I explained, "I went to a large field where I saw no one, and I gathered human bones including a skull, and correctly connected them. I applied a medicine called *hisō*[85] on the bones, bound them

---

82. This *hijiri* friend may refer to Saijū 西住, who appears in *Senjūshō* 6-4 and 6-5; for the relationship between Saigyō and Saijū, see *Senjūshō zenchūshaku*, I, pp. 582–583.

83. Here Tokudaiji refers to the Tokudaiji family, part of the Fujiwara clan headed by Fujiwara Kimizane 藤原公実. Based upon a *Kokoncho monjū* tale (15, no. 494), Saigyō is believed to have worked for the family; see *Senjūshō zenchūshaku*, I, pp. 583–585.

84. Minamoto Moronaka 源師仲 (1115–1172), a son of Minamoto Morotoki and a great grandson of Minamoto Morofusa, or the Minister of the Right of Tsuchimikado.

85. *Hisō* ひさう, 比霜 contains arsenic.

to young rattan branches with strawberry and chickweed leaves,[86] and washed them with water. After applying ashes from the burned leaves of the *mukuge* and *saikachi* plants[87] to the top of the skull for hair, I carefully laid the figure on its face on a straw mat spread on the ground so that the wind would not disturb it. I returned to the place two weeks later and practiced the *hankon* cult by burning *jin* and *ko* incense."[88]

Lord Moronaka replied, "What you did was mostly correct. But I am afraid that you did not spend enough time on the *hankon* cult. I

....

86. Strawberry is effective for relaxing the internal organs and increasing energy (*Wakan sansai zue* 和漢三才図会, 96, *ichigo*). *Hakobe* はこべ, one of the seven grasses of spring 春の七草, is edible and effectively treats sores and scabs and was used for washing the eyes and teeth (*Wakan sansai zue*, 102, *hakobe*).

87. The skin, root, and flower of the *mukuge* 木槿, a short plant belonging to the *aoi* family, are effective for correcting bowel movements. *Saikashi* 西海枝, a thorny plant belonging to the bean family, is effective for resuscitation and was believed to revive the dead (*Wakan sansai zue*, 83, *saikashi*).

88. *Jin* 沈 are tall, fragrant plants that spread from India through southeast Asia and were used as medicine (*Wakan sansai zue*, 82). *Kō* 香 generally refers to civet and other fragrance from sandalwood. The *hankon* cult 反魂術 was used by Emperor Wu (r. 141–187 B.C.) of China, who saw an apparition of Lady Li, his deceased lover, in the smoke of burning incense, called *hankonkō* 反魂香. The story in the *Hakushibunshū* (4) was brought to Japan and appears in the *Kara monogatari* (15).

learned the style of Kintō, Grand Councilor of Shijō,[89] and made a human who is now a nobleman. I do not dare tell you his name because they say that both the creator and the created would melt away if the identity of the latter became known.

"But since you have learned this much, I will tell you more. You are not supposed to burn the incense because it has the power to ward off demonic relations and invite various bodhisattvas. But bodhisattvas greatly dislike life and death. That is why a soul finds it hard to enter a created figure.

"I wonder if you should have burned frankincense and daphne incense. Also when you practice the *hankon* cult, you are supposed to take no food for seven days. If you follow these instructions, you will certainly make no mistakes." But I thought the whole thing meaningless and did not pursue the matter further.

When the Minister of the Right Tsuchimikado[90] made a figure, an old man appeared to him in a dream and said, "I control all the dead. Why did you take the bones without telling me?" The old man appeared to hold a grudge against the minister, who thought, "If I leave instructions[91] on how to create a human and if my descendants make humans by following these instructions, cursing spirits may take their lives away. That would be no good at all." So the grand councilor immediately burned the instructions. When I heard this, I felt creating a human really was impractical, and people should remember this. But then I heard that the two children of Gochiku[92] were created by a demon called Heavenly Old Man at the River Ying,[93] and they became sages.

---

89. Fujiwara Kintō 藤原公任 (966–1041) was a poet and the editor of the *Wakan rōeishū* 和漢朗詠集 and the author of the *Shinzen zuinō* 新選髄脳, a study of poetry.
90. Minamoto Morofusa 源師房 (1008–1077) was a poet and the author of the *Doyūki* 土右記.
91. *Nikki* 日記, "diary" in the text.
92. Kuretake 呉竹 may refer to Wu Zhu-jun 呉竹君, who had two intelligent sons who advised King Wu of Zhou against attacking King Zhou of Yin but were rejected. King Wu destroyed Yin around 1050 B.C. The two brothers retired to Mount Shouyang, where they died of starvation.
93. A river in Henan province.

6-1 Genjō and Shinnyo Went to India

Long ago, Genjō Sanzō¹ wanted to promote the Law, so he went to India and visited all the holy places in 130 countries.² But when he saw the remains of the Gionshōja buildings,³ wild grass growing in the dried-up White Heron Pond,⁴ and the faded letters of *taibon-gejō*⁵ on decrepit stupas, he said to himself, "This is not what I had expected." He was disheartened to see the deterioration of the Law after all the hardship he had suffered while traveling through the Taklamakan Desert and Sōrei.⁶ Genjō also lamented that he would never meet Shaka Buddha as his contemporary and wrung the tear-soaked sleeves of his priestly robe. When I hear such a story, I also shed many tears because I feel great sympathy for him.

People who devote themselves to the Way of Poetry grieve for the beautiful [cherry] blossoms scattering in the breeze—in bloom for a mere seven days. Genjō had a strong belief in the Law and so he went to India, enduring much hardship and risking his life. He saw a violent wind blowing over the Numinous Eagle Mountain,⁷ and there was no bright moon; the lonely banks of the River Batsudai⁸ did not appear so pure, and there were only foxes, wolves, and tigers at the places where Shaka Buddha once preached. Genjō must have greatly missed the ascetics who had practiced the Law with only the clouds and the wind for companionship. I also often yearn to see where Shaka Buddha was

---

1. For Genjō, see notes 9 and 10 of story 1-8.
2. See *Senjūshō* 4-8 and *Daizōkyō* 大蔵経, 50, p. 221.
3. Gionshōja 祇園精舎, or Jetavana Monastery, where Shaka Buddha lived and preached for more than twenty years; see note 3 of story 4-8 and note 21 of story 6-2.
4. See note 7 of story 4-8 for the White Heron Pond. The *Daitōseiiki* 大唐西域記, 6 (*Daizōkyō*, 51, p. 899) states that the places Genjō visited in the seventh century were already ruined.
5. *Taibon* 退凡, "rejecting common people," and *gejō* 下乗, "dismounting." When King Bimbisāra made stone steps to cross valleys and mountains to facilitate travel to the Numinous Eagle Mountain to hear Shaka Buddha's preaching, two stupas with these letters were erected on the way.
6. Sōrei is in the present-day Himalayan region of Pamir. The same expression appears in *Senjūshō* 4-8.
7. The mountain is Gṛdhrakūṭa (Ryōjusen 霊鷲山), known as Vulture Peak as its shape resembles a vulture. It is located to the east of Rājagṛha, where Shaka Buddha preached many sermons.
8. Shaka Buddha entered nirvana on the western bank of this river.

born and once preached the Law. It is especially gratifying to hear of the Buddha's presence in the Numinous Mountain.

Now in this country of Japan, after suffering many sad experiences, Prince Nagaoka,[9] the crown prince of Emperor Heijō, became Master Dōsen's[10] disciple and received the tonsure with the Buddhist name Shinnyo. Superior in learning and virtues, he studied the Sanron teachings.[11] Confining himself in a room belonging to Sōzu Shūei[12] in Zenrinji Temple, he contemplated the water at the Deer Park[13] in order to wash away the dirt of his delusions. He also attained the state of "Seeing in One's Mind"[14] while staying in the Denpōin of Great Virtuous Shūen.[15] Finally, he extended his knowledge to the Shingon teachings of Great Master Kōbō.[16]

Dissatisfied with the learned monks of Japan, Shinnyo went to China, but he declared there, "I see no outstanding teachers here either." He decided to travel to India. The Chinese emperor was impressed by Shinnyo's strong conviction in the Law and offered him various treasures before his departure. But Shinnyo regarded them all as futile and

---

9. This prince was the third son of Emperor Heijō 平城 (r. 806–809) and was called Prince Takatake 高岳親王 (799–865); he was also called Prince Nagaoka 長岡親王 (later Shinnyo 真如). He received the tonsure after the Kusuko Revolt in 809 and lost his status as crown prince. His journey to India appears in the opening of the *Kankyonotomo*.
10. Dōsen 道詮律師 (d. 876), a scholarly monk of Hōryūji Temple.
11. The Sanron School 三論宗 propounded the three treatises *Chūron* 中論, *Jūnimonron* 十二門論 (by Nāgārjuna), and *Hyakuron* 百論 (by Deva); all are based on the theory of *kū* 空 (*śūnyatā*, or nothingness).
12. Shūei 宗叡僧都 (809–884) received the tonsure at the age of fourteen, studied the Hossō and Tendai teachings, went to China in 862, and brought back many Buddhist writings. His stories appear in the *Genkō shakusho* (3), the *Shingonden* 真言伝 (3), and the *Honchō kōsōden*. He died at Zenrinji Temple 禅林寺 (located in present-day Sakyō-ku, Kyoto), a headquarters of Shingon-mikkyō; it later became Eikandō 永観堂.
13. The Deer Park 鹿谷薗 (or 鹿谷苑), where Shaka Buddha gave his first sermon to his ascetic colleagues. The remark appears in the *Ryōjinhishō* 梁塵秘抄 (2 *Agonkyō*, no. 47) and *Shasekishū* 5-4.
14. *Kakuchi isshin* 覚知一心, "seeing and knowing [everything] in one's mind in order to leave the life-death cycle" (see note 10 of story 5-13); see *Gumei hosshinshū* 愚迷発心集 (*Shisō taikei*, p. 21).
15. Shūen 修円大徳 (771–835) was a scholarly monk of Kōfukuji Temple who later built Denpōin 伝法院 in the compound of Kōfukuji (*Honchō kōsōden*, 5, in *Dainihon bukkyō zensho*, 63, p. 47).
16. Kōbō Daishi 弘法大師 was the posthumous name of Kūkai 空海 (774–835), the founder of the Shingon Sect in Japan (*Senjūshō* 5-13).

returned them to the emperor except three tangerines, which he kept for his journey. Hearing a story like this greatly moves me.

Shūei returned to Japan, but Shinnyo, who had gone with him to China, did not accompany him.[17] So his people inquired after him and from China someone reported, "While traveling to India, Prince Shinnyo was attacked by tigers in Ceylon.[18] When the tigers tried to eat him, he said to them, 'I don't begrudge you my life since I uphold the Law. Do not err.' He defended himself with a staff, but in vain. This is what we have heard." On receiving this sad news, the emperor and the courtiers in his presence shed so many tears that they had to wring out their sleeves.

Shinnyo, too, was obviously attracted to India. Alas, how could his people have guessed that, leaving behind his golden brocade bedding, the prince would shave his head? How could anyone have thought of his leaving his bones in the wild grass of a strange country? This story surely teaches us that life is futile.

Quietly closing our eyes and recalling the past, we see this life like a vague dream in which both happiness and sadness are transient. Secretly counting the people in olden times on our fingers, we feel most sad to find neither the wise nor the foolish have survived. Only their names remain.

In the depths of a distant sea where waves reared up as broad as clouds with smokelike spray, there were three divine mountains[19] on which grew many medicinal herbs granting immortality. The stories of the Shin and Kan emperors, who every year sent Taoist *hōshi* to these mountains to collect the herbs, are now mere legends. Where is King Boku of Shū,[20] who galloped around the world on his eight stallions?

The sun sets today and will set again tomorrow. Months and years have passed and only names remain. Meanwhile, bones have turned to dust and disappeared under the sun in the wild fields.

....

17. In the *Kankyonotomo*, Shūei went to Mount Wu 五台山 to worship Boddhisattva Monju 文殊菩薩, but this *Senjūshō* tale does not explain why he and Shinnyo were separated.
18. 師子州.
19. Hōrai 蓬莱, Hōjō 方丈, and Eishū 瀛州 are the three legendary mountains of China. Emperor Shi 始 (259–210 B.C.), the first emperor of the Shin 秦 dynasty, sent *hōshi* (Taoists who practiced the *shinsenjutsu* 神仙術 cult) to Mount Hōrai to obtain the immortal medicine; he appears in the *Shiki* 史記 and the *Konjaku monogatarishū* (1-1).
20. 周穆王. The king neglected governing his kingdom while galloping around the world on his eight stallions (*Hakushi bunshū*, 4). The story also appears in the *Genpei seisuiki* 源平盛衰記 (4), the *Taiheiki* 太平記 (13), and the *Sangoku denki* 三国伝記 (1-14).

6-2　The Death of Emperor Go-Reizei

About the middle of the fourth month of Jireki 4 (1068), we heard that retired Emperor Go-Reizei[21] was ill. He suffered for only five days and then passed away on the evening of the nineteenth day of the month. While we were grieving, we learned that his mother[22] had also passed away at dawn on the same day. The mourning courtiers wet their flowery sleeves[23] with their dewlike tears, while attendants and servants could not stop crying all day long.

In distant China, on an autumn night of the seventh moon in the Tenpō period (742–756), Emperor Gensō and his consort, Lady Yōkihi,[24] pledged to each other, "In the sky, we will be like birds flying with their wings side by side, and like the trees on the ground spreading their branches side by side." But their deep pledge was vainly broken by Rokuzan,[25] and the couple were separated from each other. What happened to their pledge? It was most sad that the imperial mother [in Japan] had appeared quite well the previous evening but then took her last breath the following dawn.

On the day Emperor Go-Reizei died, Emperor Go-Sanjō[26] was enthroned. Thus there was both joy and grief as one person took the throne and two others were caught by death.[27] Happiness and sadness were commingled at that time; joy was in grief and grief was in joy. In our own lives we know that grief has its bounds and rejoicing, too, comes to an end. Happiness and sadness are so changeable that we can never find peace in our hearts.

After Emperor Go-Sanjō took the throne, people both high and low enjoyed much happiness thanks to his capable governing. But only six

---

21. Go-Reizei 後冷泉院 (1025–1068), the first son of Emperor Go-Suzaku (r. 1036–1045).
22. Jo'in 女院 was a retired consort of a former emperor.
23. Here the dew, *tsuyu*, refers to tears in relation to the flowery sleeves, or the sleeves with floral designs.
24. The romance of Emperor Xuan Zong and Yang Gui-fei appears in the *Hakushi bunshū* (12).
25. Rokuzan (Anrokuzan 安禄山, An Lu-shan) (705–757) spoke six languages and was favored by Emperor Xuan Zong. He later revolted against the emperor and was finally killed by his second son.
26. Go-Sanjō 後三条 (1034–1073) was the second son of Emperor Go-Suzaku.
27. "The two" refers to the deceased emperor and his mother. Here the expression *mujō no oni* 無常の鬼, "demon of transience," means death.

years later, in the Enkyū era (1069–1074), the emperor fell ill toward the end of the year. Finally, in the early part of the fifth month [of the following year], he passed away accompanied by the weeping birds who led him on the mountain path of death.[28] Hundreds of officials grieved just as deeply as when the two emperors Engi [Daigo] and Murakami died. Commoners outside the court lamented even more than at the time of Emperor Nintoku's death.[29] It was most pitiful to hear that the late emperor was only forty years of age. Who at court could grasp the reality of it? They all must have felt as if they were dreaming.

It is impossible to describe the deep grief of the imperial consort,[30] who had shared the emperor's bed, and of those who had attended the imperial bed chamber. They must have felt as if the sky had suddenly darkened, as if the sun and moon had lost their light.

28. *Hototogisu* (cuckoos) are believed to guide departed souls through a steep mountain to the Land after Death.
29. Emperor Daigo 醍醐 (r. 901–923) and his son, Emperor Murakami (r. 946–967), were regarded as benevolent rulers, as was Emperor Nintoku 仁徳 (r. 313–399), who was long remembered for suspending taxation for three years.
30. The term *kokubo* 国母, an imperial consort who gave birth to an emperor, here refers to Shigeko 茂子, who was a daughter of Fujiwara Kiminari and the mother of Emperor Shirakawa 白河 (r. 1072–1086).

It was especially pitiful to see the *unohana*, once in full bloom on the hedges but now blown by the wind and withered in the rain.[31] Sadness filled the imperial palace as well as all the capital. The happiness of the six years of the late emperor's reign disappeared in a moment and was replaced by grief. When they delivered [the deceased emperor] to the mountain at the Rendaino burial ground in the northeastern corner of Kōryūji Temple,[32] many *hototogisu* birds were heard as if their cries guided the emperor's soul along the way of death. Some people said the birds quickened the emperor's death because their cries sounded so sad. Birds weep when recalling someone in the past, so others surmised they might have been crying because they missed the late emperor, who was already in the past. Everyone must have felt the same.

People spent days and months earnestly reminiscing over old times. Before their tear-soaked mourning robes[33] were dry and the mourning period was over, they heard that the Grand Minister of Uji[34] had died. On whom could they rely now that they had lost the minister who had been a shining example of the good old days? While people were still lamenting the succession of recent misfortunes, the Great Lord of Nijō[35] died in the autumn of the following year. Such tragedies continued for three years until the third anniversary observance of Emperor Go-Sanjō's death was held; it was performed with great sadness. How pitiful it is that no one can live forever in this life. Ōbo's[36] wish for a life of ten thousand years sounds like a dream.

---

31. The small white blossoms of the *unohana* 卯の花 (deutzia) open in April and May. The blossoms in season withering in the rain imply the emperor's early death in May and anticipate the following sad incidents.
32. *Miyama okuri* 御山おくり refers to a funeral. Rendaino 蓮台野 is present-day Murasakino. The *hyakki* 百鬼 (a hundred demons or spirits) enter and leave via the *kimon* 鬼門 (demon gate) in a northeast direction.
33. *Fujigoromo* 藤衣, "wisteria robe," refers to a grey mourning robe.
34. Uji no Daisōkoku 宇治の大相国 (prime minister), or Fujiwara Yorimichi 藤原頼通 (992–1074), was the first son of Fujiwara Michinaga 藤原道長.
35. Dainijōdono 大二条殿, or Fujiwara Norimichi 藤原教通 (996–1075), was a younger brother of Yorimichi.
36. This is a reference to Seiōbo 西王母, a legendary Chinese recluse with a leopard's tail, a tiger's fangs, and disheveled hair who lives in the west and sometimes appears as a beautiful woman (see the *Sankaikyō* 山海経). A tale in the *Kara monogatari* (16) tells of a Chinese emperor who wished for longevity and received three peaches from her peach tree, which blooms and bears fruit once every three thousand years (*Tōbōsaku* 東方朔; in the *noh* text *Yōkyoku taikan*, 3).

[A mother composed this poem, expressing feelings about her death to her son:]

Kawaran to
Omou inochi ha
Oshikara de,
Satemo wakaren
Koto zo kanashiki

I don't begrudge
Exchanging my life
For yours.
But how sad it is
To be separated from you.[37]

The mother prayed for her son to the Bright Deity of Sumiyoshi Shrine. I wonder if he lived for a hundred years. If he did, his one hundred years would have passed as quickly as a dream and he surely must have faced a sad end. The life span of the old and the young is variable;[38] both may die today or tomorrow regardless of their age. People know the futility of life because it is not difficult to understand. Why then do they not do something for their future life instead of spending their time so vainly? If they don't understand, then there is nothing to say to them. Young people may be more concerned about their future. But why don't folk with white hair see the futility of life? In this life even young ones are not sure of tomorrow.

Watching gossamer floating in the air and morning glories opening in the sun, we know their life is as short as ours. They wait for the brief period of an evening, unaware of their [impending] disappearance in the morning.

Glory and pleasures do not last long and come to an end. Eikō,[39]

---

37. Akazome-emon 赤染衛門 prayed to the deity of Sumiyoshi Shrine 住吉神社 (in Osaka) for her sick son. Her poem appears in the *Akazome-emonshū* 赤染衛門集 (no. 50), the *Konjaku monogatarishū* (24-51), and the *Jukkinshō* (10-15).

38. *Rōshōfutei* 老少不定: the time of death is unknown for both young and old.

39. Eikō, or Rong Gong 栄公, of the Shunjū period (770–403 B.C.) in China propagated the Three Pleasures: being born as a human being, being born as a man, and achieving longevity.

who proposed the Three Pleasures, died of old age in the ninth month of the first year of the Rintoku period (664–666). Anrokuzan, who danced around and around,[40] died at the hand of his son as quickly as blossoms on a tree scatter in the wind. Wealthy Shudatsu's Seven Rare Treasures perished along with his life. If transience were overcome by high rank, only emperors would survive forever in this life. If transience were afraid of warriors [and weapons], would Anrokuzan have been killed by a sword? And if wealth were unaffected by feelings of futility, wealthy Shudatsu would have been immortal in this life. Close your eyes, calm your mind, and quietly ponder life. Then you will clearly see that all who are born will die and what begins inevitably ends.

On a spring day, while you sing songs in the Yoshino mountains, you see mist rising before you know it. The tree branches appear young and weak, the wind becomes soft and breezy. Trees and flowers come into bud. Once a spray of blossoms opens, spring arrives in the capital. Flowers bloom everywhere and the people enjoy singing and drinking at home. Then a strong wind blows away the fully-opened plum blossoms on the south-facing branches and the half-opened ones on the northern branches. Soon the tree is left with only light green leaves. The flowers wither in the rain or are scattered by the wind.

When you look around Sagano Field[41] in the second month, you see the entire area covered with grass wet in the spring rain. You also see bracken emerging; if you watch it casually as time passes, you will see it growing tall and dark, and eventually it will look entirely different.[42]

When summer comes, you look forward to hearing the *hototogisu* birds crying for fragrant citrus. You want to hear them calling on nights of early summer rain and anticipate their visits in the clouds of the dawning sky. While thus anxiously waiting, suddenly one day you hear them no more. Meanwhile, you secretly wish to see flowers on the grassy fields. One day you see them blossoming and the fields are covered, looking like sheets of brocade. You want to spend the whole

---

40. An Lu-shan danced in front of Emperor Xuan Zong, spinning around as fast as a gale (*Hakushi bunshū*, 3).
41. Sagano 嵯峨野 is northwest of Kyoto and is a popular *utamakura* place for poems about autumn plants and insects.
42. Various seasonal changes, including growing bracken, suggest the transience of life.

day in such fields, for you well remember someone saying, "Sixty years have passed but I never tire of gazing at them." Time passes quickly and you find yourself at the end of autumn with its chilly nights. In the cold frost, you see pampas grass disappearing in withered fields, while colorful leaves scatter away and finally snow falls on bare branches. The melting snow reminds you of the ups and downs of this futile life and its constant changes.

If you understand the reason for this life and always recite the Buddha's name, then you will not fail to attain the great gift of deliverance. In general, it is most desirable to devote yourself to the Way by leaving everything behind, even your wife and children. But if you cannot manage this, then having a strong desire and conviction for the Way is most important. Whatever you do, you should never neglect this conviction but always keep it in your mind. How tragic it would be if you were caught unawares in this life while your house was destroyed by flames.[43] But there is nothing unfair in whatever the buddhas do.

6-3　Sōzu Rinkai

Long ago Sōzu Rinkai of Tōin,[44] a man of great virtue, served for many years as the abbot of Yamashina Temple. One day in the tenth month when he was young, he watched a strong wind blow red leaves into a heap in the garden. Suddenly the sky grew dark; a shower of hail fell on the leaves then instantly disappeared. Perhaps as a result of past karmic relations, Rinkai immediately realized the futility of life. Dampening his sleeves with tears, he hurried to his parents and earnestly entreated, "Please let me become a monk!" To his confused parents he explained, "Everything appears pitiful when I see the futility of life. Following the Way of the buddhas, I would like to receive the tonsure for the sake of my future life and to guide others in the Way." His parents were most

---

43. A *kataku* 火宅, "burning house," is compared to this life, which is full of suffering. The parable is from the Chapter of Parables in the Lotus Sutra.
44. Rinkai 林懐 (951–1025), a scholarly monk of Kōfukuji Temple, became the *bettō* director, or abbot, of Yamashinadera (Kōfukuji) in Nara. He was also a lecturer at the Yuimae Meeting in 998 in the Tōin 唐院, a branch temple of Kōfukuji. He appears in the *Kasugagongen-kenkie* 春日権現験記絵, 10 and 15 (*Nihonemaki zenshū*, 15).

impressed, so he became a disciple of Kūsei,[45] the abbot of Yamashina Temple, in the spring of his thirteenth year.

Whenever Rinkai heard anything, he learned ten things and understood one hundred. In addition to his natural talent, he was able to endure hunger and lack of sleep as he applied himself to his studies. He read the ten rolls of *yuishiki* writings by the light of the moon, the light reflected on the snow near his window, and the light given off by fireflies. As a result of his efforts, he was promoted and eventually became abbot of the temple.

When Rinkai was still young, he accompanied Great Virtuous Chūsan[46] to Kumano.[47] As soon as Chūsan nobly recited the *Shingyō* sutra[48] at the base of Nachi Falls, Rinkai saw the water flow upward and a thousand-handed Kannon[49] appeared at the top of the falls. People said they praised not only Chūsan's virtue but also Rinkai's virtue, which allowed him to worship the Kannon.[50]

Rinkai's receiving the tonsure was very noble and extraordinary. There are some in this futile life who composed poems in the evening while they admired the moon and are buried on Mount Tai,[51] while others who appreciated flowers in the morning are blown away by a transient wind[52] in the evening. Intoxicated by the drinks of the ignorant[53] and bound by worldly attachments, we vainly pass the time until we have wrinkled foreheads and white hair. This is the usual way our minds work.

---

45. Kūsei 空晴 (878–957) was a scholarly monk of Kōfukuji Temple and a teacher of Abbot Shinki 真喜, who was Rinkai's master. His name appears also in *Senjūshō* 7-4.
46. Chūsan 仲算 (899–969 or 935–976) was a scholarly monk of Kōfukuji Temple and a disciple of Kūsei. He appears in *Senjūshō* 7-4 and 7-5 and *Konjaku monogatarishū* 28-8.
47. Kumano 熊野, south of the Kii peninsula, has been a popular religious site; the Nachi Falls and the Kumano sansha 熊野三社 (Kumano Three Shrines) are located there.
48. *Hannya shingyō*; see note 10 of story 1-8.
49. *Senju kannon* 千手観音 has an eleven- or twenty-seven-faced head and forty hands. Each hand contains one eye and will help sentient beings in the twenty-five worlds (*nijūgoukai* 二十五有界); for the Kannon, see note 8 of story 1-8 and *Senjūshō* 5-8, 7-5, 7-11, and 8-35.
50. *Namami* 生み, "in life," meaning that he actually saw Kannon with his eyes, not in a dream or delusion.
51. Here, Mount Tai 泰山 in China was a burial ground.
52. *Mujō no kaze* 無常の風, "death."
53. Ignorance that confuses our minds is compared to *mumyō no sake* 無明の酒, the *sake* of no light.

But Rinkai was different—even when he was not much more than ten years old. As soon as he saw the leaves blown by the wind and the hail disappearing before he could catch it in his hands, he realized the futility of life and shed tears of deep sadness. This does not seem to be the result of a shallow karmic relation but of something far deeper and more meaningful.

How does anyone realize the futility of life? Why do I vainly lose my way? If someone young [like Rinkai] found the Way, why can't I find it when my hair becomes as white as snow and my eyebrows look like frost? Why can't I realize the penetrating truth of futility, which should bring tears to my eyes? I regret much of my life except for one pleasing experience. While I was serving at the court of Emperor Toba,[54] I performed my duties as best I could, trying to outdo others and invite no criticism. Enduring the summer heat, I worked all day long, wiping away the perspiration. Enduring the severe cold of snowy winter, I prostrated myself on the sandy ground in the blustering wind just to worship the imperial face and wished for nothing contrary to his will. I met and became familiar with a beautiful lady [at court][55] and grieved greatly when we were separated like clouds on a summit blown by a violent wind. I forgot neither her face nor our pledge. But who could tell me if it was all a dream or real as I stood alone in a grassy field? Seeing the dewdrops on my sleeves changing their color,[56] I grew dejected in that frost-withered field. Unaware of the passage of time, I vainly spent the following days and months playing with the moon and flowers.[57]

Suddenly one day toward the end of the Chōshō era (1132–1135), I felt the futility of life deeply in my heart. I soon left my office at court and also my wife and children and finally became a wandering monk. My wife, the woman with whom I had once made a pledge, shaved her

---

54. *Sendō* 仙洞, a retired emperor's palace, refers here to the palace of Retired Emperor Toba 鳥羽 (r. 1107–1123). Saigyō served the emperor as a samurai before receiving the tonsure; for his personal story, see *Senjūshō* 5-10 and 6-5 and the *Saigyō monogatari* (*Saigyō zenshū*, p. 961).

55. Unidentified. Saigyō was attracted to Lady Mifukuin, the imperial consort of Emperor Toba, in the *Saigyō no monogatari*, *Shin Nihon koten bungaku taikei*, 54, pp. 372–391; for an English translation, see Yoshiko Dykstra, "Saigyō no Monogatari," *Journal of Intercultural Studies* 28: 29–41. For Saigyō's life, see Mezaki Tokue, *Saigyō no shisōteki kenkyū* (Tokyo: Yoshikawa kōbunkan), 57–58.

56. *Iro kawaru tsuyu*, "color-changed dew," refers to tears of sadness, or *kōrui* 紅涙, "red tears."

57. *Usobuku*, "pretending to play," here implying criticism of passing the time frivolously.

head and is now living in a *bessho* on Mount Kōya.[58] I heard that my daughter remained in the capital with her relatives. Thus we are separated, living in three different places as if we had never exchanged any friendly talk.

There is an old proverb: "Horses from the north neigh in the north wind and birds from the south gather on branches facing the south."[59] Ignoring the criticism of others, I went to see my old home. It was most pitiful to see the crumbled earthen wall and the leaning gate. I went inside; the old dwelling was dilapidated because no one was living there. The wind blew lightly over the moss under the eaves and the vines on the hedge. Both moonlight and rain could enter the house through the broken thatched roof, and insects sang among the grass, which grew in profusion. The place where I had once slept was now a nest for insects. I felt the entire place seemed pitiful, yet it so suited my taste that I wanted to live there again. I recalled the saying "Your body is like your old house." The dilapidated state of my old house reminded me of the transient state of my life, and I finally left there with my sleeves soaked with tears.

6-4 Holy Man Nishiyama and Saijū's Death[60]

At the start of the eighth month, Holy Man Saijū[61] of Nishiyama and I passed by Naniwa Bay.[62] We saw some fishing boats floating on the waves like leaves, for it was an especially fine day with no wind. I said to my companion, "I wonder how many fish have been caught? How tragic! Let's board a boat and pray for the fishes' afterlife!" Saijū replied, "Indeed. Let's do it!" So we waded through the shallow water to a boat and said to the fisherman, "Please, let us come aboard."

---

58. *Bessho* 別所, "separate place," refers to the halls and huts built at a distance from the main Kongōbuji Temple of Mount Kōya. A tale in the *Hosshinshū* (6-5) narrates how Saigyō's wife lived as a nun in Amano at the foot of Mount Kōya (the western valley of Mount Kōya in Kii province) and later her daughter joined her.

59. *Kouma* 湖馬, horses from the northern Hu region, and *etsuchō* 越鳥, birds from the southern Yue region, including Vietnam, appear in the *Bunsen* 文選 (*Shinkanbun taikei* 新漢文大系, 29). The expression refers to people's nostalgic feelings toward their old dwellings.

60. This story is related to the following one, 6-5, which has no title.

61. Saijū 西住, a close friend of Saigyō; see story 6-5.

62. *Naniwa no watashi* 難波の渡し refers to Osaka Bay. Naniwa is the old name for Osaka.

The fisherman refused, saying, "This boat is for fishing, not for carrying passengers. What's the use of coming aboard?" But we insisted and forced our way onto the boat. We secretly recited the Buddha's names for the poor fish and then sailed to several beaches to watch the fishing. Meanwhile, I casually recited a poem:

Naniwabito
Ikanaru e ni ka
Kuchihaten

The fisherman of Naniwa,
I wonder in which bay
He will die?

Saijū pondered the last portion of the poem as he rested his chin on his hands. But immediately the old fisherman added the last two lines:

Au koto nami ni
Mi o shizume tsutsu[63]

Without meeting [the Buddha] among the waves,
He will sink [into the sea].

I felt his contribution was very interesting and was delighted to hear such an unexpected poem after we had forced ourselves onto his boat. My joy was indeed great. The old man stopped fishing and concentrated on composing linked verses. Because I was impressed by his abilities, I began another poem:

Fune no uchi
Nami no shita nizo
Oinikeru

---

63. *Nami* 波, "waves," are associated with *nami*, or *nai* 無い, "lacking," "without." Thus the last two lines mean the fishermen with no chance of meeting a buddha will sink into the sea of life and death as they repeat the sufferings of the life-death cycle. A similar poem by the Regent Prime Minister in the *Shinkokin wakashū* 新古今和歌集, or *Shinkokinshū*, (18, no. 1704) has the second line *nami no ue*, "above the waves."

While in the boat
I am aged
Under the waves

The old man thought for a while and then added:

Ama no shiwaza mo
Itoma nano yo ya[64]

The work of fishermen
Allows no rest in this life.

While we were exchanging poems, the sun began to set behind the western mountain. We rowed back to the old fisherman's shack and bade him farewell, telling him that we had no particular destination in mind. He replied, "It's already dark," and insisted that we remain, so we decided to spend the night at his place.

Later, the old man began to reminisce: "I am a descendant of

---

64. A similar poem by the Regent Prime Minister appears in the *Shinkokinshū* (11, no. 1077) as a love poem with the last line *mi o tsukushi tsutsu*, "devoting or exhausting oneself."

Middle Councilor Yamakage.[65] My father used to live in Higashiyama in the capital but moved to this area owing to difficulties in his life. He befriended a woman of Naniwa Bay, and I was born. My parents died when I was only three years old. From that time my grandmother, my mother's mother, took care of me, but she died when I was twelve years old. I did not know how to survive except by fishing. Although I have thought of shaving my head and living somewhere else, I have been unable to abandon this life. Life is very hard for me. It is sad to take so many lives to make a living. Even now, several times a day, I think of cutting my hair, and whenever I think of it, tears fill my eyes.

"I found some poetry among my father's belongings and have been consoling my heart by composing poems. I have no wife or children and am now more than fifty years old. I am very envious of you. I wish I could join you." Then the old man cut his hair on the spot and gave his house, where he had lived for a long time, to a close friend. He joined us after naming himself Gyōjū, and he later became a fine ascetic.

Gyōjū went to the capital, lived in a hut in Nishiyama, practiced the Way, and was respectfully called the Holy Man of Nishiyama. He did not come from a lowly family, but to survive he had worked hard and without rest, boiling seawater for salt, collecting seaweed, and catching fish with his nets. In this way he had spent fifty years before suddenly taking the tonsure. Wasn't this most noble of him?

Some years later I went to the capital and visited Gyōjū's hut in Nishiyama. His hut was located in a shady place on a mountain with a stream of pure water flowing nearby. In front was a vast, wild field with an unobstructed view of the four directions. Wild foxes lived in the thorny bushes and owls hooted in the pine trees. Gyōjū looked most impressive as he sat quietly practicing meditation in his neatly arranged dwelling with the buzzing insects and deer as his friends.

He said to me, "Thanks to you at our last meeting, I am as you see me now and most happy, praying for my present and future lives. How can I reward you? By delivering myself as soon as possible."

I know Gyōjū had been aware of the futility of life since his youth. When a disciple asked him, "What is the best way to obtain my future life?" the holy man replied, "Relax your mind and feel the transience of life."

---

65. Perhaps this refers to Fujiwara Yamakage 藤原山陰 (d. 888), a son of Takafusa. The old fisherman in the story is unidentified. The story of Yamakage's saving a turtle appears in *Konjaku monogatarishū* 19-29, *Jikkinshō* 1-5, and *Hasedera kenki* 長谷寺験記 3-13.

6-5 [Untitled]

When I heard that Holy Man Saijū was ill, I left my place on Mount Kōya and went to the capital to visit him in his hut. He was so ill that he could hardly speak. As soon as he saw me, he said tearfully, "I'm so happy." I felt so much pity for him that I also shed tears. He continued, "I am the one who should console you in your lonely life. And I feel all the sadder as I think how much you will grieve when you are left alone after I am gone." As he said this, he squeezed his tear-soaked sleeves. Greatly overwhelmed, I stayed with him that night, talking about our afterlives, but I was afraid his last moments were fast approaching. Finally at dawn, the holy man passed away, reciting the Buddha's names and facing west.

While preparing the funeral, I heard that the middle councilor of Kazan'in[66] wanted to see me, so I called on him because I wanted to talk about Saijū. When I told him about my deceased friend, the councilor tearfully said, "Last spring I went to the Higashiyama flower-viewing[67] with him and that was last time I saw him." He then recited a poem:

Nare nare te
Mishi ha nagori no
Haru zo tomo,
Nado shirakawa no
Hana no shita kage[68]

Familiar with the springs,
But farewell to the last one,
How did I miss the shadow
Under the blossoms
In Shirakawa?

---

66. Unidentified.
67. *Hana* 花, "flower," "cherry blossom." Higashiyama 東山, the eastern part of Kyoto, is famous for its cherry blossoms.
68. *Nare nare*, "familiar with," suggests his familiar friend, Saijū. *Nagori* 名残り implies separation (by death) or farewell; *nagori no haru* 名残りの春 means "farewell in the spring." *Shira* of Shirakawa implies "to know" and *nado shirakawa* suggests "why" or "how not to know." Shirakawa is a river flowing in the north of the capital and is also a region that includes Higashiyama and east of the Kamo River. *Kage*, "shade" or "shadow," implies death (of his friend). The poem by Fujiwara Masatsune appears in the *Shinkokinshū* (16, no. 1456).

His poem truly touched my heart. On my way home, the color of my black robe grew faded with the dew and [my tears]. Since I began serving at court and relying on the Buddha,[69] Saijū had accompanied me whenever I asked him to come. But now he was gone, leaving me behind. I felt it almost impossible to go on living.

I became sad merely looking at trees and plants. The moonlight's dim appearance [as my eyes clouded with tears] darkened my feelings. Moreover, when the wind, lightly blowing over the leaves of the *shino* plants, dispersed the dew, I felt like a plover, its cries sounding so pathetic. When I heard the faint call of geese flying in the sky, my heart ached so much that I felt as if I were severing my intestines in the *kōkyū* palace.[70]

After I returned to Mount Kōya, I dreamed of Saijū, who said, "I was reborn in the Outer Palace of the Tosotsuten,"[71] and then I awoke. It was sad that he had not been reborn in the Inner Palace, but then the Outer Palace was just as fine. If I had served in the imperial palace in this life, how could I be reborn in the Outer Palace in heaven? In my old life, by arranging my hairstyle and dressing properly, I was allowed to come and go at the palace and enjoyed a most splendid lifestyle thanks to the imperial blessing. But now I am aged and have cut my hair and shaved my head and am dressed in a shabby hemp robe. People may think I look ridiculous. But this is the true heart of [an ascetic practicing the Way].

This life is futile and transitory, but people will allow themselves to get caught up in the desire for profit and fame and will sink into the Three Evil Realms[72] forever. Isn't that most regrettable? The lord on whom you depended cannot help you; your relatives, including your wife whom you loved and children whom you raised with so much

---

69. *Gaō kie* 鵞王帰依, "putting faith in the Buddha," or receiving the tonsure.
70. The plover's sad cry. The expression "cutting intestines" (*danchō* 断腸) conveys extreme sadness, chagrin, regrets, and vital actions. *Kōkyū* 行宮 refers to a temporary palace where emperors stay during an outing. The expression is based upon a poem by Bo Ju-i, which narrates how sad the moon appears viewed from a temporary palace and that the cry of a monkey on a rainy night sounds as sad as cutting one's intestines (*Hakushi bunshū*, 12, *Chōgonka*).
71. Tosotsuten 都卒天, or Tuṣita Heaven, the fourth of the six heavens in the World of Desire (*kārma dhātu*) located high above Mount Sumeru. There are two palaces in this heaven: Gein 外院, "Outer Palace," and Naiin 内院, "Inner Palace," where Miroku Buddha (the future Buddha) resides.
72. The Three Evil Realms, or Worlds (hell, hungry ghosts, and animals), are known variously as *sanzu* 三途, *san'akudō* 三悪道, and *san'akushu* 三悪趣.

care, cannot accompany you on the journey after death.[73] You will grieve alone and will be confused alone. This is what usually happens to people in the afterlife.

So wouldn't it be more pleasant to leave your [worldly attachments, including your] wife and children, visit interesting places, and practice the Way at various temples in the mountains? When you leave secular life, you have no desires. Without desires, you have no frustration. With no powerful lord to serve, you are free from his anger. Without a wife and children to love, you have neither delusions nor attachments. Carrying no treasures with you, you are not fearful of thieves when you sleep in fields or on mountains. Being a recluse, what enemies do you have? And you are no longer concerned about rising and falli ng in your afterlife.[74]

6-6 Lord Fuke and the Oracles of the Kasuga Deity

During the reign of Emperor Toba (1107–1123)[75] lived Lord Nyūdō Fuke,[76] a grandson of Lord Kyōgoku[77] and a son of Lord Gonijō.[78]

---

73. *Chūu* 中有 is the intermediate existence after death and before rebirth in another world. The periods vary but usually extend for seven, thirty-five, and forty-nine days, during which time services are held.
74. *Goshō no shōchin* 後生の昇沈, "rise and fall in the afterlife," refers to the alternative possibilities of being reborn in a better place (the heavens) or falling or sinking into bad places (the hells). If a person is completely free of attachment, he does not even concern himself with being reborn in a Buddha land or falling into hell.
75. Toba 鳥羽 (1103–1156), crown prince of Emperor Horikawa. After Former Emperor Shirakawa died in 1129, Toba was involved in *insei* 院政, or cloistered government, for twenty-eight years. Later he turned against Retired Emperor Sutoku and led the Hōgen Revolt. He excelled in playing the flute, and his poems appear in imperial anthologies such as the *Kin'yō wakashū*.
76. Nyūdō Fuke 入道富家, or Fujiwara Tadazane 藤原忠実 (1078–1162). Since he lived in the Fuke district, east of Uji, he was called Lord Fuke. *Nyūdō* is an honorific title for a tonsured person. After his father, Moromichi, died, he was adopted by his grandfather, Morozane. He became a regent in 1107 and prime minister in 1112. The *Chūgaishō* and the *Fukego* record his conversations.
77. Kyōgoku 京極大殿, or Fujiwara Morozane 藤原師実 (1042–1101), was a son of Yorimichi and a grandson of Michinaga. He became a regent in 1086 and prime minister in 1088. He excelled in poetry, music, and calligraphy. His poems appear in various imperial anthologies such as the *Goshūi wakashū*. His writings include the *Kyōgoku kanpakushū* 京極関白集 and the *Kyōgoku kanpakuki* 京極関白記.
78. Gonijō 後二条, or Fujiwara Moromichi 藤原師通 (1062–1099), a son of Morozane, became *kanpaku* regent in 1094. His diary is titled *Gonijō Moromichiki* 後二条師通記.

There is no need to describe the great respect in which he was held by officials because, as a scion of the Fujiwara clan, he knew how to manage political affairs well. Many days and months passed, and Lord Fuke's hair became as white as snow and his eyebrows like the frost. He wanted to take a leave of absence from his duties and receive the tonsure.

One day he visited the Bright Deities of Kasuga Shrine, where he saw a young boy of eleven or twelve years of age. Suddenly the boy appeared most noble and lovable [as if possessed] and said to him, "Although all phenomena are within one's mind,[79] the inner consciousness[80] has *kyō*[81] senses and *shin* [mind]. When the mind arises, it completely depends on inner consciousness. How interesting this is!"[82]

Feeling this to be a most extraordinary occurance, Lord Tadazane [Fuke] remained silent and the boy continued, "I am the third deity of

---

79. 不離識: not separate from *shiki* 識 (consciousness).
80. *Naishiki* 内識: "inner-consciousness."
81. *Kyō* 境 are things sensed by the eyes, ears, nose, tongue, body, and will. The idea reflects the concept of consciousness only.
82. 心起必託内境生故: This is because mental activity (*shin* 心, "mind") is activated (*ki* 起, "arises") through its necessary dependence on inner consciousness; see *Daijō hōon girinshō* (*Kokuyaku daizōkyō, shūkyōbu*, 18, p. 57).

Kasuga Shrine[83] and am very glad you are visiting me today. I appreciate with tears that you realize the futility of life and have decided to receive the tonsure. In order to show my appreciation, I have given you this oracle. Never forget the transience of life and keep it always in your mind. That is what I esteem most.

"You have two sons[84] who will eventually become the leaders of your clan. Master Tadamichi manages political affairs honestly. Skillful in calligraphy, music, and poetry, he is popular among the people, but I don't agree with him because he has no faith in pursuing the Way. His younger brother, Master Yorinaga, excels in Confucian studies, manages worldly affairs, and is most clever in judging people's good and bad qualities. He will be an outstanding man in the future. But unfortunately he ignores the buddhas and deities and causes trouble in temples, so I don't regard him highly either." With this the boy finished. Appearing to recover his senses, he then left. When I heard this story, I was most impressed.

They [the gods and buddhas] are very pleased with people who have faith in them. The gods and buddhas care for all sentient beings, much more than parents care for their children. They feel most sad when they see us immersed in the flames of delusion. They feel most happy when they help us realize the futility of this life, abandon delusions, and turn to the Way.

A parent thinks of his only child so much that he doesn't mind sacrificing himself for his child's sake. If he sees the child run into a fire and choke in the smoke, doesn't this cause him terrible grief? Is a mother relieved to see her child escape the flames and make for a safe place? The gods and buddhas are just like caring parents.

But in spite of such divine help, we ignorant humans only compete

---

83. See *Senjūshō* 6-3 for the Kasuga Shrine. Prince Ame no koyane no mikoto is enshrined as the third deity of the shrine and as the tutelary deity of the Fujiwara clan; also see *Senjūshō* 9-1.

84. Fujiwara Tadamichi 藤原忠通 (1097–1164) was the first son of Tadazane. He became *kanpaku* regent and head of the clan in 1121. In 1150, his father stripped him of his rank and office and gave them to Yorinaga, his younger brother. From that time the brothers fought each other. After Yorinaga died in 1156, Tadamichi regained the position of clan head. His poems appear in the *Kin'yō wakashū*; he also wrote a diary, the *Hōshōji kanpakuki* 法性寺関白記. Fujiwara Yorinaga 藤原頼長 (1120–1156), the second son of Tadazane, was adopted by Tadamichi. Later Yorinaga sided with Retired Emperor Sutoku but was defeated in the Hōgen Revolt and died. His diary, the *Daiki* 台記, reveals his scholarship in Chinese and Buddhist studies (*Zōho shiryōtaisei*, *Daiki*, 1, pp. 98–100).

against each other and try to get ahead, which results in nothing but hardship in the future. How dreadful this is!

The Kasuga Deity's oracle is found in the *yuishiki* chapter of a sutra.[85] How can a shallow person understand a deep mind? Disregarding the meaning of the oracle's text, I repeatedly recite the verses [of the oracle]. My mind becomes pure as tears fill my eyes. Because it is such a noble text, even an ignorant mind [that finds it] is drawn to the Way. What the text means is this: We should not become attached even to our own consciousness. This is the highest level of understanding[86] of the *yuishiki*.

6-7 Sōzu Eshin at Kamo Shrine

Sōzu Eshin[87] of Yokawa was a monk of great learning.[88] His long-accumulated merits and virtues exceeded those of others, and his miraculous revelations benefited many people like the blessings of the Law.

One day in the tenth month of a certain year, Eshin visited Kamo Shrine.[89] His heart felt purified as he spent an entire night in front of the shrine. A sudden shower fell and a stormy wind hid the moon behind the clouds. The villagers seemed to enjoy the moonlight as the clouds cleared away. While gazing at the dew on the grass in a withered field, Eshin thought of the transience of life and became sad and miserable. Then he heard a noble voice coming through the shrine doors, reciting this verse:

Tsune naki yo niwa
Kokoro todomuna

---

85. For the *yuishiki* concept, see *Senjūshō* 5-4.
86. *Kanpō* 観法, "to observe, understand, realize the Law," can also be translated as "practicing meditation."
87. Eshin 恵心, or Genshin 源信 (942–1017), was a monk of the Tendai Sect. He studied under Master Jikei 慈恵大師 (Ryōgen 良源) on Mount Hiei and established the Pure Land Sect in Japan. Since he lived in Yokawa, he was called Sōzu of Yokawa. *Sōzu* 僧都 is a priestly title below *sōjō*, or abbot. Yokawa 横川 is located to the north of Konponchūdo on Mount Hiei. Ryōgen built Eshin'in 恵心院 Temple in Yokawa and lived there.
88. *Chisha* 智者, a learned person, is related to *chishiki* 智識, or *zenchishiki* 善智識, a good teacher who leads others to the Way.
89. Kamosha 加茂社 in Kyoto has two shrines: Kamo Wakeikazuchi and Kamo Mioya.

Do not rest your heart
On the transient life

Immediately Eshin recited the following two lines:

Gekka no nasake mo
Hate wa araba koso

The feelings of the flowers and the moon
Have their limitations.[90]

The shrine began to shake with a frightful noise and Eshin heard the same voice cry out, "How moving!" I heard that Naiki Nyūdō,[91] who [also] witnessed this and heard the voice, was filled with awe.

The shrine deity was greatly impressed by Eshin, whose poem expressed his true feelings about the futility of life and was a most wonderful blessing of the Law. If the feelings of the flowers and the moon had lasted forever, he would have retained his heart in this life.

6-8 The Holy Men of Sanonowatari

Around the eighth month in the year of Eiryaku (1160–1161), I went to Sanonowatari in Shinano province.[92] I decided I could not simply pass through the district after seeing the flowers blooming so beautifully and hearing the melodious chirping of the insects. While wandering in a field there, I found a path[93] in the trodden grass beside the usual route. I wondered, "What kind of path is this?" I followed it until I saw a monk sitting in a hut made of plants and grasses such as *susuki*, *karukaya*,

---

90. In other words, since the flowers and the moon are as changeable as this life, I will not attach myself to such transient matters.
91. Naiki Nyūdō 内記入道, or Yoshishige Yasutane 慶慈保胤 (931–1003), was a son of Kamo Tadayuki, who was a Yin-Yang master. His writings include the *Nihon ōjō gokurakuki* and the *Chiteiki* (*Senjūshō* 5-3). His association with Genshin is mentioned in *Senjūshō* 7-6.
92. Sanowatari is perhaps somewhere in present-day Nagano prefecture (near Yamanouchi-chō, Shimotakai-gun).
93. *Tamaboko* 玉ぼこ *no yukikau michi* refers to a path of coming and going. *Tamaboko* is a pillow word, or *makurakotoba*, to introduce *michi*, "path."

hagi, and *ominaeshi.*[94] When I looked inside I saw paper labels attached to the plants that had been brought into the hut. A poem was written on a label attached to the door, which was made of pampas grass:

Aki no yokaze no
Susuki shigeru
Ika naran
Yoru naku mushi no
Koe no samukesa[95]

How does the night wind
Pass over the pampas grass
In the autumn field?
There is the night's coldness
In the insects' chirping.

Another poem was written on a label attached to a *karukaya* blind:[96]

Yamakage ya
Kurenu to omoe[97] *ba*
Karukaya no
Shita oku tsuyu mo
Madaki iro[98] *kana*

As I thought of the sunset

---

94. *Susuki* is Japanese pampas grass; *karukaya*, a lemon grass; *hagi*, Japanese bush clover; *ominaeshi*, a perennial plant with small yellow flowers. All are popular plants associated with autumn in the *waka* poem tradition.
95. The following six poems, all related to autumn, appear in the *Tsuchimikadoin hyakushu* 土御門院百首 (One Hundred Poems by Retired Emperor Tsuchimikado [r. 1183–1198]), nos. 38–43.
96. A *shitomi* is a board attached to a framed lattice to block out sunlight; it was used as a screen or an outdoor fence. In this poem, a *shitomi* made of *karukaya* is used as a blind or screen.
97. In these poems, I have used modern readings for the original *kana*, such as *omoe* for *omohe*, "thinking."
98. *Madaki*, "premature"; *iro*, "color" (the autumn color). This means that the dew appears to prematurely have autumn color. The poem hints at the subtle approach of autumn.

In the mountain shade,
I saw the dew already resting
Under the *karukaya*
In early autumn color.

Yet another, written on a *fusuma* door made of *fujibakama* plants:[99]

Tsuyu no nuki[100]
Ada ni oruchō
Fujibakama
Aki kaze matade
Tare ni kasa mashi

To whom shall I lend
The wisteria skirt
Vainly woven by the dew
Without its waiting
For the autumn wind?

On a door made of *ogi* blossoms:[101]

Yuu sare ba
Magaki no ogi ni
Fuku kaze no
Me ni minu aki o
Shiru namida kana

I shed tears in the dusk
As I feel autumn
Approaching invisibly

---

99. *Fusuma* is made of paper. *Fujibakama* (wisteria skirts) is a thoroughwort belonging to the chrysanthemum family; it grows to a meter in height and has small, pale purple blossoms. It is one of the Seven Autumn Grasses (*aki no nanakusa* 秋の七草). In this poem the plant is treated as a pair of *hakama* skirts of wisteria color.
100. *Nuki* refers to *nukiito* 貫糸, a horizontal thread in weaving and implies another word, *nugu*, "to take off."
101. *Ogi* 荻 is a common reed about 1.5 meters high belonging to the rice plant family. It grows by the water and has silky ears; it was used to thatch roofs.

In the wind passing
Over the *ogi* in the hedge.

On a label attached to a blooming *ominaeshi* plant:[102]

Ominaeshi
Ueshi magaki no
Aki no iro
Hana o shirotae no
Tsuyu zo kawaranu

The *ominaeshi* blossoms
Planted in the hedge
Are as beautiful as
The white silky dew
Of autumn color.

And finally a poem for *hagi* blossoms:[103]

Hagi ga hana
Utsurou[104] *niwa no*
Aki kaze ni
Shitaba mo mata de
Tsuyu wa chiri tsutsu

The *hagi* blossoms
In the autumn garden
Are blown by the passing wind,
The dew is scattered away
Before resting on the lower leaves.

---

102. *Ominaeshi* 女郎花 blooms in the summer and autumn with small umbrella-like yellow blossoms and is one of the Seven Autumn Grasses. In the poem, *aki no iro* 秋の色, "autumn color," implies an autumn atmosphere and scene. *Shirotae*, "white silk," refers to something beautiful. *Tsuyu* 露, "dew," in *tsuyu zo kawaranu*, "not a bit different": I have translated this as "as beautiful as."

103. *Hagi* 萩, a member of the bean family, is 1.5 meters high with reddish purple or white tiny blossoms; it is one of the Seven Autumn Grasses.

104. *Utsurou*, "changing," "transient"; it implies the futility and short life of the blossoms and the dew.

The monk was sitting quietly absorbed in meditation. Feeling most impressed and inspired by the monk, I asked him, "Who are you and where do you come from?" He simply replied, "I have been here since spring." He remained silent and ignored all of my other questions. Meanwhile, the sun began to set, and even though I felt very sad to leave him, I tearfully bade the monk farewell. I took off my hemp robe and left it with him as I hoped to establish a relationship[105] with him.

While heading west, I came to a very steep mountain with a running stream of fresh water. The appearance of the rocks was most unusual. The mountain scenery was more impressive than any painting and attractive enough to capture a person's eyes and heart. I walked upstream for about one *chō* and saw a monk of about sixty years of age sitting among the leaves. I thought here is another man [in meditation]. Feeling excited, I quickly approached him. I discovered that while sitting in an elegant posture, as if sleeping, he had expired. A poem was written on a label tied to a tree branch beside him:

Murasaki no
Kumo matsu mi ni shi

---

105. *Kechien* 結縁, "binding a relationship," means to establish a friendship or relationship with someone who can lead one to the Way.

Arazareba,
Sumeru tsuki o zo
Itsumade mo miru[106]

Being unable
To wait for the purple clouds,
I only remain
To gaze forever
At the clear moon.

I felt most sad and full of pity, thinking that this monk must belong to the same practice as the holy man in the hut. I hurried back to the hut and explained about the monk in the mountains. "Most sad," said the holy man. Reaching for his ink stone, he wrote this poem on a sheet of paper:

Mayoi tsuru
Kokoro no yami o
Terashi koshi
Tsuki mo ayanaku
Kumo gakure nuru[107]

The moon that
Illuminates the darkness
Of the distressed heart
Also vainly hides away
Behind the clouds.

After finishing the poem, the holy man breathed his last breath; it was as if he had fallen asleep with the writing brush still in his hand. Filled with pity, I clung to his sleeves and cried. Then, worrying about the monk in the mountains, I tearfully hurried back there and saw him still seated with his head bent forward.

---

106. The author of the poem is unidentified. *Murasaki no kumo* 紫雲, "purple clouds," signifies the Pure Land of Amida, who comes riding on purple clouds to receive his devotees at their last moments. *Mi ni shi arazareba*, literally, "because I am not the one," means the protagonist is not yet qualified to wait for the purple clouds, implying a humble attitude in his faith.

107. The author of the poem is unidentified. The term *ayanaku*, "unreasonably" or "worthlessly," in the poem suggests a regretful feeling as well as the futility of life.

Since I could not leave him as he was, I decided to cremate him, so I took a flint and prepared to burn the body. But I was too sad to do so [immediately] and decided to draw a portrait of him before the cremation. Wiping away my tears, I sketched him in the hope that his portrait would keep me company in my lonely life. As soon as I finished it, I cremated him and returned to the hut in the field. There the holy man was also sitting with his head bent forward. I made a drawing of him as well and then cremated him. I remained there in the field, reciting the Buddha's name throughout the night and praying for the holy man's rebirth in the Pure Land. At daybreak, I collected all the poems in the hut and left there in tears.

Indeed, the control these two monks exerted over [their] lives and deaths was most unusual and truly noble. They were probably able to do this because they had been fine Zen monks. And their poems were truly extraordinary in this degenerate age. The places where they lived appeared so [peaceful] that they must have purified their hearts and minds there. Living far from the village and possessing almost nothing, how did they survive even for a short while? After I renounced the world, I traveled around various provinces and met many noble people, but I have yet to meet anyone like these monks.

I met them at their last moments and cremated them. I climbed up to Mount Kōya,[108] left their bones and ashes in proper fashion in the mountains, then copied their writings and recited their poems. I feel happy knowing that with their powers they will lead me to the Pure Land. Their poems and writing style are quite superior to anything in this degenerate age.

6-9 Monk Eon and Mount Rozan

Long ago, Monk Eon lived on Mount Rozan[109] in China. He was a

---

108. Mount Kōya refers to Kongōbuji Temple. Depositing ashes and bones there was regarded as proper and respectful.

109. Mount Lu in the south of Jiang-xi province and Kōro Summit (香炉峰) are well known from the poems of Hakukyoi 白居易 (772–846). Eon 恵遠, or Hui-yuan 慧遠 (334–416), was a Chinese monk of the Eastern Jin dynasty who retired from secular life at the age of thirty-one and practiced the Way on Mount Lu. He built Dong-lin Temple (東林寺) there and established a religious group, the White Lotus Society (Byakurensha 白蓮社), which was dedicated to Pure Land practices. A similar story appears in *Shishū hyaku innenshū* 3-5, *Sangokudeki* 3-5, *Shasekishū* 10-1, *Taiheiki* 12, and *Ainōshō* 3-5.

disciple of Zen Master Ekaku,[110] who was so distinguished that all the brave generals in the region greatly respected him.

Rinfu, a general of the country of So,[111] had five sons. He thought, "My first son should inherit my profession. I will therefore send another son to Master Ekaku to make him a monk so he will pray for my future life." So the father sent his second son to Ekaku.

About a hundred days later, a messenger from Ekaku came to the parents and told them, "Your son did not study well and died this morning while being punished. Do not grieve for him." Such appalling news made the parents so sad that they remained in tears before they finally replied to the message. Several days passed, but they were still grief-stricken. In time they agreed that their original plan [to make one of their sons a monk] should not have ended as it did. While stroking the hair of their third son, then thirteen years old, they decided to send him off to become a monk as well. So they sent him to Master Ekaku despite their sadness at the loss of their second son and greatly missing their third. Truly, their hearts were admirable.

About five months passed and the parents received a message [from Ekaku] saying, "I thought this boy was different from your other son, but he had a bad nature and he did not take the teachings seriously. So we beat him to death as a punishment." At this shocking news, the parents felt as if they were dreaming and sank into deep grief. They regretted ignoring their earlier sad experience and sending away their young son.[112]

But again the parents rose [from their sadness] and said [to each other], "We cannot leave the matter as it is. Let's send our fourth son!" So the fourth son, just eight years old, was summoned. "Please send him away only after my life has ended," his wet nurse tearfully begged. But her tears and entreaties were in vain and the son, accompanied by the messenger, was sent to Master Ekaku.

From that time on, the parents remained apprehensive, fearing they might receive another sad message about their fourth son's death. Every morning and evening, whenever they heard someone knocking

---

110. 恵覚 could be Ekaku, or Hui-jue 慧覚, a high-ranking monk of Sui, but his lifetime does not correspond with that of Eon.
111. So 蘇 was an ancient Chinese country that was destroyed by the barbarian Di during the Chunqiu period (770–403 B.C.).
112. *Ni-hachi* 二八 in the text means twice eight, that is, sixteen. Here the expression simply means being very young.

at the front door, they thought, "Now, again..." But in time they heard that their fourth son had received the tonsure at the age of thirteen, and their joy was indescribable.

When their son returned home for a visit, they joyfully hurried to him and asked, "Now that you [have become a monk], you must know the Law well. Tell us how we can save ourselves in our future life." The son replied, "Be aware of the transience of life and understand that everything is only a dream or an illusion." As soon as the father heard this, his faith increased. He renounced the world and received the precepts from his son. Some thirty days later his mother also cut her hair [and became a nun].

This is [the story of] Monk Eon. According to the *Meiki* of Han,[113] Eon was eventually reborn in the Inner Palace of Tosotsu Heaven,[114] while his parents were delivered to the Western Pure Land [of Amida Buddha]. When I read this story, I was overwhelmed by tears. Today, masters do not kill their disciples because of their idleness in learning. And no parents would continue to send their sons to a master after losing two other sons to him. If their loving child died while in his charge, parents would certainly hold a strong grudge against that master.

To be sure, Eon's parents were extraordinary! With such strong hearts, how could they fail to be reborn in the Western Pure Land? I never fail to be impressed by their noble hearts.

6-10 Monk Shōkū

Long ago, Monk Shōkū[115] lived in a mountain temple in Shosha, Harima province. He had been Chūta Kosaburō,[116] a samurai serving Great Councilor Tokitomo, who was a grandson of Safu Tokihira of Hon'in.[117]

---

113. Unidentified.

114. See note 6 of story 6-5.

115. Shōkū 性空 (910–1007) was a monk of the Tendai Sect. He received the tonsure at the age of thirty-six, built a hut on Mount Shosha 書写山 (in the present-day city of Himeji), and built Enkyōji Temple there. He was often called Holy Man Shosha. A similar story appears in *Konjaku monogatarishū* 19-9.

116. 仲太小三良.

117. Fujiwara Tokihira 藤原時平 (871–909), a son of Mototsune, gained political power by slandering Sugawara Michizane. He compiled the *Sandai jitsuroku* 三代実録. Great Councilor Tokitomo is unidentified.

Tokitomo had a very fine ink stone, which had been handed down from his ancestors. He used to take it out of its brocade bag and admire it only when he received a promotion, so it was rarely removed from the bag. When Tokitomo was promoted to great councilor, he took the ink stone out of the bag and placed it in a *zushi* case.[118] Wishing to see the ink stone, Chūta talked to Tokitomo's ten-year-old son. While secretly holding it [in his hands] and admiring it, Chūta heard loud footsteps [approaching the room]. While hastily trying to put the stone back into the bag, he dropped it, breaking it in half. In the confusion, the young prince said to him, "Don't worry. I will tell my father that I did it. If he hears that I did it, he may forgive me." Greatly relieved and rubbing his hands together in gratitude, Chūta happily left the room.

When the great councilor saw the broken ink stone, he became furious and asked, "Who did this?"

"I did it, sir," answered the young prince in tears.

The councilor scolded him loudly, saying, "When Daishokukan[119] visited Sumiyoshi Shrine, the Great Bright Deity appeared to him and said, 'I have been living here for a long time, but no one as reliable as you has come here. Now, to my great pleasure, you have visited me. As a token of my appreciation, I will give you an ink stone that reflects my image. Look at it when something important happens in your life.' With this revelation, the ink stone was slipped into Daishokukan's left sleeve. Since then it has been kept in the brocade bag. Anyone who breaks it must be punished!" And with this, the councilor cut off the young prince's head.

When he heard what had happened, Chūta was struck with grief and regret. To pray for the prince's future life and to atone for his sinful deeds, he cut his hair and called himself [by the Buddhist name] Shōkū. Since that time, he tearfully felt the transience of life, purified his Six Roots,[120] and recited the Lotus Sutra. He built a hut on Mount Shosha in Harima province and purified both his mind and body, thanks to the merits gained by reciting the sutra.

....

118. *Zushi* 厨子, a case or large container to store items such as Buddhist images and books.

119. Daishokuhan, or Taishokukan 大織冠, Fujiwara Kamatari 藤原鎌足 (614–669), was the founder of the Fujiwara clan. He and Emperor Tenji destroyed the Soga clan and established the Taika Reform.

120. *Rokkon shōjō* 六根清浄, "purifying the six roots of eyes, ears, nose, tongue, body, and mind," i.e., parts that recognize things.

From the time Chūta received the tonsure, he practiced the Way with a firm conviction [and prayed for the prince's future life]. So the young prince surely must have been reborn in the Pure Land of the Sacred Mountain.[121] The prince lost his life by taking the blame for another's misdeed. This was truly extraordinary, especially since he was only ten years old. It is most touching to think what sort of person he would have become if he had lived.

Now Shōkū said to himself, "I have finally purified my heart and body, thanks to the merits gained by reciting the sutra. But it is my greatest regret that I still have not seen Bodhisattva Fugen[122] in this life." He prayed for seven days, and at dawn on the seventh day a heavenly boy[123] appeared to him in a dream, saying, "Worship the principal courtesan of Muro.[124] She is the true Fugen." After delivering this message, the boy disappeared.

Feeling this message was most strange, Shōkū wanted to leave for Muro without delay. It would have been improper to visit a courtesan in a black robe, so he changed into a white one and took with him to Muro five monks wearing the same white robes. When they arrived at the senior courtesan's house, she appeared and poured *sake* for Shōkū. Saying, "Since you insist . . . , " she began to sing and dance.

"The wind visits the mountain stream of Mitarashi in Suō."

The attending courtesans followed her in chorus: "Small waves rise, *yare ka tottō*."

During the performance, Shōkū wondered, "Is this the real image of Fugen?" He closed his eyes to concentrate. Then the gentle and handsome Fugen, riding on a white elephant, appeared in his mind and sang, "In the purified Great Sea of the Law, the Fugen's blessings shine like moonlight." When Shōkū opened his eyes, the courtesan was singing, "Small waves are rising . . . " As soon as he closed his eyes once more and concentrated on the words of the Law, the courtesan

---

121. *Ryōzen jōdo* 霊山浄土 refers to the Vulture Peak, or Luminous Mountain, the Pure Land of Shaka Buddha.

122. Fugen Bosatsu 普賢菩薩 appears on the right side of Shaka Buddha. He rides on a six-tusked white elephant to help Shaka save sentient beings.

123. *Tendō* 天童, heavenly beings (*tennin* 天人), appear in the human world as young boys who assist and protect the Law.

124. Muro, or Murotsu, in present-day Hyōgo prefecture was a port town where many courtesans gathered.

appeared again as Fugen. Feeling most blessed and impressed, he [and the other monks] bade farewell to her and left. When they had walked about one *chō*, the courtesan suddenly passed away.

She had spent months and years as a courtesan. Who would have believed she was [an incarnation of] Fugen? People thought she was just a common woman. It was truly wonderful that she was the bodhisattva.

All the buddhas of the three generations show themselves in this life in different forms and figures. But we fail to recognize them because of the thick clouds of delusion covering our eyes, just as we cannot discern the true appearance of the clear moon. It is most unfortunate to see only a courtesan when you are really looking at a noble bodhisattva. It is regrettable to hear a song of "small waves" when you should be hearing the wonderful words of the Law. Why did the courtesan pass away so suddenly? Was it because she had revealed her true nature as Fugen? Or was it because Holy Man Shōkū worshipped the true Fugen as he had hoped?

This story appears in the *Shuishō*.[125] I did not disregard it and

---

125. The story in the text is not included in the *Shūishō* 拾遺抄, the imperial anthology compiled by Fujiwara Kintō 藤原公任 in 997.

wrote it down here. The enlightened person hears the wonderful Law in the winds and the waves. This was practically proved by [Shōkū], who heard the words of the Law in the courtesan's song.

How I wish I could be enlightened for just a little while. Then I would realize how foolish people are when they cling to this life. They are attached to this life because they fail to see it as a burning house.[126] If they knew this, then why would they choose to stay in this life? When I think of the capital and other places that I have never seen, I wonder how many people live in this country of Japan? How many of them live forever? Reaching the age of eighty is quite rare.

After they die, where do they go? Where do they stay? They are born and reborn, but they don't know the beginning of their births and they repeat death without knowing the end of their deaths. The *sanzu* worlds[127] are not their final destination. All the places they go to are only temporary; they are like balls bouncing up and down and carts circling around a yard. In what permanent place can we rest our minds for a while? Human beings are not in an unchanging state. Born as humans, we assume the appearance of humans; if we were born as birds because of previous karmic relations, we would appear as birds.

Thus we should not cling to our transient lives. Enlightenment is the only eternal place and only a buddha's body[128] is free of transience. It is most foolish to dwell in this futile body in this temporary life and ignore the buddha body of enlightenment.

6-11 The Holy Man of the Musashi Field

Recently, when I passed through Musashi Field,[129] I saw that it was covered in profusely growing grass and blossoms and resembled a piece of rich Chinese brocade. Impressed by its vastness, I composed a poem:

---

126. *Kataku* 火宅 refers to this chaotic life. The same expression appears in *Senjūshō* 6-2.
127. *Sanzu* 三途 refers to the three worlds, or the realms of hell, animals, and hungry ghosts.
128. *Busshin* 仏身; as opposed to *ninjin* 人身, a human body.
129. Musashino 武蔵野 included the present Tokyo area and the southern part of present-day Saitama prefecture.

Musashino wa
Yuke domo aki no
Hatezo naki
Ika naru kaze ka
Sue ni fuku ran[130]

O Musashi Field,
No matter how far I go,
I can see no end to autumn,
What kind of wind
Is blowing at the end?

I went farther into the field until I saw a monk of fifty years of age in a house [decorated] with flowers. He was sitting before a flower desk.[131] A roll of the Lotus Sutra was on the desk and he was reciting a verse from the sutra in a most noble voice: "Thinking of the Buddhist Way deep in the mountains."[132]

Curious to know what kind of a person he was, I approached and questioned him. He replied, "I was once a samurai attending Lady Yūhōmon'in.[133] After she passed away, I realized the transience of life, so I cut my hair, received the tonsure, and left the capital. But I didn't know how to practice the Way and wandered until I came upon a man preaching the Lotus Sutra. He said, 'The Lotus Sutra tells us that in the Buddhist world, there is only One Vehicle,[134] not two or three. Nothing is more marvelous than the teachings of the One Vehicle.' Because I agreed with his preaching, I began to read the sutra, continuing to recite it diligently for my future life. Thanks to the merit gained from reciting the sutra, I have not been attacked by wolves[135] even though I live alone in this wild field. As for food, a noble heavenly boy visits

---

130. The poem appears in the *Shinkokinshū*, Autumn Section, no. 378.
131. *Hanazukue* 花机: sutras and items for religious services are placed here; the desk is set before Buddhist images.
132. The verses appear in the introduction to the Lotus Sutra.
133. Yūhōmon'in (1076–1096), a daughter of Emperor Shirakawa, lived with her father in Rokujōin until she died at the age of twenty-one. She attended various poetry meetings held at her father's palace.
134. *Ichijōmyōten* 一乗妙典: the Lotus Sutra.
135. The term *korō* 虎狼 can refer to tigers or wolves, but it mainly refers to wolves.

me now and then, carrying something white as snow. But before I eat, I don't feel hungry."

How extraordinary! This monk must have been a *sennin* hermit.[136] Reciting the sutras and the names of buddhas will surely benefit ignorant people. This holy man, who began as an ignorant ascetic, was able to attain the status of *sennin* through his recitations of a sutra.

Thanks to my relationships with many distinguished people, I have gained some discernment and this gives me much pleasure. In secular life [serving at the imperial court], I was constantly looking up at the distant clouds[137] [in search of promotion] and paying attention to the color of my robes, which indicates title and rank. The smoke [of frustration] in my heart was comparable to that of Mount Fuji, and the dew on my sleeves was like the swift waves of Kiyomigata Bay.[138] For days on end my mind was never clear.

Finally, I realized the futility of my life and received the tonsure. I yearn to gaze at the moon from a lotus seat[139] and for the coming of the holy people of the Pure Land.[140] As for my few good deeds, I want to use them to benefit all the sentient beings of the buddha world as I pray [for birth with them] on the same lotus seat.

When Amida Buddha was the Wheel King,[141] we might have lived in his country and been able to establish a relationship with him. Probably on account of this relationship, we still think of him as being very noble and depend on him. Everybody—including those lamenting and grieving, those suffering from love, the poor and the lonely living in miserable homes where all light has been extinguished, solitary folk chilled by the cold autumn wind—all of us depend on Amida as we chant his name. We know that we commoners have a deep relationship with the Buddha.

---

136. A *sennin* 仙人 is a hermit or recluse who has obtained, thanks to his ascetic practices, special powers, such as the ability to fly.

137. *Kumoi* 雲井 here refers to a distant higher place, that is, the imperial palace or promotion at the court.

138. The beach is near Kiyomi Temple in present-day Okitsu in Shizuoka prefecture; it is one of the *utamakura*, or poetic sites.

139. *Rendai* 蓮台: lotus seats for those reborn in the Pure Land.

140. *Shōjū no raigō* 聖衆の来迎: receiving and welcoming the holy ones, including buddhas and bodhisattvas from the Amida's Pure Land, who come to receive devotees at their last moments.

141. Amida Buddha was called Tenrin'ō 転輪王 or Mujōnen'ō 無上念王 in a past life.

6-12 An Ascetic in Holy Man Mitaki's Hut

Soon after I had received the tonsure, I wanted to establish a relationship with Holy Man Mitaki Kankū,[142] so I went to visit him. He was absent at the time so I decided to wait for him. I went through the east-facing *tsumado* door[143] and rested inside. Meanwhile, someone who was trying to conceal his noble background, came along. His head was recently shaved as if he had just received the tonsure. Paying no attention to me, he gazed at the flowers in the garden and composed poems. He appeared very elegant and noble. He examined the dew that had just fallen on the sleeve of his monk's shabby robe. Because of his noble appearance I didn't think he was a commoner and so I composed a poem:

Tsuyu o dani
Ima wa katami no
Fujigoromo[144]

The dew [on the sleeve]
Of the wisteria robe
As a token [of the deceased]

The monk immediately added the last two lines:

Ada nimo sode o
Fuku arashi kana

But the stormy wind
Vainly blows it away.

---

142. Unidentified. Mitaki refers to the vicinity of Ganjōji Temple in present-day Bessho in Wakayama prefecture.
143. *Tsumado* 妻戸, the door to a yard or garden, is located at the end of a building.
144. *Fujigoromo* 藤衣 is a wisteria vine robe or a monk's coarse robe. The poem is by Fujiwara Hideyoshi 藤原秀能 (1184–1240), who composed it as he recalled his deceased father. The poet wished to keep the dew (his tears) on his sleeve in memory of his father, but the stormy wind ruthlessly blew it away (*Shinkokinshū* 8, no. 789).

Because I felt his addition was most interesting, I asked, "Who are you? I would like to hear about your life before you had your head shaved."

He answered, "I closely served Emperor Konoein.[145] Every year, I gazed at the autumn moon from Seiryōden Hall in the imperial palace and at the red leaves of Mount Kōya.[146] When I had just reached the Third Rank,[147] the emperor passed away prematurely.[148] I realized the transience of life, left the palace without taking anything except his relics, which I have kept for some time. I am not doing anything particular now." After I heard this, I shed many tears.

Everyone knows that this life is futile, for we can be born in the morning and die in the evening. But we mingle with our friends today without noticing the sun setting, we work tomorrow without hearing the bell tolling the transience of life. While we ignored the smoke rising from the burial ground of Mount Toribe, this young man of the

---

145. Konoein 近衛院 (1139–1155), a son of Emperor Toba, died at the age of seventeen. His early death became one of the causes of the Hōgen Revolt.
146. Seiyōden 清涼殿 is the imperial residence hall. Koyasan 古射山 refers to the retired emperor's palace.
147. *Wazukani kurai mishina* 僅に位三品, "barely the Third Rank," meaning the protagonist was still a young official.
148. *Honobono* ほのぼの: "slight." The emperor died at a "slight" age, that is, while still young.

Third Rank suddenly realized the futility of existence and left secular life. Surely that was most extraordinary.

People say dew is the most futile thing, but didn't you see the morning glories that bloomed this morning, only to die before the dew settled on them? Is the gossamer blown by the wind covering the banana leaves going to disappear before or after the leaves are broken? Both are as mutable as we are. Which disappeared first, the person who composed a poem about a flower on a spring morning or the flower itself? On an autumn night when someone views the moon, is he going to perish before or after the moon hides behind the clouds? Leading a life as short as lightning, we boast of ourselves and speak ill of others while we ignore the slow pace of sheep [as they move toward the slaughter house].[149] Isn't this a most shameful attitude?

The Buddha granted me understanding to realize the futility of life, but I am not talented enough to fully comprehend the depths of his teaching. Still I can avoid [secular life] and desire deliverance in my future life. Master Kōya[150] says, "A crooked *yomogi* plant will become straight of its own accord if it is placed among the hemp."[151] Is this not true? Associating with someone who understands the futility of life and listening to what he says will naturally purify my heart and mind and help me see the transience of life.

---

149. See the preface and *Senjūshō* 7-14.
150. A reference to Kūkai 空海 (774–835), who wrote this sentence in his *Sangōshiki* 三教指帰, I, (*Nihon koten bungaku taikei*, p. 88). Yomogi 蓬, a perennial plant with fragrant leaves, grows as high as one meter and is often mixed with rice to make rice cakes.
151. In other words, if you associate with someone correct and straight, you will eventually become straight under his influence.

7-1 Teishi Meets a Skeleton

Long ago in China, a man called Teishi[1] was a government official similar to a *daifu*[2] in our country. He served at the imperial court during the Ryō dynasty.[3] Winter days turned dark early as the setting sun sank as fast as the Running White Horse[4] behind the western mountains and the sun of the Golden Crow[5] rose over the eastern summits.

Teishi finished his duties late one night. Despite the time, he decided to return home because he [had something] to do there. Accompanied by an attendant, he mounted his horse and started the long way home. Since it was so late, there were no dogs barking in the village to warn [off intruders]. A stream, not yet frozen, made a lonely sound as it flowed through the rocks in the valley. As they rode farther from the village, Teishi and his attendant felt most bleak and

1. Unidentified.
2. *Daifu* (or *daibu*) *no shi* 大夫の史: an officer of the Fifth Rank.
3. There were three Liang dynasties: the first began in 362 B.C.; the second, 502–557; the third, 907–923. We are not told in which of these dynasties this story took place.
4. *Hakku* 白駒, "white horse," is a metaphor of time passing as fast as a galloping horse.
5. *Kin'u* 金烏: According to an old Chinese belief, a three-legged golden crow lives in the sun.

desolate; they heard no mountain temple bells to console their lonesome hearts.

They saw a faint light ahead of them. This made them very happy, and they hurried toward it. When they arrived at its source, they found themselves facing a house with crumbling walls. Inside a noble-looking woman was playing a *koto,* her [long] hair swaying as she played. Wondering who she was, Teishi became most curious. He quickly knocked at the gate, calling out, "Please let us stay here." After a while, the woman replied, "That's quite unthinkable," and then she ignored him. But Teishi persisted until she said hesitantly, "Very well," and showed him in.

The outside of the dwelling appeared terribly dilapidated, but the inside was in good order with a tall stand holding a burning taper and a cloth screen placed beside it. As Teishi approached the woman, he grew enchanted by her [beauty]. Her *koto* music was most tasteful and purified his heart. He asked her, "Why do you live in this wilderness?" She replied, "I have been here for three years."

The moon in the dawning sky became shadowy as the eastern sky brightened. His head resting on a pillow, Teishi faintly heard a distant temple bell. Then cocks began crowing clearly and cheerfully, and finally he awoke. Lo and behold, he found himself in a wild field of pampas grass, lying next to a skeleton! Appalled, he quickly mounted his horse and galloped to a neighboring village. After he relayed everything that had happened to the villagers, they said to him, "That is quite possible. Once in this village, there was a man called Baidō[6] who had a beautiful daughter who played the *koto* constantly. She died before her parents and her corpse was abandoned in that field. At night her bones transform into a woman and she plays the *koto.*" This was the story they told him and it sounded most mysterious.

What does it all mean? The daughter was deeply attached [to playing the *koto*]; even after her death she wandered through the field in search of her bones so she could assume the form of a woman and play the *koto.* When I heard the story, I first felt it was very frightening, but later it came to fascinate me. I wonder if it is telling us that we should not become overly attached to anything.

---

6. Unidentified.

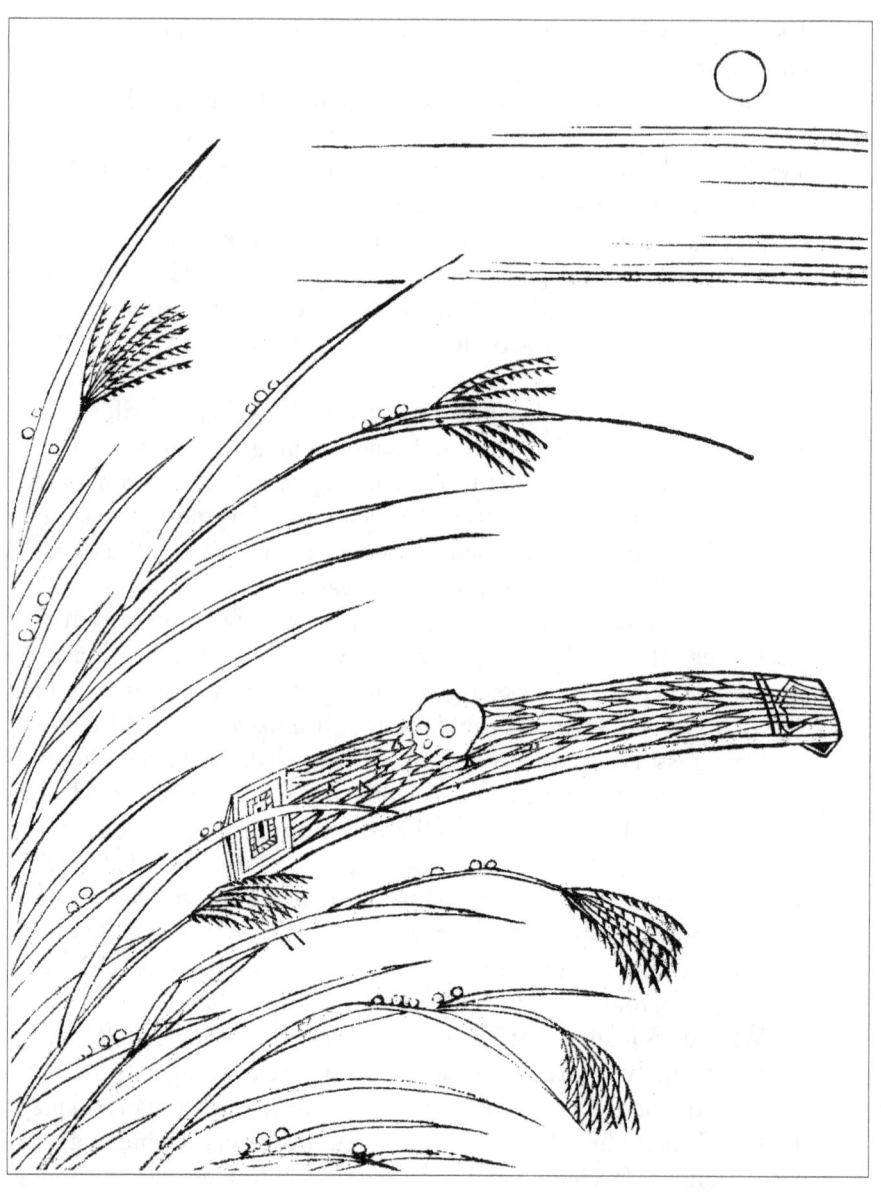

7-2 Lord Kyōshin Meets a Monk Who Composes Linked Verse while Flower-Viewing

Some time ago, Lord Kyōshin,[7] the Sochi Great Councilor, wanted to view the cherry blossoms in Nishiyama.[8] He took his court with him, which was made up of men of great taste. When the party arrived at the Ōi River,[9] the courtiers stayed on the bank and admired the blossoms on the many cherry trees. Their hearts ached to see the petals drift on the water, swallowed up by the ripples and mixed with the weeds, and they lamented and grieved over the heartless stormy wind [that had scattered the blossoms].

After a while, they boarded a raft and made for the opposite bank. There they enjoyed themselves, climbing to the top of a hill before descending into a valley, where they came across a monk of about fifty years of age. He was wearing a one-layer kimono and sat under a tree practicing meditation. The party gathered around him and asked, "What are you doing? Where do you come from and who are you?" But the monk did not reply. After a while, he finally asked the visitors, "Why have you come here?" Lord Kyōshin answered, "We have come to view the blossoms." "So have I," said the monk.

Believing that he was a man of deep thinking, Kyōshin said to him, "Please give us a verse from a text that will clear our minds." The monk recited, "Delusion is enlightenment, life-death is nirvana."[10] "Just as I thought, he is no ordinary man," Kyōshin said to himself and asked the

---

7. Kyōshin 経信 (1016–1097), a son of Minamoto Michikata and the father of Toshiyori, excelled in playing the *biwa* lute and became the founder of the Katsura School of *biwa* music. He was promoted to great councilor in 1091. He was *sochi* (or *sotsu* 師), a full-fledged director, of the police headquarters at Dazaifu in Kyushu. His writings include the *Sochiki* 師記 and the *Dainagon kyōshinshū* 大納言経信集. His name appears in other *Senjūshō* tales: 2-4, 8-27, 8-31, and 8-32. For an article about Kyōshin, see Watanabe Nobukazu, "*Senjūshō* ni okeru Minamoto Kyōshin," in *Chūkyō daigaku bungakubu kiyō* 15, no. 3 (January 1981).

8. Nishiyama 西山 refers to the mountains to the west of Kyoto.

9. The Ōikawa 大井川 flows near Arashiyama in Kyoto.

10. The verse means that our daily activities are all delusions and the cycle of life-death in this life is real and true. Wisdom, understanding, and enlightenment are born from the awareness of delusion, therefore the delusion itself is enlightenment. These phrases popularly appear in various Buddhist writings; see the *Kanshin ryakuyōshū* 観心略要集 by Genshin 源信 (*Dainihon bukkyō zensho*, 39, p. 54).

monk to explain the meaning of the verse. The monk obliged so well that the people in the lord's party were freed of delusion; they all wanted [to receive the tonsure and] practice the Way with the learned monk.

They said to him, "It is fine to live alone on this mountain and attain the Way without being disturbed by others. But benefiting yourself while benefiting others is the practice of a bodhisattva,[11] so why don't you come to the capital and become a teacher?" But the monk appeared to ignore their suggestion. Reluctant to leave him there, they did not return home but stayed with him through the night, asking him questions about the holy texts while seated in clean robes[12] on the rugged mountain ground.

At dawn, they knew they could not stay there forever, so they tearfully bade the holy man farewell, promising him, "We will return." Lord Toshiyori[13] recited two lines of a poem:

Nakite zo kaeru
Haru no akebono

In the spring dawn
Leaving in tears

Immediately, the monk added three more:

Mata mo kon
Aki o tanomu no
Kari dani mo

I will come again
As the geese return

---

11. *Jiri rita* 自利利他: *jiri*, "to benefit oneself by practicing for oneself"; *rita*, "to benefit others by helping others." The combination of the two concepts is the ideal of Mahāyāna Buddhism; see the *Myōgyō shin'yōshu* by Genshin (*Dainihon bukkyō zensho*, 39, p. 247).
12. A *jōe* 浄衣 is a clean robe and refers to a monk's robe. Here it means the people with pure hearts. The passage suggests that the party wanted to establish a relationship with the monk.
13. Minamoto Toshiyori 源俊頼 (1055–1129), the third son of Kyōshin, excelled in poetry; he compiled the *Kin'yō wakashū* and wrote the *Toshiyori zuinō* 俊頼髄脳.

To the autumn fields.[14]

The members of the party were deeply impressed [by the poem]. Later, they returned to the monk, but their visit was in vain. This was most moving.

Living deep in the mountains, the monk with his pure heart understood the truth of life.[15] His heart would never have become clouded even if the water of the Kiyotaki River[16] turned muddy. This is indeed noble.

In general, secular matters are in the Truth [the Law]: It is said, "Everything in this world is in the Law." But to those who are not enlightened, there is a great difference between the truth and the secular truth. Goodness and non-goodness are interchangeable. It was truly noble that the [monk] understood this concept.

Unwilling to leave the Law [the monk], Lord Kyōshin and his party spent the night [with the monk] on the rugged mountain. They used rocks for pillows and spread their robes on the mossy ground. This was also truly noble. They must have established good relationships [with the monk]. Alas, in today's world, such people seldom exist.

7-3 A Monk of Ōba in Sagami Province

Long ago, a monk lived in a humble hut in Ōba Field in Sagami province.[17] Now and then, he supported himself by begging for food and working as a servant in the village. An epidemic broke out and both the high and the low fell sick. Among them was an impoverished widow, who lay extremely ill in bed. Even before the epidemic, she had found it difficult to survive. Now she was helplessly ill and about to die. When the monk heard the villagers talking about her, he secretly went

---

14. The poem appears in the *Shinkokinshū* (13, Love Poems, 3, by the Regent Prime Minister). It is divided into two parts, composed by Toshiyori and the monk in the *renga* 連歌 style (linked verse). *Tanomu* 田の面, the surface of a rice field, implies *tanomu* 頼む, "relying," or "depending on." *Kari* 雁, "geese," is associated with *kari* 刈り, "crop."
15. *Ri* 理 (Absolute Truth) and *ji* 事 (Conventional Truth, or truth in the secular world) are *sokuichi* 即一, "one and the same." For this concept of Tendai teaching, see Hirota Tetsumichi, *Chūsei hokekyō chūshakusho no kenkyū* (Tokyo: Kasama Shoin, 2005).
16. The river runs to the north of Kyoto and joins the Hotsu River.
17. Ōba is in present-day Kanagawa prefecture.

to her place at night and found her suffering greatly and unconscious. He tried various means to care for her and, when she recovered consciousness, he helped her recite the Buddha's name. As she gradually improved, the monk urged her to eat something to prolong her life. Since the poor woman possessed nothing at all, the monk went around the village begging for money and rice and supported her without telling anyone. Meanwhile, he cultivated her mind by advising her to recite the Buddha's name.

People said that because the holy man had deep sympathy and mercy for all suffering beings, he constantly shed tears; his eyes were always swollen and his sleeves never dry. Reaching the end of his wanderings, the monk died in his hut at dawn on the twenty-fifth day of the third month of the Enkyū era (1069–1074). They said that when he attained deliverance, music was heard in the sky and an unusual fragrance filled his hut. This was recorded in a biography. When I read the article about him in the *Shūiden*,[18] I shed many tears. I felt most moved to learn that the monk overcame sleep and forgot hunger when he practiced meditation, that the Buddha's mercy filled his hut, and that the Buddha's sacred vows to save the unfaithful last forever. I wish I could raise my heart as high as he did.

---

18. An unidentified work.

7-4 Monk Chūsan

Long ago, Daitoku Chūsan,[19] a monk of great learning, lived in Matsumuro in Yamashina Temple.[20] He was a disciple of Sōzu Kūsei of Kita-in[21] and was regarded as an incarnation[22] [of the bodhisattva] who had appeared in flowing water.

When Chūsan was still living in Kūsei's room, Holy Man Kōya[23] visited Kūsei to ask about a text. Kūsei was out; the young boy[24] Chūsan was alone in the room and received Kōya. When Chūsan explained that his master was absent, Kōya was sorry that a young boy should be left on his own. He entered the room and said to Chūsan, "Bring the *go* board here. I will show you how to play the game." Chūsan tried to lift the board, but it was too heavy for him to move.[25] Seeing this, Kōya said to him, "Place these *nenju*[26] beads on the board." As soon as Chūsan put the beads on the board, they wound around the board's legs of their own accord and brought the board to the holy man [Kōya].

Nothing attracts our attention more than the Law. Kōya was the fifth son of Emperor Engi[27] and is on record as an incarnation [of a buddha] in the Seikanshi.[28] There is nothing mysterious about an enlightened and virtuous man [like Kōya] having the power to move lifeless beads.

---

19. *Daitoku* 大德, "great virtue," was often used as a title. Chūsan 中算 (935–976) was a scholarly monk of Kōfukuji Temple. Stories about him appear in the *Konjaku monogatarishū* (28-8), the *Honchō shinsenden* (24), the *Hosshinshū* (3-12), the *Zōdanshū* (7), and the *Sangoku denki* (12-24).
20. For Kōfukuji Temple, see *Senjūshō* 1-8, 5-1, and 5-4. Chūsan lived in Matsumuro, living quarters located northeast of Ichijōin in Kōfukuji Temple.
21. Kūsei 空晴 (876–957), a son of Fujiwara Takamitsu, was a scholarly monk. He appears again in *Senjūshō* 6-3. Kitain 喜多院 is a pagoda in Kōfukuji Temple.
22. Here *kenin* 化人 means an incarnation. Buddhas and bodhisattvas appear in this life to save sentient beings. For Chūsan, Bodhisattva Kannon, and water, see *Senjūshō* 6-3 and 7-5.
23. Kūya, or Kōya 空也, (903–972) traveled widely, built roads and bridges, repaired temples and halls, and popularized the chanting of Amida Buddha's name. He was the founder of *odori nenbutsu* 踊念仏, the dancing and chanting of the Buddha's name, and was called Amida Hijiri 阿弥陀聖, Amida Holy Man.
24. *Warawa* 童: young boy servants who were employed in temples and noblemen's mansions.
25. A *go* board (*goban* 碁盤) is 4–5 inches thick with four short legs.
26. 念珠.
27. Emperor Daigo is here referred to by the name given to one of his reign periods, Engi. Kōya also appears in *Kankyonotomo* 1-4 as a son of Emperor Engi.
28. Unidentified.

7-5 [Untitled][29]

At the end of Emperor Engi's reign, Chūsan went north with many other ascetics to practice the Way. It was so hot that all the springs had dried up and Chūsan's people were all tired and thirsty. Thanks to the mercy of the buddhas and bodhisattvas, a mountain spring in Ōmi province was still producing fresh, cold water, and many people were coming from far and wide to retrieve it.

Chūsan stopped a woman who was carrying a bucket [of water] on her head and said, "We are all tired [and thirsty]. Please give us just a little bit of your water." The woman retorted, "You look like a holy man. Why don't you create a spring for yourself and your people? I don't see why we should give you our [precious] water when we all have come from distant places to fetch it." Chūsan replied, "You are right. I should produce water for myself."

He ran to a cliff in the mountains and cut off a part that was jutting out with his sword. Fresh, cold water gushed out like a waterfall. The spring was called the Fresh Water of Samegai.[30] The villagers thought this most extraordinary and were all greatly excited and amazed. Since then the spring has never dried up even during periods of drought.

Several days later, Honorable Jōzō[31] passed by the place, heard about the [new] spring, and wished to establish a good relationship [with Chūsan]. When Jōzō cut into the side of the cliff next to the [new] spring, another smaller spring gushed out and so it was called Smaller Samegai.

What wonderful men they were! It is recorded in a text[32] that Chūsan once appeared as a One-Thousand-Armed Kannon,[33] climbed into a waterfall, and disappeared. But there is nothing surprising about

---

29. The tale has no title but is obviously a continuation of the previous story about Chūsan.
30. Samegai is in present-day Shiga prefecture.
31. Jōzō Kisho 浄蔵貴所: *Kisho*, the residence of a nobleman, may also be understood to mean "honorable." Jōzō (891–964), a monk of Enryakuji Temple, was blessed with miraculous powers; he subjugated Taira Masakado and cured Emperor Suzaku.
32. Unidentified.
33. Chūsan and the Kannon appear in various tales including *Senjūshō* 6-3, *Hosshinshū* 1-4, and *Shishū hyaku innenshū* 9-16.

his marvelous deeds because he was a Nyorai buddha[34] who had been enlightened long ago.

Jōzō was the eighth son of Prime Minister Zen.[35] He straightened the crooked Yasaka Tower[36] with his prayers. After his father ended his karmic relation in this life and passed away, Jōzō engaged in *kanpō* practice[37] at the foot of Ichijō Bridge[38] and revived his father. This was most extraordinary. The bridge is called Modori-bashi, or Returning Bridge, because of this story about the revived minister.

Yukinobu[39] mentioned that the Bridge of Going and Coming in the

---

34. Nyorai 如来 means the One (*tathāgata*, 如) who has come (*rai* 来) to save sentient beings. Nyorai is also one of the ten honorific titles of a buddha.
35. Miyoshi Kiyoyuki, the father of Jōzō, was a doctor of letters.
36. 八坂の塔: Yasaka Tower or Pagoda, east of Kyoto, is one of present-day Japan's Important Cultural Assets. The five-storied pagoda built by Prince Shōtoku (574?–622) was repeatedly burnt down and restored. The present pagoda was rebuilt in 1440. The stories of Jōzō and the Yasaka Tower appear in various tales, such as the *Konjaku monogatarishū* (20), the *Hōbutsushū* (5), the *Genkō shakusho* (10), and the *Sangoku denki* (6-9).
37. *Kanpō* 観法 is one of the practices for attaining enlightenment by concentrating on the Absolute Truth.
38. The Horikawa Bridge is in present-day Ichijō, Kamigyō-ku, Kyoto-shi.
39. Unidentified.

Uji chapter of the *Genji*[40] is based on the Returning Bridge. I wonder if it is a mistake to call it Uji Bridge?

7-6 Sōzu Eshin and the Water Practice

Long ago, Sōzu Eshin[41] of Enryakuji Temple engaged unceasingly in *kanpō* practice[42] and acquired the power to change himself and his room into water. Once, Naiki Nyūdō Yasutane[43] visited Eshin to discuss enlightenment. He opened [the door of] his room; it was full of water, but Eshin was nowhere to be found. Thinking that there must be some meaning to it all, Yasutane [grabbed a nearby pillow and] threw it into the water. Then he left.

Yasutane returned to the room on the following day, and Eshin told him, "Someone threw a pillow on my chest and I feel very uncomfortable. Would you please remove it?" Yasutane was intelligent and immediately understood what he had done the previous day. He replied, "There is no need to mention it." "I am glad," Eshin answered and closed his eyes for a while. Then his body turned into water, which began to fill the room with large waves, but Yasutane did not become wet at all. He took the pillow floating on the water and threw it past the sliding doors [of the room]. After a while, Eshin came out of the room. This was indeed mysterious.

Mastering *kanpō* practices is truly wonderful. Since [Eshin's] faith in the Law was so profound and he never neglected meditation practice, he produced flames from his body when he concentrated on the

---

40. Here the "Uji chapter" may refer to the ten Uji chapters in the *Genji monogatari*, but Yukinobu's mention of the bridge is not found in these chapters. A quotation from this *Senjūshō* story appears in *Jinten gainōshō* 5-51.

41. Eshin 恵心, or Genshin 源信 (947–1017), was a scholarly monk who lived in Eshin'in of Yokawa 横川 on Mount Hiei. He studied under Master Jikei 慈恵大師 (Ryōgen 良源), avoided wealth and fame, and established the Pure Land Sect of Japan. His many writings include the *Ōjō yōshū* 往生要集.

42. See note 8 of story 7-5. Here the protagonist concentrates on *suisōkan* 水想観, thinking of the pure water found in the Pure Land.

43. Naiki Nyūdō Yasutane 内記入道保胤, or Yoshishige Yasutane (d. 1002). *Naiki* 内記 were chroniclers of the imperial court and the position was awarded to a man skilled in writing. *Nyūdō* 入道 refers to those who practice the Law while remaining in secular life. Since Yasutane was *Dainaiki*, Great Chronicler, he was popularly called Naiki Nyūdō after receiving the tonsure. He went to Yokawa and practiced the Way with Eshin. His writings include the *Nihon ōjō gokurakuki* and the *Chiteiki*; see *Senjūshō* 5-3.

Flame Practice.⁴⁴ When he engaged in the Water Practice, he always produced water. This has nothing to do with the Correct or Degenerate Ages⁴⁵ nor with one's birth and status in this life. A person is able to acquire such marvelous powers solely because of his faith in the Law. Everyone knows this, but having such resolute faith is as difficult as taming wild deer; the dogs in our houses, however, are too tame and familiar with us to remove our delusions. Alas, I wonder when I will ever acquire true faith in the Law.

7-7 Monk Musō

Some time ago an unknown monk lived in a humble hut by the Tone River in Shimotsuke province.⁴⁶ He was not attached to anything; naturally gentle, he was very pure-hearted. Since the villagers had never seen him angry, they called him Musōbō,⁴⁷ Monk of No Thoughts.

About two years later, in the fifth month, the river flooded and suddenly many possessions were washed away and many people drowned. The villagers thought of Musō and lamented, saying to each other, "How sad! He was such a devoted ascetic. He must have perished [in the flood]." Among them was a very devoted patron of Musō. Concerned for his master and wishing to see what had happened to his hut, he swam with a few men out to Musō's dwelling.

When they arrived, they found the hut gone, but Musō, with his eyes closed, was quietly sitting on the water. They thought it most extraordinary. Quickly, they swam closer and said to him, "Let's go back!" but Musō ignored them and said nothing. After a while, he told

---

44. *Kashō zanmai* 火生三昧: fire-raising *samādhi*. A reference to the *sanmai* (*zanmai*), *samādhi* 三昧 is the state of mental concentration of Fudōson 不動尊 (Acala), who appears in flames produced from his body to destroy delusions.

45. *Jōdai matsudai* 上代末代: *Jōdai* includes the ages of *shōhō* 正法 (Correct Law) and *zōhō* 像法 (Imitative Law, the ages when the Buddha's teachings were still popular and active). The period of ten thousand years after *zōhō* is *mappō* 末法, the Degenerate Age, when only the Law remains. In Japan the *mappō* period began in 1052.

46. Shimotsuke province included present-day Tochigi-ken. The Tone River, the largest river in the Kanto plain, runs through five prefectures (Gunma, Tochigi, Saitama, Ibaragi, and Chiba) and to the Pacific Ocean at Chōshi.

47. Musōbō 無相坊, a monk with no attachments. The Sanron 三論宗 Sect teaches that everything in life is *śūnyata*: emptiness (*kū* 空), nothingness (*mu* 無). Sō 相 is a state of mind, while bō 坊 is a monk.

the villagers, "I will come back later by myself. You look after yourselves so that you do not come to any harm. Go back quickly!" The villagers thought that the monk should not be left alone, and so they tried to take him by pulling his sleeves, but Musō would not move at all. Although he was sitting on water, his clothes were not at all wet. No matter what they said, he would not listen to them. They became exhausted and returned without him. Later when the sun was high, the monk finally arrived back at the village.

"He is indeed a noble buddha," said the villagers who came to worship him. But Musō denied this and asked, "How can I be such a buddha?" Nevertheless, many people who heard about him came running to worship him. Then suddenly one evening the monk disappeared.

The grieving villagers searched for him in vain. Finally, they invited a *busshi*[48] to make an image of Musō, and they built a hut on the site where his dwelling had been. Since he had disappeared on the eighteenth day of the month, they gathered at the hut on the eighteenth of each month to recite "Namu Musō, faith in Musō" and to establish a relationship with him.

This was extremely unusual. The villagers believed that an

---

48. *Busshi* 仏師: a sculptor who specializes in carving Buddhist images.

incarnation of the Kannon [as Musō] had appeared to save sentient beings. The monk disappeared on the eighteenth of the month and the *Higekyō* sutra[49] mentions that the eighth and the eighteenth of the month are Kannon days. Moreover, the flood took place on the eighth of the month. The villagers had surely been saved and felt closer to those who perished in the flood as they worshipped the monk's [Kannon's] image.

7-8 Kakuban

In recent times a holy man called Kakuban,[50] who had mastered the Shingon teachings, lived on Mount Kōya. Among spring blossoms he instantly attained the Way by making a *mudra* sign,[51] all the while quietly transferring the flowery fragrance[52] onto his robe, which was as thin as [spring] mist. Under the autumn moon, he practiced meditation, joining the palms of his hands[53] as he reflected the clear moonlight on his pure heart.

Kakuban built Denpōin Temple, modeling it on [Kongōbuji Temple, which had been built by] Master Kōbō.[54] He waited for the Three Meetings of the Dragon Flowers[55] and finally attained the Way. People were greatly impressed.

49. The *Higekyō* 悲花経, a sutra in ten volumes, does not mention this. A tale in the *Kokoncho monjū* (20, no. 711) mentions that the fifteenth and the eighteenth of the month are the special days for Amida and Kannon.
50. Kakuban 覚鑁 (1095–1143), or Kōkyō Daishi, built Daidenpōin and Mitsugon'in, subsidiary temples of Kongōbuji on Mount Kōya, in 1132. He became the *zasu*, or abbot, of both establishments in 1134 but moved to Negoro in Kishū province in 1140. His writings include the *Kōyōshū* 孝養集 and the *Mitsugon shohishaku* 密厳諸秘釈. For a study on Kakuban, see Kushida Ryōkō, *Kakuban no kenkyū* (Tokyo: Yoshikawa kōbunkan, 1975).
51. *Ichiintonjō* 一印頓成: instant enlightenment by making an *in* 印, or *mudra* hand sign. The idea also suggests the instant opening (*tonsei* 頓成, "accomplishment") of cherry blossoms.
52. *Nioi* 匂 refers to the fragrance or color of flowers; translated here as fragrance, it suggests incense offered to the Buddha.
53. *Zenshin gasshō* 禅心合掌: meditating by joining the palms of the hands. The autumn here evokes a contrast with *ichiintonjō* in the spring.
54. 弘法大師, or Kūkai 空海 (774–835), who introduced Shingon teaching from China and built Kongōbuji Temple on Mount Kōya, the headquarters of the Shingon Sect in Japan.
55. Ryūgesan'e 龍花三会: The Three Meetings, or Sermons, of the Dragon Flower held by Bodhisattva Miroku under the Dragon Flower Tree to rescue the sentient beings who failed to be saved while Shaka was alive.

Ignorant visitors from the western provinces came to the temple by rowing up and down the Takase River, while the wild men of the east galloped from afar to Mount Ausaka[56] to visit the temple. Thus a crowd of high and low alike created a market area [in front of the temple], making it difficult to locate the place. Needless to say, the situation became noisy and chaotic.

Some monks of the main temple[57] gathered and discussed the situation: "In more than sixty provinces in this country, no one has ever attained the Way except the Great Master [Kōbō]. Especially in the generations [following the Master], who on this mountain can emulate him and attain the Way, regardless of the virtuous merits he has accumulated? Let us attack Denpōin and stop Kakuban!" And with this, they attacked the temple.

Unable to defend themselves, Kakuban's disciples ran away. When the assailants entered the cell where Kakuban was practicing meditation, they saw two Fudōson images.[58] The first was one that Kakuban worshipped, and the second was Kakuban himself. Since the attackers could not distinguish between the two, one of them touched the images and found the second image to be warm. "This is the one," he said and tried in vain to cut the image down with his sword. After he tried a second time, Kakuban emerged from his meditation and was attacked and injured. The attackers quickly fled to their main temple in the valley.

Kakuban later said to himself, "This is not what I wanted. I will not stay here any longer." He eventually moved to Negoro,[59] where he built a hut and settled. Just as he had expected, he entered nirvana on the

---

56. Ausakayama 合坂[逢坂]山, or Ōsakayama, the boundary between present-day Kyoto and Ōtsu-shi in Shiga prefecture; it was an important barrier protecting the capital, Kyoto.
57. A reference to Kongōbuji Temple. Kakuban, an innovator in the Shingon Sect, was strongly opposed by conservative factions. Conflict between the main temple and Daidenpōin continued after he formally moved to Negoro in 1140 and even after his death.
58. Fudōsan 不動尊, or Fudōmyōō 不動明王 (Acalanātha, the non-moving *deva* king). He is usually depicted with a fearful expression; he holds a sword in his right hand, a rope in his left, and has flames on his back to frighten and destroy delusions. For Kakuban and Fudōson, see Yamada Shōzen, *Saigyō no waka to bukkyō* (Tokyo: Meiji Shoin, 1987), 160.
59. Negoro lies a short distance to the west of Mount Kōya in present-day Wakayama prefecture.

third day of the third month at the age of seventy-two.[60] It was reported that his last moments were most splendid: Music was heard in the sky and flowers fell to the ground.

Kakuban left some writings in which he recorded, "I will not think ill of those who attacked and slandered me during my meditation. I will benefit both those who trust me and those who criticize me." His words indeed sound most noble. A buddha thinks, "Everyone should imitate me," but we are usually too ignorant to follow him. But this holy man, emulating the Great Master, tried to attain enlightenment. People should have been pleased with his efforts, but some were hostile. This is most upsetting.

Holy Man Kakuban was not an ordinary man. Once, when Former Emperor Shirakawa[61] wished to see an incarnated buddha, he prayed for seven days. On the seventh night, the emperor had a revelation in a dream: "Tomorrow at such and such time, a monk will visit you from Mount Kōya. Worship him because he is really Amida Buddha incarnated." From the time he awoke, the emperor waited anxiously and wondered what kind of man would visit him. Finally, Kakuban came to see him about building Denpōin on Mount Kōya. When he appeared before him, the emperor thought he saw a light shining from Kakuban's forehead and remembered his mysterious dream. It is said that the emperor immediately granted Kakuban five manors.

It is foolish to say that Amida Buddha was incarnated as a common man to lead ignorant people like us to his peaceful world[62] and to establish a relationship with us. As I hear about these events, my tears wet my sleeves, making them difficult to keep dry. I wonder if Kakuban in his previous lives met the Buddha when he was the Wheel King[63] and established a deep relationship with him. I feel very happy as I think of this. Whenever I am grieving, I recite the Buddha's name; when I am cold and hungry, I reflect on my situation and recite the

---

60. The *Genkō shakusho* states that Kakuban died at the age of forty-nine on the twelfth day of the twelfth month in 1143 (*Dainihon bukkyō zensho*, vol. 87).

61. After Emperor Shirakawa 白河 (1053–1129; r. 1072–1086) retired, he began the *insei* 院政, or cloistered government system, and controlled politics during the reigns of the three succeeding emperors: Horikawa, Toba, and Sutoku. Five manors were granted to Kakuban during the time of Emperor Toba (r. 1103–1123) (*Negoro yōsho*, pp. 486–487).

62. An'yōkai 安養界: Amida's paradise.

63. Mujōnen'ō 無上念王, or Tenrin'ō 天輪王 (*cakra-varti-rāja*, Wheel King).

Buddha's name. I hope that in this way I have established a deep relationship with him.

7-9 Yoshikazu Hires a Monk

Long ago, a shabby monk came to Ichijō Jirō Yoshikazu,[64] a warrior of Shinano province,[65] and told him, "I would like to serve you." Yoshikazu asked, "Where do you come from?" The monk replied, "I come from a distant place. I looked after my wife for many years, but since she died, I found nothing to rely on in my life and have been living as a beggar." Yoshikazu felt sorry for the monk and took him into his service.

The monk ate only one bowl of food at noon and nothing else. When someone offered him more and better food, he would not accept it. He worked so diligently and without saying much that his master thought there could be no one else like him. Everyone appreciated him and said, "He is such a considerate man!" One day for some unknown

---

64. Unidentified.
65. Shinano province is present-day Nagano prefecture.

reason, the monk suddenly disappeared. His master and retainers lamented and again exclaimed, "He was such a nice man!" But there was nothing they could do.

In the monk's room, they found a diary written in a most beautiful style. They were curious to know its contents so they opened it and read, "On a certain day, in order to dispel any delusion, I recited the Buddha's name three hundred times and practiced meditation from the Hour of the Dog until the Hour of the Dragon.[66] On the following day, I engaged in the Purifying Practice,[67] and the Consciousness Only Practice at some other time." Everyone was most impressed that the monk had recorded nothing but his *kanpō* practice in the diary, and they all shed tears.

What kind of a wise man was he, working as a servant[68] and hiding his virtues? People remember him fondly and wonder if he could have been Monk Genpin[69] of olden times. The monk must have had a deep faith to refuse more food. He must have had such a pure and noble heart!

It is truly sinful that we have limitless delusions rising one after another in our minds, attaching ourselves to worldly affairs, but we do nothing to leave this defiled world. I wonder where the monk purified his heart? His time corresponded with that of Genpin, but there is nothing to identify him. What a noble and attractive heart he had!

7-10 A Hut in Yoshino

At the end of the Chōshō era (1132–1135), I received the tonsure as I had wished[70] and longed to visit sacred and interesting places. So I

---

66. From 8 p.m. to 8 a.m.
67. *Fujōkan* 不浄観: a practice to observe and purify delusions.
68. *Tsubune* つぶね. Monks who deliberately worked as lowly servants to hide their learning and virtues often appear in the *Senjūshō* stories, such as Gyōsei in 2-8, Shōjikibō in 3-8, and Eishō in 5-1. These *tsubune* tales seem to have been inspired by retired recluses such as the high-ranking monk Genpin 玄賓 (734–818).
69. Genpin studied the teaching of the Hossō Sect in Kōfukuji Temple and became the most learned monk in the capital, but later, avoiding fame and wealth, he retired to Yukawa Temple in Bitchū province.
70. According to this text, the protagonist Saigyō received the tonsure no later than 1135, the last year of Chōshō. According to the articles in the *Daiki* 台記 (*Shiryō taisei*, p. 64) and the *Hyakurenshō* 百錬抄 (*Kokushi taikei*, p. 62), Saigyō received the tonsure either in 1140 or 1142. Based upon these discrepancies, Nishio Kōichi concluded that Saigyō was not the author of the *Senjūshō*; see Nishio Kōichi, *Senjūshō* (Tokyo: Iwanami Shoten, 1976), 351.

climbed Mount Yoshino and spent three years there.[71] The appearance of the mountain, the color of its flowers, its trees, its serenity—everything was much superior to what I saw and experienced in the capital. It was most extraordinary to observe a strong storm wind wildly shaking oak leaves deep in the mountains, then watch it weaken as it passed over the pampas grass. Or to see the snow [on the trees] replaced by [cherry] blossoms. The sight of the pagodas[72] and the buildings in the upper and lower parts[73] of the mountain were so impressive that even ignorant folk could not ignore them. So, strongly attracted to the place, I remained on the mountain for three years.

About the third month of a certain year, when the cherry blossoms were scattered elegantly in front of my hut, a very shabby monk in his fifties with some rice in his sleeve came and rested under a cherry tree. I felt sorry for him and thought, "What a pity. With no faith in the Way or means to live, he has to stand at someone's gate and spread his sleeves [to beg]." So I deliberately began to recite loudly the name of the Buddha. As I saw him leaving, I thought again, "Buddhas and bodhisattvas pity all living beings and would certainly not ignore this man. Besides, they would not in the least discriminate against him thanks to his buddha nature."[74] So I said to the monk, "Please stay and admire the blossoms." The man replied, "I'm glad you said that. But this is how I feel:

Sakanumamo
Satekoso sugure
Yamazakura
Sanomiya hana no
Kage ni kurasamu

O mountain cherry blossoms,
I have been waiting
For you to open,

---

71. Mount Yoshino 吉野山, located in the central part of Nara prefecture, is famous for its cherry blossoms. Saigyō lived in a hut on the mountain and his poems about the cherry blossoms and Yoshino often appear in his anthology, the *Sankashū* 山家集.
72. *Anzen hōtō* 安山宝塔, "bejeweled towers of peaceful mountains," refers to pagodas.
73. *Kami-shimo no gozen* 上下の御前 suggests the noble buildings of Zaō Gongen in the upper and lower parts of the mountain.
74. Busshō 仏性: buddha nature; the possibility of cultivating enlightenment.

But now that you are open,
Should I stay under the shade of
Your blossoms?"[75]

When I heard his moving poem, I realized that he was not a common person, and I replied with:

Sakanuma wa
Hana o nomi matsu
Tabibito no
Sakeba nado teka
Nagame zaruran

A traveler who waits
Only for the opening
Of the blossoms—
But once they bloom,
Why doesn't he stay to gaze on them?

The man seemed to be well disposed[76] toward me and said, "I have left the secular world and retired deep into these mountains. Come and see where I live." So he took me to his place. The hut was built under four or five cherry trees and had a pine [thatched] roof and was surrounded by pine trees. He possessed nothing except the single-layer cotton robe he was wearing. The hut was located far away from any villages, and it was such an ideal place for him to clear his thoughts and mind that I was envious.

"Now tell me how to shed my anxiety[77] about life after death," I said. He replied, "I believe in the idea of *sanze fukatoku*, that is, nothing is certain in the Three Ages."[78]

---

75. The poem suggests the futility of sheltering under blossoms that scatter away. This poem and the following one are found only in this *Senjūshō* tale.
76. *Kokoroyose* 心よせ (*kokoro*, "heart"; *yose*, "closer"): that is, feeling friendly and trusting. While exchanging the poems, the man seems to feel friendly toward the protagonist.
77. *Yami* 闇: darkness; implies the protagonist's anxiety about life after death and whether he would assuredly be reborn in paradise or not.
78. *Sanze fukatoku* 三世不可得 (*sanze*, "the three periods of past, present and future"; *fukatoku*, "unobtainable"): that is, nothing is certain in the three generations.

Up to that point I had thought of him as a poor monk, but now I realized that he was an extraordinary ascetic practicing the Way. I promised to visit him, informing him that I, too, lived in these mountains. And then I left. As a result of our meeting, I concluded that he was an admirable ascetic pursuing the Way. It was extremely impressive that this man, living deep in the mountains, understood Nothing in the Three Ages.

7-11 Sōjun of Mount Hiei

Long ago, Sōjun[79] lived on Mount Hiei.[80] When he visited the Kannon of Hase[81] in a dream, the Kannon called to him, "Sōjun!" Sōjun respectfully sat up and the Kannon said, "After you return to your great temple,[82] a strong wind will cause the bell to fall. It will destroy many buildings in the living quarters. Many people, including you, are destined to die because of the wind. But since you have a deep faith in me, you will be saved." As soon as the Kannon finished speaking, Sōjun woke up, wondering how it was possible for a firmly hung bell to fall. He returned to Mount Hiei.

A few days later, the temple bell was suddenly blown down by a strong wind, which was later known as the Wind of Eiso.[83] Scores of houses, including Sōjun's living quarters, were destroyed and many people lost their lives because it happened so unexpectedly. Ajari[84] Sōjun was practicing the Way in the *jibutsudō* hall[85] when the bell fell. Although the hall was destroyed, Sōjun was unhurt because a life-sized Kannon statue fell over him as if to protect him. It was most mysterious. His dream at Hase had come true.

---

79. Unidentified.
80. Mount Hiei 比叡山 is located between Kyoto and Shiga prefecture and generally refers to Enryakuji Temple 延暦寺, founded by the monk Saichō 最澄 in 788 as the headquarters of the Tendai Sect; see note 2 of story 1-1.
81. Hase (Hatsuse) no Kannon 初瀬の観音 refers to the Kannon of Hasedera Temple in present-day Sakurai city in Nara prefecture; see Yoshiko Dykstra, "Tales of the Compassionate Kannon: The *Hasedera Kannon Genki*," *Monumenta Nipponica* 31, no. 2 (1976): 113–143.
82. Ōdera 大寺 refers to Enryakuji Temple.
83. The great wind blew on the thirteenth day of the eighth month in 989 (the Eiso era).
84. *Ajari* or *ācārya* 阿闍梨, meaning a teacher or correct conduct, is a title for a monk of high virtue.
85. *Jibutsudō* 持仏堂: a private hall housing Buddhist images.

The Kannon's skillful means to benefit his devotees are truly remarkable. The Kannon of Hase together with the Kannon of Sōjun's hall must have worked together to save him. Since then, the hall has been named Hase Hall because of Sōjun's dream at Hase Temple. There is no need to mention the great powers of buddhas to cultivate us.[86] This was a most marvelous incident.

7-12 Bright Deity Daichi and Mount Daisen in Hōki

There was once a shrine dedicated to the Bright Deity Daichi[87] on Mount Daisen in Hōki province. Bodhisattva Jizō[88] was the original

---

86. *Daishō no keyō* 大聖の化用: *Daishō*, "great," "sacred," i.e., buddhas; *keyō*, "cultivating sentient beings," i.e., buddhas helping and benefiting all beings.

87. *Daichi no myōjin* 大智の明神: the Bright Deity of Great Wisdom. The shrine was comprised of three minor shrines including Nankōin, Seimeiin, and Chūmon'in, forming Daisenji Temple; it was very popular from the eleventh century. Mount Daisen is in the west of present-day Tottori prefecture.

88. *Jizō bosatsu* 地蔵菩薩, or Bodhisattva Kṣitigarbhara, saves all beings after Śakyamuni and before Maitreya, or Miroku 弥勒, appears. To save sinners, he often appears in hells as a monk with a jewel ball in his left hand and a staff in his right. Faith in the bodhisattva was popular in Tang China and Heian Japan; see Yoshiko Dykstra, "Jizō, the Most Merciful: Tales from *Jizō Bosatsu Reigenki*," *Monumenta Nipponica* 33, no. 2 (1978): 179–200.

entity[89] of the deity and its power was as great as the sun rising from the mountainside.

One day Toshikata, an expert archer, set out to hunt deer and other animals. There were so many deer he was able to shoot as many as he wanted. When he went to retrieve them, he saw many five-inch-high Jizō statues pierced with his arrows. From a distance, he thought they were deer, but he now saw that they were some of the thousand Jizō images that he kept in his private worship hall. Greatly shocked, Toshikata held the images while shedding tears. Soon afterward he cut his hair, changed his house into a Buddhist hall, and stopped hunting in that area.

During the reign of Empress Shōtoku, an oracle pronounced that the hall should be changed into a shrine, so it was called [the shrine of] Bright Deity Daichi.[90] Its power was so great that sand flowed uphill in the evening to visit the shrine before flowing back down the next morning. All the pines on the hill faced the shrine to show their faith. It was most extraordinary that inert sand and plants placed their faith in the deity.

When Bodhisattva Jizō lived as [a woman called] Kōmokujo,[91] she firmly made a great vow to her mother, Shirazengen,[92] to save many beings with various vows. She practiced the Way and fulfilled her vows. Thanks to her merits, Jizō attained the highest rank of bodhisattva. Which other buddhas and bodhisattvas are superior to Jizō? A sutra mentions "[the bodhisattva's] long and great vows of mercy" and states that "[Jizō's] courageously devotional practices excel those of other bodhisattvas."[93]

Once, at the foot of Tōriten,[94] Shaka Buddha, Jizō's master, told

---

89. *Hontai* 本体. For Buddhist-Shinto syncretism, see notes 4 and 6 of story 1-2.

90. In 954 Emperor Murakami issued an edict establishing the shrine of Bodhisattva Daichimyō (*Zoku-gunshoruijū* 28, I, p. 210). Empress Shōtoku reigned from 764 to 770.

91. 広目女. The *Jizōbosatsu hongankyō* 地蔵菩薩本願経 identifies Kōmokujo 光目女 as Jizō (*Daizōkyō* 13, p. 781).

92. Shirazengen is identified as the father of Kōmokujo in the *Jizōbosatsu hongankyō* (*Daizōkyō*, p. 779), the *Sanbō kanō yōryakuroku* 三宝感応要略録, II, 32 (*Daizōkyō*, 51, p. 854), and the *Sangoku denki* 三国伝記, 5-1 (*Chūsei no bungaku*, p. 251).

93. *Daijōdaijū jizō jūronkyō* 大乗大集地蔵十論経 in *Daizōkyō*, 13, p. 726.

94. Tōriten (Trāyastriṃśa) is located at the top of Mount Sumeru in the center of which Śacra Deva (Taishakuten 帝釈天) lives.

him to save all the beings living between the times of the two Buddhas [Shaka and Miroku].[95] Jizō wholeheartedly devoted himself to fulfilling the vow. It was most wonderful that Jizō, possessing the Buddha's knowledge and the merciful heart of the bodhisattvas, first appeared as a deer and then revealed himself as a noble image to stop a wicked hunter from taking lives.

7-13 Bright Deity Kashima

During the Jishō period,[96] I visited a shrine dedicated to the Bright Deity Kashima in Hitachi province.[97] The shrine faced south with the sea before it and a mountain behind it. The roofs were lined one after another and the floor of its corridors squeaked[98] under the eaves. At high tide, the waves came up to the front of the shrine, while the sandy beach expanded for three *ri* at ebb tide.

Looking south, during the day [visitors] could watch row boats make their way across the limitless expanse of the sea and at night view the moon reflecting on the waves. Facing the mountain in the north [behind the shrine], they could listen to the cries of cuckoos among the cedars. It was most bleak and lonesome to hear deer crying at night with the dew on the grass, monkeys howling at dawn, and the wind from deep in the mountains blowing through the pines. East and west of the shrine were fields of colorful flowers, resembling rolls of brocade. Most interesting to see were the blooming cherry blossoms above the shrine, falling into the garden and the water at high tide. They floated here and there in bunches of scattered petals as they drifted toward the beach and into the bay.

A noble voice reciting a sutra, "Contemplation of the Way in a deep mountain," was heard in the corridor and soon stopped. Because [the

---

95. Stories of Jizō helping sentient beings after Shaka and before Miroku appear in *Shasekishū* 1-6 and *Sangoku denki* 5-1.
96. Saigyō was sixty to sixty-four years old during the Jishō 治承 period (1177–1181).
97. Kashima Myōjin 鹿島明神; the Kashima jingū 鹿島神宮 is in present-day Ibaragi prefecture. Since olden times it has been a tutelary shrine of the Fujiwara clan and related to the Kasuga Great Shrine 春日大社 in Nara. Among the four Kasuga shrines, Kashima Bright Deity is accorded first place.
98. *Kishireri* 軋れり: making a grinding noise. The wooden floors of the corridors made squeaking sounds as people walked on them.

visitors] wished to hear more, a *miko*[99] medium beat a hand drum saying, "We wish to hear more of the sutra." She also revealed various oracles to prove the existence of the deity. Among them was the revelation: "In the past Jingokeiun era,[100] I moved to Mount Mikasa[101] to protect the Hossō teachings. But I will not abandon this place and will constantly protect it."

Riding on the waves at high tide, many fish came to the shrine and then returned to the sea as it receded; thus they visited the shrine three times a day. It is most noble that they greatly benefited thanks to their relation to the deity. Another related deity, Isakawa,[102] is enshrined away from the main shrine, and this deity made a vow to protect all the beings in the world.

Cranes fly for a thousand *ri* and eagles ascend to the clouds, but neither have ever been outside this world. What other birds and animals are without the benefits of the buddhas and the gods? So many

---

99. *Kannagi* or *miko* 巫女: maiden or female mediums in the service of Shinto shrines.
100. Jingokeiun (767–770) was the reign of Empress Shōtoku. The passage is found in the preface of the *Kasugagongen kenkie* 春日権現験記絵, 1.
101. Mikasayama 三笠山: Mount Mikasa in Nara, where the Kasuga Shrine is located.
102. Isakawa Jinja 卒川神社 is not found among the twenty-two minor related shrines of Kashima, but the name often appears, for example, in *Kasugagongen kenkie*, 10-4.

buddhas and gods regard us as their own children and are determined to save and help us. But alas, our minds are so thickly clouded with delusions that they are never clear enough to receive their help. What a pity to have such useless hearts! There are ways to rid ourselves of delusions, but we are too lazy to find them. We are so ignorant that we even waste the Five Śīlas,[103] which we once observed. What shall we do?

7-14 Seeing [a Monk] Save a Man while Practicing the Way in a Northern Province

During that same Jishō period, I traveled to Koshi[104] to practice the Way. I saw the snow-capped summits of Shirane and Kai,[105] the lonely smoke rising from Mount Asama,[106] the snow falling on grass-thatched roofs, and the lower leaves of trees matching the color of a desolate, wild field.

I found such scenery attractive as I continued my way to see the Mano Log Bridge[107] and the valley stream that never froze and never seemed to end. After walking along a steep path under trees growing among the summit rocks, I crossed the Kiso Hanging Bridge.[108] I wish to keep everything I saw then a memory of my life and to take it with me after my death. I had heard the eastern route[109] was interesting but not so attractive as this one.

As I passed a mountain temple and saw flowers blooming here and there, I became more melancholy than when I passed through

---

103. *Gokai* 五戒: the five precepts that forbid Buddhists to kill, steal, commit adultery, use false words, and drink.
104. Koshinokata こしの方: the region including present-day Ishikawa, Fukui, Toyama, and Niigata prefectures.
105. Shirane 白根 and Kai 甲斐 summits span the three prefectures of Yamanashi, Nagano, and Shizuoka.
106. Asamayama 浅間山 is a volcano spanning Gunma and Nagano prefectures.
107. Mano is unidentified. まろき橋, "round bridge," is a bridge made from a log.
108. The bridge linked Agematsu and Fukushima stations in Shinano province (Nagano prefecture).
109. Azumaji 東路, the eastern route from the capital, included the Musashino plain and Mount Utsu. The text compares the eastern and the northern routes.

the grassy fields of Musashino.[110] Walking along this mountain path cleansed my heart more than following the narrow, ivy-covered path of Mount Utsu.[111] I heard there was no shade in which to rest in Sano Field.[112] I wondered if the wind was blowing through the pampas grass on the thatched roofs in Shinano. Reflecting on such things brought tears to my eyes.

I approached the Basket Ford,[113] and there I saw a monk and a man by the mountainside. The man appeared so strange that I could not ignore him. I asked, "What is the matter with you?" The man replied, "Well, just as . . ." and said nothing more. I persisted, "Why are you so afraid? Don't hold anything back. Tell me everything." Then the monk intervened, saying, "Well, the thing is this. I am a traveling ascetic, carrying a big *oi* container[114] on my back. I don't know who this man is; I just happened to meet him on the way. But I did learn that he has terrible enemies who are waiting ahead for him. He has no defenses and tried to turn back, but he has no chance of escaping them. Thinking of their own safety, his servants left him along the way, so he has been abandoned without any help. I feel sorry for him and cannot leave him in this plight. I tried to think of some means to aid him but am unable to think of anything. I feel as sad for him as for a sheep heading to the slaughterhouse, and now the sun is setting."

The monk finished in tears. The man also wept, saying, "I have known this monk only for one day, but he has been so sympathetic that I will never forget his kindness. How can I reward him for his kindness?" In these pitiful circumstances, the three of us remained there, weeping without words.

Since we could not remain where we were for too long, we decided to hide the man in the *yamabushi*[115] monk's big container and continue

---

110. Musashino 武蔵野: the Kantō plain including the present-day Tokyo area.
111. Utsunoyama 宇津の山: Mount Utsu, located between Okabe-cho, Shita-gun, and Maruko, Shizuoka-shi.
112. Sanononobe 佐野の野辺 is found in various places, so it is hard to determine which place is intended. The sentence in the text, *sode haraubeki kage mo nashi*, "no shade to shake a sleeve," means "no shade under which to shelter".
113. *Kago no watari* かごの渡り: crossing a river in baskets hung by ropes.
114. An ascetic carried an *oi* 笈 container on his back for his clothes, eating utensils, and Buddhist items.
115. *Yamabushi* 山伏: a mountain ascetic, referring to the monk in the text.

on our way. Soon we met about ten men armed with swords and bows and arrows. "Have you seen such and such a man on the way here?" they asked. The monk calmly replied, "Yes, we met such a man as he was going to cross at the Basket Ford. But someone told him, 'Your enemies are waiting for you that way,' and so he turned back toward Echigo."[116] Hearing this, the men said to each other, "Too bad! We've missed him. Let's go after him!" They quickly mounted their horses and galloped away.

Finally, we reached Ecchū[117] province, and so the man was saved. The monk tried to persuade the man to stay with him, but he would not listen and left. The monk also urged me to remain, but I thought "Why should I when the man he saved would not?" So I also left him.

What a splendid heart that monk had! The man's attendants, who had served him for a long time, abandoned him, but the monk, unknown to him, showed him much kindness. He hid the man in his container and confronted the man's enemies to save him. Such a heart is most impressive. Meeting this person on the road, the monk could have exchanged just a few words with him. Who else would show such sympathy to a stranger? The monk's kindness was as great and deep as the Kannon's mercy. He felt other people's sadness and joy as his own. That is the true Buddhist Way, for it is said, "Benefiting others as well as oneself[118] is the true service of buddhas."[119] Everyone should keep this in mind.

7-15 A Nun in Ise Province

Not long ago a very thin and emaciated nun lived in a brushwood hut in Ise province.[120] She constantly shed tears while reciting the Buddha's name. Her face, hands, and feet were so dirty that the local people admonished her, saying, "You seem to be a person with deep thoughts. So why are your face, hands, and feet so dirty? You don't have to keep them that dirty." The nun replied, "You are right. You must indeed

---

116. Present-day Niigata prefecture.
117. Present-day Toyama prefecture.
118. *Jiririta* 自利利他.
119. *Shin kuyō butsu* 真供養仏.
120. Present-day Mie prefecture.

think I am very dirty. But if I look like other women, [men] may say something unbecoming to me. So I have deliberately neglected my appearance. The reason I constantly weep is because I am afraid of what will happen to me after I die."

The nun's recitation of the Buddha's name never ceased. People respected her, saying, "Surely she will be reborn in paradise," so they helped her to survive.

One day the nun announced, "Someone whom I cannot refuse wants to see my hut so I am going to invite him here. Please do not come here for the next five days." The villagers then began to despise her, saying to each other, "It is just as we thought. Women are untrustworthy. We believed that she was concerned only about her future life. But she has a husband whom she secretly allows into her place."

So no one approached the hut for five days. The villagers heard her recitations until the fourth day, then nothing was heard from the dawn of the fifth day. Feeling this was strange, they went to the hut only to find that the nun had passed away, facing west with her hands joined in prayer. Thus she was saved just as she had wished.

A person of the nun's social status usually does not think of life after death, so her strong concern for her future was most extraordinary. Amida's vows are not prejudiced. He vowed to save all who depend on him. So how could this woman fail to be saved? She shed tears as she thought about her life and death. She believed in Amida and never neglected to recite his holy name. Such a heart is indeed most impressive. When I imagine her last moments, I am so moved that I break out in a sweat.

On whom should we rely[121] to enter the Pure Land of Amida? How can we avoid the flames of the scorching hell and the ice of the freezing hell?[122] It is so sad that we do nothing about this. Whatever we think will become the causes of life and death. We create bad karma for our future life, and we waste the Five Precepts, which we once observed. It is also quite useless to plant the seeds of suffering for such a long

---

121. *Kataudo* 方人: someone reliable, a friend.
122. *Shōnetsu jigoku* 焦熱地獄 ("scorching hell") and *guren jigoku* 紅蓮地獄 ("freezing hell"): where the skin is torn and becomes bloody like the red *guren* lotus flower. These two hells are among the Eight Great Hells described in the *Ōjō yōshū*.

time,[123] trying to support a life as transient as the dew on morning glories or foam on the water.

When Genjō Sanjō[124] went to India, he was attacked by pirates.[125] When Genjō saw them, he asked, "Why do you plant the seeds of long suffering for a life as brief as lightning and as transient as dew on morning glories?" Hearing this, the pirates became enlightened, shaved their heads, and served Genjō.

Genjō was truly a wonderful guide to the Way. Unlike trees and stones, people have hearts. Once their hearts are moved, they will be saved. While they may not be able to join [the priesthood], they earn merits by raising their hearts toward the Way. If they recite the Buddha's name just once while thinking of their future lives, how can Amida ignore them? He must surely have been moved by the pure heart of the nun in Ise.

---

123. *Asōgiyajōya* 阿僧祇耶長夜: an unaccountably long period. *Jōya*, "long night," is compared to the long, dark night of the ignorant state.

124. For Genjō Sanjō 玄奘三蔵, see *Senjūshō* 6-1.

125. For the story of Genjō and the pirates, see *Konjaku monogatarishū*, 6-6.

8-1 How Takamura Was Appointed Councilor Thanks to His Poetry

Long ago, Emperor Saga,[1] who was called Lord Saga, built a palace by the Ōi River in Nishiyama.[2] It was splendidly constructed, and its garden—with trees, a pond, and hillocks—was especially attractive.

Around the tenth day of the second month, the emperor, accompanied by Ono Takamura,[3] visited the palace for the first time. He called Takamura to him and ordered him to "compose a poem about the scene before you." So Takamura immediately recited his poem: "Purple-dust bracken[4] looks like the fist of a melancholy person,[5] while a jade-green reed in the cold resembles a gimlet jutting through a sack."[6] The emperor was so impressed by Takamura's poem that he immediately appointed him councilor, bypassing many other courtiers. It was truly an honor for Takamura to be promoted to this position.

After Takamura passed away, some poems by Hakurakuten[7] arrived from China. One of them read: "The bracken looks like the fist of a melancholy person, while the reeds in the cold resemble gimlets piercing through a bag." The heart of the poem was the same as Takamura's, but Hakurakuten used slightly different expressions. The intellectuals of the day praised it, declaring, "Takamura's poem is still wonderful."

---

1. Emperor Saga 嵯峨 (786–842), a son of Emperor Kanmu, excelled in the Way of Poetry and ordered the compilation of the *Shinsen shōjiroku* 新選姓氏録, the *Ryōunshū* 凌雲集, and the *Bunka shūreishū* 文華秀麗集.

2. Ōigawa 大井河 runs near Arashiyama in Kyoto. The upper stream is called Hotsugawa and the lower stream, Katsuragawa. Nishiyama 西山 refers to the mountainous area that includes Arashiyama and Atagoyama in the west of Kyoto.

3. Ono Takamura 小野篁 (802–852) excelled in poetry. When he received an imperial order to go to China, he disliked the ambassador so much that he did not board the ship, and so he was exiled to Oki. After he was pardoned and returned to court, he was promoted to the office of councilor. He compiled the *Ryōgige* 令義解 and the *Takamurashū* 篁集; see also note 27 below.

4. *Shijin* 紫塵: bracken covered with purple dustlike hair.

5. *Monouki* 㛧: "melancholy"; the bending bracken resembles melancholy persons lowering their heads.

6. *Hekigyoku kanro* 碧玉寒蘆: a jade-green reed in the cold season. *Kiri fukuro o dassusu* 錐嚢脱: a gimlet piercing out of its bag. The verses appear in *Wakan rōeishū*, I and Sōshun, 12.

7. 白楽天; see *Senjūshō* 2-3 and 6-2.

Indeed, the heart and words [of Takamura's poem] are truly interesting. Bending purple bracken resembles the fist of a melancholy person: The Great Master of Kōya[8] said, "Someone who is melancholy looks as if he is bending [bowing]." The reeds growing as green as jade in the cold appear [sharp] like gimlets piercing through a bag: By contrasting purple with jade-green and comparing the melancholy bracken to the [spirited] reeds in the cold, the poet exhibits impeccable taste.[9]

The heart of the emperor who promoted Takamura to councilor was as clear as a mirror free of dust; it brightened the world by discovering such talent. This was most extraordinary. When the emperor promoted Takamura, passing over many others, no one criticized him.

---

8. Kōbō Daishi (Kūkai). The origin of the saying in the text is not known.

9. The softness of the bending (round) bracken contrasts against the sharpness of the piercing (straight) jade-green reeds. The colors purple and green are in interesting contrast.

8-2 Miyako Yoshika and the Two Verses

During the reign of Emperor Uda,[10] there was a distinguished scholar called Miyako Yoshika.[11] Around the time of the fourth month, he and his friends visited Chikubu Island in Ōmi province.[12] They climbed the mountain and went to the shrine. The view from the top of the mountain was most impressive in all directions, so Yoshika composed a poem, declaring, "The Three Thousand Worlds are all before us."[13]

Suddenly, the shrine began to shake violently, and everyone clearly heard a solemn voice reciting the verse, "The Twelve Karmas in the mind are all futile."[14] It was most impressive.

Because he was atop a mountain on a clear day, it was quite natural for Yoshika to recite a few lines praising the view. And the verse coming from the shrine was indeed noble. Everyone wondered, "Who else but a deity could have added such a verse?" Truly, talents [in poetry and music] are valuable.

It was also very admirable that Yoshika went on to recite the verse composed by the deity three times a day, and thanks to this recitation for his future life, he passed away understanding the meaning of the verse. This was indeed noble.

---

10. Emperor Uda (867–931) was also called Teishi-in, Suzaku-in, Rokujō-in, and Uda-in. He employed the scholar Sugawara Michizane (845–903) to end the despotic politics of the Fujiwara clan. He favored poetry and literature and compiled the *Shinsen man'yōshū* 新撰万葉集 and the *Kudaiwaka* 句題和歌.
11. Miyako no Yoshika 都良香 (834–879) excelled in poetry in the Chinese style and was promoted to Lower Junior Fifth Rank in 873. He compiled the *Montoku jitsuroku* 文徳実録.
12. Chikubushima 竹生嶋 is the island in Lake Biwa in Shiga prefecture. Chikubu Bright Deity is enshrined on the island. The beautiful scenery surrounding the shrine popularly appears in *yōkyoku* 謡曲 and *kyōgen* 狂言 dramas.
13. *Sanzen sekai* 三千世界: the Three Thousands Worlds, meaning the whole world in the Buddhist concept. The view from the mountain on Chikubu Island is said to be as beautiful as if one were commanding a view of the entire world.
14. *Jūni innen* 十二因縁: the Twelve Karmas. *Kokoro no ura ni munashi* 心裏に空し, "futile in mind," meaning that when one sees a beautiful view from an island, all the karmas of suffering in the mind become futile and empty. These two verses appear in *Wakan rōeishū* II, no. 583; *Gōdanshō* 4-33; *Jukkinshō* 10-6; and *Kokon chomonjū* 4-113.

8-3 [Untitled]

Around the tenth day of the second month at the beginning of the Engi period,[15] Miyako no Yoshika[16] was on his way to the imperial palace. Seeing some green willows swaying in the spring breeze by Suzaku Gate,[17] he composed an opening verse [in the Chinese style]: "On a fine day, the spring breeze sways new willows like combing hair."[18] Trying to compose the closing verse, Yoshika stopped to think for a moment. A fearful red demon wearing a white loincloth appeared above the gate and loudly recited, "Ice melts and ripples wash old moss like beards."[19] And with that the demon vanished.

These two verses are vastly superior [to others] in their meaning and wording. When the wind blows in the great sky, the air becomes clear, and new willows sway like hair combed in the breeze. Since it was the early spring, "new willows" is most appropriate for this poem.

15. The Engi period (901–923) was one of the eras in Emperor Daigo's reign.
16. See *Senjūshō* 8-2.
17. Suzakumon 朱雀門 is a large gate facing Suzaku Avenue to the south of the imperial palace.
18. This verse appears in the *Wakan rōeishū*, I, Early Spring, 13.
19. The verse composed by the demon appears in *Gōdanshō* 4 and *Jikkinshō* 10-6.

The verse composed by the demon is likewise extraordinary. River water covered by ice [in winter] never touches the moss on the banks. But in the spring, when the air is clear and the new willows are swaying in the breeze, the melting ice sets the water free and its ripples wash over the roots of the moss, [which resembles beards].

By comparing willows with hair and moss with beards, the poem expresses the hearts of plants from their roots to their leaves. It is most interesting.

8-4 Lord Seishin

Long ago, during the reign of [Emperor Daigo],[20] Lord Seishin[21] was middle councilor. The emperor sent him an edict promoting him to General of the Left, but Lord Seishin declined, saying [in Chinese-style verses], "The clouds over Mount Long[22] are still dark. General Li[23] remains at home. The waves of the River Ying[24] are quiet. Cai Zheng-lu[25] is not yet in service."[26]

The emperor was deeply impressed by Seishin's reply and promoted him to the office of grand councilor; the lord later received First Rank. This was all thanks to his splendid poem. If he had declined the rank of General of the Left without composing the verses, he would not have received such honors.

---

20. Emperor Daigo (r. 898–930) is here referred to *Engi no gomon* 延喜の御門, Honorable Gate of Engi.
21. Lord Seishin 清慎公, or Fujiwara Saneyori 藤原実頼 (900–970), was the first son of Tadahira. He served four emperors: Daigo, Suzaku, Murakami, and Reizei. He actually declined the rank of General of the Left in 955, which was not during the reign of Emperor Daigo. The verses in the story appear in various writings including *Honchō monzui* 本朝文粋 5-140; *Wakan rōeishū* II, Shōgun, 684; *Gōdanshō* 8-6; *Jukkinshō* 10-7; and *Kokon chomonjū* 4-117.
22. Mount Long 隴山 is located between the provinces of Xiaxi 陝西 and Gansu 甘肅.
23. 李将軍 (?–119 B.C.), a general of Han China; see *Shiki* 史記, Ritsuden, 49 (*Kanbun taikei*, p. 215).
24. River Ying 潁川 runs through Henan province.
25. Cai Zheng-lu 蔡征虜 (?–33) conquered the Hebei region and was promoted to the rank of general; see *Mōkyū* 蒙求, p. 300.
26. The verses imply that since more talented men such as the generals Li and Cai were not in active service, he should decline such a high position.

8-5 Lord Yashō's Poem about Returning

Long ago, during the reign of Emperor Ninmyō, Lord Yashō was exiled to Oki province as punishment.[27] He composed a poem [in the Chinese style]: "Traveling to the east for ten thousand miles, I wondered when I would return [to the capital]. Gazing at the western [sea] for the rest of my life would bring such sorrow."[28]

When the emperor heard the poem, he decided to pardon Yashō. But the edict had already been issued, so he was helpless and had to send Yashō away. When the lord returned to the capital the following year, the emperor told him that, thanks to his excellent poem, he had been pardoned. His poem is truly exceptional. It would have been

---

27. Emperor Ninmyō, or Fukakusa (810–850), was the son of Emperor Saga. Lord Yashō 野相公, or Ono Takamura 小野篁 (802–852), was appointed vice-emissary to China in 834 but did not go to China as he was against Ambassador Fujiwara Tsunetsugu; as punishment he was exiled to Oki Island (in present-day Shimane prefecture). He excelled in writing both Chinese and Japanese poems. His Chinese-style poems appear in the *Keikokushū* 経国集 and the *Honchō monzui* 本朝文粋; his *waka* poems in the *Kokinshū*. His story appears in *Senjūshō* 8-1.

28. The poem appears in the *Wakan rōeishū*, II, *Senbetsu*, 635; and *Gōdanshō* 4-84. According to a note to the poem in the *Wakan rōeishū*, the poem was composed on the way to the capital and was given to a Chinese guest.

most unfortunate for him to travel thousands of miles, drifting on the waves, to remain in the west[29] for the rest of his life.

While Yashō was exiled in Oki, he often watched the fishermen's boats sail far away and disappear behind the islands. He composed this poem:

Wata no hara
Yaso shima kakete
Kogi idenu
Hitoni wa tsuge yo
Ama no tsuribune[30]

O fishermen
On your boats,
Tell people that
I have rowed away
To the many islands of the great sea.

Excelling in poetry, Lord Yashō composed *waka* poems as well [as Chinese-style verses]. It is most remarkable that his poems show such taste.[31]

8-6 Lord Asatsuna's Poem and His Becoming Councilor

Long ago, Lord Asatsuna[32] was sent to Hitachi province[33] as lieutenant governor. On the way, he stayed in Shinano province, where he had a

---

29. "Remain in the west" refers to being in exile.
30. *Watanohara* 大海原, "a great sea"; *yasoshima*, or *yasojima* 八十嶋, "eighty islands," meaning many islands. The poem appears in various collections: *Kokinshū* 9, travel poems, 407; *Wakan rōeishū* II, travel, 648; *Konjaku monogatarishū* 24-45; *Hōbutsushū* 2-164; and the *Hyakuninshu hitoyogatari*, Sangi Takamura.
31. Lord Yashō's two poems, one in *waka* style and the other in Chinese style, convey his yearning for the capital. Especially in the second one, the poet wishes the fishermen to tell his feelings to the people in the capital and at the imperial court, including the emperor.
32. Ōe Asatsuna 大江朝綱 (886–957), appearing as Nochino Gōshōkō 後江相公 in the text, was a doctor of letters and received the Lower Fourth Rank. His appointment as lieutenant governor of Hitachi is not officially recorded.
33. Hitachi is present-day Ibaragi prefecture.

dream that some misfortune befell his home [in the capital]. He anxiously sent a messenger home to inquire and composed a poem in the Chinese style: "I send my thoughts on a journey to a remote place as the evening clouds gather over Mount Ganzan. My tears at dawn wet the strings of my crown in the Kōro Hall as our reunion will be in the distant future."[34] Before the messenger reached the capital, Asatsuna's library burned down. This unfortunate incident must have been what he had foreseen in his dream.

When the emperor heard Asatsuna's poem, he summoned him back to the capital, made him a councilor,[35] and granted him Iyo province.[36] By that time Asatsuna had traveled as far as Kōzuke province,[37] but he returned to the capital without ever reaching Hitachi province. His appointment as councilor with a province to govern was a great honor for him.

The style of Asatsuna's poem is remarkably tasteful. Traveling to a remote place, he sent his heart to the evening clouds over Mount Ganzan and looked forward to meeting his friends in the distant future. This was what his poem expressed.

8-7   Hakurakuten's Poem

Long ago in China, on account of his blunt speech, Hakurakuten[38] was exiled to the region near the Jin'yō River.[39] There he composed the verse: "I will decline any promotion in government service, and I

---

34. The verses were composed at the farewell party in the Kōro Hall 鴻臚館 for the envoys from Bokkai 渤海, a country in northeastern China, which from 727 maintained this link with Japan. Mount Ganzan 雁山, or Goose Mountain, is located north of Shanxi province. The last verse compares the Bokkai envoys, who were returning to their country in the north, with the geese also returning north. The two verses convey the poet's wish to return to the capital. The verses were popularly quoted at farewells and appear in various writings including *Wakan rōeishū* II, Senbetsu, 632; *Gōdanshō* 6-11; *Kokon chomonjū* 4 (112); *Heike monogatari* 7; *Genpei seisuiki* 32; and *Taiheiki* 12.
35. In 953 Asatsuna was appointed *sangi* 参議, or councilor.
36. Iyo province is present-day Ehime prefecture. In 936 Asatsuna was said to have become lieutenant governor of Iyo province, but no official records verify his appointment.
37. Kōzuke 上野国 is present-day Gunma prefecture.
38. The poetry of Hakurakuten 白楽天, or Bo Ju-I 白居易 (772–846), a Chinese poet, greatly influenced the literature of Heian Japan; see note 2 of story 6-2.
39. This is the Yangzi River 揚子江, which runs through Jiangxi province.

will say nothing about secular matters."⁴⁰ A dragon appeared from the water, shedding tears, and exclaimed, "What a pity! If the world were just . . . " before disappearing into the waves.

Indeed, if his lord had possessed a pure mind, Hakurakuten would have been much favored; instead, he was exiled. People were greatly disappointed and thought China an inferior country.

8-8   Minister Kitano

Long ago, during the Engi period,⁴¹ Minister Kitano⁴² was exiled to a western province because of a certain incident. Moreover, he and his children were separated and forced to live in five different places. The minister was so sad that he could not see his reflection in a mirror

---

40. This poem appears in *Wakan rōeishū* II, Kankyo, 618.
41. The Engi period, 901–923, corresponds to the reign of Emperor Daigo.
42. Kitano Daijin 北野大臣, or Sugawara Michizane 菅原道真 (845–903), a doctor of letters, was a most tragic figure who was exiled to Dazaifu in Kyushu owing to the slander of Fujiwara Tokihira 藤原時平. To appease his aggrieved spirit, he was posthumously enshrined as the deity of Kitano Tenmangū Shrine 北野天満宮 in Kyoto and is popularly known as Tenjin-sama 天神様 for his scholarship.

because of his tears,⁴³ and he felt as if he were wandering in darkness. Then one day he faintly heard the cries of geese⁴⁴ flying in distant clouds and he composed a poem [in the Chinese style]: "You are the visiting guests while I am an exile. Both of us are wandering travelers. At night, while resting on a pillow, I think of my return flight. I wonder whether I can return, whereas you will most surely go back [home] in the coming spring."⁴⁵

His poem is most touching. Indeed, both the geese and the minister were travelers; the former were welcome guests, while the latter was in exile. When the minister quietly pondered at night his return journey, he knew the geese would surely go back the following spring. But he did not know when his own return would be. It is indeed pitiful that he passed away while still in exile.⁴⁶

During the last year of the Ōwa period (964), a verse arrived from China: "Three or four months have passed since I left home. With many tears streaming down my cheeks, I sometimes look up at the blue sky and feel everything is like a dream."⁴⁷ The poem was attributed to Minister Kitano. Who in China could have recited this poem when it was unknown in Japan?

The benevolent Emperor Daigo was known for his virtue even outside Japan, and his blessings were as abundant as the plants and grass on Mount Tsukuba.⁴⁸ I wonder why he mistakenly exiled the innocent minister to such a distant place.

---

43. *Kōkyō* 紅鏡, a red or crimson mirror, refers to the sun and is also related to *kōrui* 紅涙, red or painful tears. The sentence can be translated as "He was so sad he could not see the sun through his tears."
44. *Hatsukari* 初雁 refers to the first flock of geese flying from the north; this was a popular poetic subject in the autumn.
45. The poem appears in *Kankegoshū* 菅家後集 480, *Shintōshū* 神道集 9-49, and the *Kitano tenjin engi* 北野天神縁起.
46. Michizane died in 903 as a deputy of the director of the Dazaifu Police Office in Kyushu.
47. "Looking up at the blue sky" implies his innocence. The poem appears in *Kankegoshū* 476, *Gōdanshō* 4-11, and the *Kitano tenjin engi*.
48. The passage appears in *Wakan rōeishū* II, Tenō, 658; *Gōdanshō* 6-22; *Shasekishū* 10-11; and *Shintōshū* 9-49.

8-9 Naomoto

Tachibana Naomoto, a doctor of letters,⁴⁹ was about to be exiled owing to a false accusation. He heard the imperial edict would be issued the following day. Naomoto thought everything was due to karmic relations in his former life, nevertheless he was sad to leave his loving wife and children and his home in the capital. Hoping that the Kitano Tenjin Deity⁵⁰ would come to his aid,⁵¹ he went to the shrine and tearfully prayed to the deity throughout the night.

Toward dawn, a loud and noble voice calling, "Dōfū, Dōfū,"⁵² came from within the inner shrine. Then Naomoto heard Dōfū's voice, saying, "This grieving man, Naomoto, is innocent. I will give him a letter asking for his pardon." At this splendid revelation, Naomoto felt his hair stand on end, and he remained at the shrine in tears. Soon an oblong folded letter was tossed out to him from the inner shrine. He quickly opened it and read: "It is most pitiful that Tachibana no Naomoto, doctor of letters, is accused falsely. The Tenjin Deity desires his pardon, so Ono no Dōfū has written this letter." Greatly pleased, Naomoto hurried home, wrote a message explaining exactly what had happened at the shrine, and sent it to the emperor with Dōfū's letter.

When the emperor read what Naomoto had sent him, he was greatly surprised and immediately referred to an appeal written [by Dōfū] on the tenth of the first month in Tentoku 2 (958) asking for the governorship of Ōmi province. Dōfū had written: "I added seven pieces of calligraphy about the sages to the sliding doors of Shishinden Hall.⁵³ During the Great Daijōe Meetings,⁵⁴ I twice made paintings for the standing screens. I have remained in this country,⁵⁵ serving three

---

49. Tachibana Naomoto 橘直幹, a Chinese-style poet, became a doctor of letters in 948.
50. For Sugawara Michizane, see *Senjūshō* 8-8.
51. This implies that Michizane also suffered from a false accusation.
52. Ono no Dōfū 小野道風 (894–966) was one of the Three Calligraphers (*sanseki* 三蹟) along with Fujiwara Sari 藤原佐里 and Gyōsei 行成. He served three emperors: Daigo, Suzaku, and Murakami.
53. The hall is in the imperial palace.
54. The Daijōe Meeting 大嘗会 was held for the first crop of a new emperor's reign.
55. *Shinchin* 身沈, "sinking oneself," means to stay or remain. The poem appears in *Honchō monzui* 本朝文粋 6-151.

virtuous emperors, and my name is also known in China, across thousands of miles of waves."

Because the emperor found the handwriting was the same on both the appeal and Dōfū's letter from Kitano Shrine, he immediately pardoned Naomoto and promoted him to deputy of the Office of Ceremony, a position Naomoto had desired for years.[56] Indeed, the Tenjin's efficacy is truly great!

8-10 [Untitled]

Long ago, when Lord Kintō, Great Councilor Shijō,[57] was elevated one rank higher than Middle Councilor Tadanobu,[58] he composed a poem:

Ureshisa o
Mukashi wa sode ni
Tsutsumi keri
Koyoi wa mini mo
Amari nuru kamo

In olden days,
Joyful feelings were
Hidden in sleeves.
But tonight happiness
Overflows my whole body.[59]

Truly, Kintō must have been very pleased because he was an ambitious man.

At one time Lord Tadanobu, director of the Imperial Guard of the Right, was promoted above Kintō thanks to his successful

---

56. Naomoto became deputy of the Office of Ceremony (*shikibu daisuke* 式部大輔) in 958. The story of Naomoto's pardon through the intercession of Kitano Tenjin is unknown.
57. Fujiwara Kintō 藤原公任, popularly called Shijō Dainagon, or Great Councilor Shijō (966–1041), was a son of Regent Prime Minister Yoritada who excelled in poetry and music. He edited the *Wakan rōeishū* and his writings include the *Kintōshū*, the *Shinsen zuinō*, the *Shūishō*, and the *Kin'yōshū*.
58. Fujiwara Tadanobu 藤原斉信 (967–1035) was a son of Prime Minister Tamemitsu.
59. The poem appears in *Wakan rōeishū* II, keiga, no. 772.

performance at the *mikagura* celebration held at Seishodō Hall.[60] Kintō then tried to resign from his office of *midō*, but the emperor sent his messenger Masafusa[61] to him, saying "Kintō's resignation is not accepted because his reason for doing so is [inexplicable]. Go quickly and offer him one rank higher." As a result, Kintō was not only saved from embarrassment, but also promoted over [Tadanobu].[62] People thought it was most auspicious and Kintō must have been very pleased. Weren't the verses "Joyful feelings were hidden in sleeves/But tonight happiness overflows my whole body" truly splendid?[63] Who could ever criticize them?

8-11 [Untitled]

When Kintō was appointed great councilor, he wished that Lord Sanjō[64] and Regent Higashi Sanjō[65] were still alive. He thought how happy and helpful to him they would have been in every way. He became sad and composed a poem:

Yo no naka ni
Aramashi kaba to
Omou hito
Naki wa ookumo
Nari ni keru kana

In this life,
Many of the people

---

60. After the Daijōe Meeting, *kagura* music and dance were offered at the Seishodō Hall in the imperial palace. Accounts of Tadanobu's excellent performance on the occasion appear in the *Kojidan* (1-46) and the *Jikkinshō* (1-31).
61. The lifetime of Ōe Masafusa 大江匡 (1041–1111) does not coincide with that of Kintō.
62. According to the *Kugehosa* 公家補佐, both Kintō and Tadanobu held Junior Second Rank in 1005, but Kintō was middle councilor while Tadanobu was deputy middle councilor (*Kokushi taikei*, p. 251).
63. *Kakinomoto* 柿本 here means an excellent poem, that is, a poem as good as one by Kakinomoto no Hitomaro 柿本人麻呂, an ancient poet sage.
64. Kintō's father, Fujiwara Yoritada (924–989), became regent prime minister with First Rank and was popularly called Lord Sanjō 三条.
65. Fujiwara Kaneie 藤原兼家 (929–990) was a cousin of Kintō's father, Yoritada. He became regent prime minister with Junior First Rank and was called Lord Higashi Sanjō 東三条.

Whom I wish
Were still alive
Have passed away.⁶⁶

People said that Lady Nakatsukasa,⁶⁷ when she overheard the poem from behind a screen, tearfully prostrated herself on the floor. Some were skeptical about her crying so much, but others thought it most understandable for her to be so tearfully moved by the poem.

Everyone must wish to have someone special with him after being promoted to a higher office.

8-12 Yukihira

Long ago Middle Councilor Yukihara⁶⁸ was exiled to Suma Beach⁶⁹

---

66. The poem appears in *Wakan rōeishū* II, Kaikyū, no. 749; *Shūishō* no. 571; and *Shūi wakashū* 20-1299.
67. Poetess Nakatsukasa 中務 (912–989?) was a daughter of Lord Nakatsukasa (the fourth son of Emperor Uda) and a wife of Saneyori, Kintō's grandfather. Her mother was the famous poetess Ise 伊勢; see *Senjūshō* 8-2.
68. Ariwara Yukihira 在原行平 (818–893) was a poet and an older brother of the renowned poet Ariwara Narihira. Yukihira's poems appear in the *Kokinshū* and the *Gosen wakashū* (*Gosenshū*).
69. Suma 須磨 is southwest of Kobe city, across Awaji Island.

because of a fault he had committed.⁷⁰ While tearfully wandering, he saw some women divers⁷¹ by Ejima Beach.⁷² Attracted to one of them, he approached and asked her, "Where do you live?" She casually replied in a poem:

Shiranami no
Yosuru nagisa ni
Yo o sugosu
Ama no ko nareba
*Yado mo sadame zu*⁷³

Being a fisherman's child
Who spends her life
On the beach where
White waves come and go,
I have no other place to settle in.

After she finished reciting the poem, she disappeared. The middle councilor was said to have been too sad to dry his tears after she left.

Making a living among the waves day and night, the woman did not want to wet [her sleeves] while she waited for the moon to shine on them. Because she spent so many moons sleeping on sleeves soaked by the waves, she was used to such a life.⁷⁴ Among the women divers who live their lives on boats and sleep on wet sleeves,⁷⁵ here was one

---

70. There is no official record of his exile. During the time of Emperor Montoku (r. 850–858), Yukihira left his position of his own accord and settled in Suma; see *Hyakuninshu hitoyogatari* II, Chūnagon Yukihira.
71. *Kazukisuru* means to make a living by diving for shellfish.
72. Ejima 絵島 is the northeastern part of Awaji Island.
73. The opening term *shiranami* しら波, "white waves," implies *shirazu* ("don't know"), meaning "you asked me where I lived and I don't know." *Yo o sugosu* 世を過ごす, "to spend one's life," also means to spend the night (夜). The last line, *Yado mo sadame zu*, "have not settled my dwelling," also implies "I have no particular man" (*yado*, "inn" or "lodging"). The poem appears in *Wakan rōeishū* II, *yūjo*, no. 721; *Shinkokinshū* 18, *zōkashita*, no. 1704; *Fūyō wakashū* 18, *zōsan*, no. 1353; and *Hyakuninshu hitoyogatari* II, Chūnagon Yukihira.
74. *Tsuki o kasanete nareshi omokage* 月をかさねてなれし面影: *tsuki* (moon or months), *kasanete* (doubling), *nareshi* (used), *omokage* (visage or image); the phrase means that she had become accustomed [to a life of sleeping on her wet sleeves] since she had spent many months doing so.
75. *Katashiku*: *kata* (one of the sleeves), *shiku* (spread); i.e., sleeping on one of the sleeves spread on the floor of the boat.

with a heart to understand such refined feelings. The middle councilor became even more moved when he thought of her, for the message of her poem was most elegant.

8-13 Lord Tameyori and a Poem[76]

Long ago Middle Councilor Tameyori[77] went to the imperial palace and approached some people whom he had known for a long time. He was noticed by a young courtier who for some reason then slipped away from the group. Seeing this, Tameyori tearfully composed a poem:

Izuku ni ka
Mi o ba yosemashi
Yono naka ni
Oi o itowanu
Hito shi nakereba[78]

Where should I place
My old body?
For there is no one
In this world
Who does not avoid old age.

Tameyori left after he finished the poem. He must have experienced deep feelings on that occasion.

It is true that people change as they grow old and become too familiar with many things and that young people do not like them. Unless a person passes through the Gate of Furōmon [without aging],[79] he cannot keep from growing old. Everyone avoids old people; Tameyori

---

76. The word *uta* 歌 (poem) appearing in the story title after the name of the protagonists in tales 8-14 to 8-28 has been omitted.

77. Fujiwara Tameyori 藤原為頼 (941–998) was a poet with Lower Junior Fourth Rank and was an uncle of Lady Murasaki Shikibu 紫式部. There is no official record of his becoming middle councilor.

78. The poem appears in *Wakan rōeishū* II, Rōjin, no. 732.

79. Furōmon 不老門 is the gate leading to the world where no one ages. In China it was the name of Luoyang city; in Japan it referred to the gate north of Hōrakuin Hall in the imperial palace.

lamented his own aging and wondered where he should go.

The elderly should make friends with other older people. But this is difficult because they wish to associate with the young. I wonder if this feeling is another unhappy sign of old age.

8-14 Lord Takamitsu

Long ago Takamitsu[80] asked for the position of *saishō*,[81] or prime minister, but he did not receive it. He was very disappointed and depressed. About that time, on the night of the thirteenth day of the ninth month, there was a poetry meeting[82] at the imperial palace. The topic was "Gazing at the Moon."[83] Takamitsu composed a poem:

---

80. Fujiwara Takamitsu 藤原高光 (939–994) was a son of Morosuke. His mother was Princess Masako, a daughter of Emperor Daigo. He held Junior Upper Fifth Rank but never became a *saishō*, or prime minister. In 961 he received the tonsure, took up ascetic practice on Mount Tōnomine, and was popularly called Tōnomine Shōshō 多武峰少将. He was one of the Thirty-Six Poet Saints, or Thirty-Six Renowned Poets (*sanjūrokkasen* 三十六歌仙). The poem appears in *Wakan rōeishū* II, Jukai, no. 764; and *Shūishō* 10, Zatsuge, no. 500. It was composed when Takamitsu became a monk; see *Eiga monogatari* 1, Tsuki no en.

81. *Saishō* 宰相, a position below the great and middle councilors, were selected from those higher than the Fourth Rank.

82. *Utaawase* 歌合.

83. *Getsu zen jutsu kai* 月前述懐: expressing one's thoughts by gazing at the moon.

Kaku bakari
Hegataku miyuru
Yononaka ni
Urayamashiku mo
Sumeru tsuki kana

In the world
That appears
So difficult to live in,
The moon looks
Enviously clear.

When the emperor heard the poem, he was so impressed that he quickly promoted Takamitsu to the post of prime minister. Takamitsu was very pleased and declared, "We should always compose poems. Unless the darkness in our minds is expressed in words, it will sink deep into our hearts and never be cleared." This is touchingly most true.

8-15 Lord Kintō

Long ago during the reign of Emperor Murakami, there was a heavy snowfall in the middle of the second month. At dawn the moon was especially bright and snow lay everywhere, as in King Ryo's garden.[84] The moon allowed one to see for a thousand *ri,* as if one had climbed Lord Yū's edifice.[85] Every tree was in bloom, and one could not distinguish between the snow and the plum blossoms.

The emperor summoned Middle Councilor Kintō and told him to bring a branch of plum blossoms with him. Kintō brought him a snow-coverd branch. The emperor asked him, "What were you thinking?" Kintō replied with this poem:

Shirashirashi
Shiraketaru yo no
Tsukikage ni

---

84. King Ryo 梁王 refers to King Xiao 孝王 of the Han dynasty who created the famous Liang Garden.
85. The edifice in Jiangxi province was built by Lord Yū when he was governor there.

Yuki kakiwakete
Ume no hana oru[86]

White and white,
On the whitened night
Under the shadow of the moon,
I trudged through the snow
And broke off a plum branch.

The emperor was immensely impressed. He was moved by the poem's fine theme and greatly praised the verses. Overwhelmed by his admiration, Kintō shed so many tears that the emperor also could not stop weeping. This was truly noble. When recalling this event, Kintō said, "This is the happiest memory," and seemed to have a difficult time drying his tears. This was indeed true and such an incident cannot be found in this degenerate age.

---

86. *Shirajirashii*, "white upon white," implies a cold feeling. *Shiraketaru yo*, "whitened night," means the dawn; *shiraketaru* also suggests a "boring" feeling since everything is a monotonous white. But the last two lines of the poem break this monotony with the breaking of a branch while thrashing through the snow. The poem appears in *Wakan rōeishū* II, Shiro, no. 803; and *Hyakuninshu hitoyogatari* 5, Dainagon Kintō.

8-16 [Untitled]

When Ōnakatomi Yoshinobu[87] visited Lord Ononomiya,[88] the lord, who was sitting behind a screen, offered him a cup of *sake*. Seeing a piece of *hikage*[89] [sun-shade] fern at the bottom of the cup, Yoshinobu quickly composed a poem and recited:

Ariake no
Kokochikoso sure
Sakazuki ni
Hikage mo soite
Idenu to omoeba[90]

I feel as though I see
The moon at dawn,
For when the cup is offered
With the *hikage* fern
It also shows the sun.

The lord was greatly impressed by the poem, and indeed, it is truly interesting. Unless the verse is referring to the moon at early dawn, how could it cause the shadow of the sun to appear? People may think that anyone can easily compose a poem like this, but quickly producing a verse on a suitable theme in front of a noble lord is a most extraordinary feat. Experts in the Way of Poetry highly appreciate such poems.

---

87. Ōnakatomi Yoshinobu 大中臣能宣 (921–991) was a son of Yorimoto, the head priest (*saishu* 祭主) of Ise Shrine. He was one of the Thirty-Six Renowned Poets and his anthology is the *Yoshinobushū*.

88. Lord Ononomiya 小野宮 refers to Fujiwara Saneyori 藤原実頼 (900–970), a son of Tadahira and the elder brother of Morosuke 師輔. He was appointed regent with First Rank and excelled in poetry and music.

89. *Hikage* 日陰 ("shade" or "shadow") is a fern and is also called *hikage no kazura*; its stem grows 2–3 meters high in shady places (also known as *hikage*).

90. *Ariake* 有明け refers to early dawn, when the moon is still in the sky. The last two syllables of *sakazuki* ("*sake* cup") are associated with *tsuki*, "moon." *Hi*, the first syllable of *hikage* (a fern), refers to the sun, while the last two, *kage*, can mean shadow. Thus the poet can appreciate the *sake* as well as view the moon and the sun, light and shadow, in the same cup. The poem appears in *Shūishō* 9, Zōjō, no. 425; *Shūi wakashū* 17, Zōshū, no. 1148; *Yoshinobushū*, no. 62; *Wakan rōeishū* II, Sake, no. 490; and *Hyakuninshu hitoyogatari*, Ōnakatomi Yoshinobu Ason.

8-17 Sosei

Long ago there was a poet-monk named Sosei[91] who lived in Ōhara,[92] outside the capital. Like a retired recluse detached from secular affairs, he enjoyed the flowers [in spring] and the red leaves [in autumn].

On a long, leisurely autumn night when he could not sleep, Sosei felt tears filling his eyes. In the early dawn, when for no reason he felt lonesome and heard some crickets crying, he recited:

Ima kon to
Tare tanome kemu
Aki no yo o
Akashikane tsutsu
Matsumushi no naku[93]

Waiting for someone
Who may perhaps come,
I find it hard to pass
The long autumn night
While the crickets are crying.

When he heard a grasshopper crying by his pillow,[94] he composed this poem:

Kirigirisu
Itaku nakiki so
Aki no yo no
Nagaki omoi wa

---

91. Sosei 素性 (844–?), a son of poet-monk Henjō (816–890), was one of the Thirty-Six Renowned Poets and was active at the imperial court. The anthology of his poems is the *Soseishū* 素性集.
92. Ōhara 大原 is part of present-day Sakyo-ku in Kyoto.
93. *Matsumushi* 松虫: crickets. *Matsu* of *matsumushi* is a pine but also means "to wait"; *mushi* is an insect. The final line of the poem, *matsumushi no naku*, "the crickets are crying," implies the poet is also weeping. The poem can be understood to mean, "I am waiting for someone who told me 'I will come soon'; I spend the long night crying just like the crickets." The poem appears in *Wakan rōeishū* I, Mushi, no. 332.
94. *Makura no shita*, "under the pillow," in the original text.

SECTION EIGHT 225

Warezo masaru[95]

Don't cry so hard,
O grasshopper,
For my feelings
Will last longer than
This autumn night.

Both of these poems show much taste.

8-18 The Fan Meeting

Long ago some people[96] gathered for a Tanabata Festival[97] Fan

---

95. The poem appears in *Wakan rōeishū* I, Mushi, no. 333. Both poems are listed as Sosei's compositions in the *Senjūshō*, but the attribution of the second verse is not completely certain; see *Senjūshō zenchūshaku* II, pp. 406–407.
96. *Sarubekihito*, "certain persons," here refers to poets at court.
97. Tanabata 七夕 is the annual star festival held on the seventh night of the seventh month, when the herd boy star (Kengyūsei 牽牛星) and the weaver star (Shokujosei 織女星) meet across the Heavenly River (Amanogawa 天の川). A magpie spread its wings to make a bridge over the river for the two stars to meet, so it is called the Kasasagibashi, or Magpie Bridge.

Meeting[98] at Lord Kujō's mansion.[99] Lady Nakatsukawa[100] wrote this poem on her fan:

Ama no kawa
Kawabe suzushiki
Tanabata ni
Ōgi no kaze o
Nao ya kasamashi[101]

At Tanabata
Should we send
More breezes with fans
To the cool banks
Of the Heavenly River?

The lord and the participants handed the fan to each other and read the poem. They were all deeply impressed by the verses. Shortly afterward, Motosuke[102] turned in his fan, on which this poem was written in a most tasteful style:

Ama no kawa
Ōgi no kaze ni
Kiri harete
Sora sumi wataru

---

98. *Ōgiawase* 扇合 is a contest of poems written on fans. The poems listed in the text were presented at the Fan Meeting of En'yūin 円融院扇合, which was actually held after Lord Kujō's death.
99. Lord Kujō 九条, or Fujiwara Morosuke (908–960), Minister of the Right with Second Rank, was a son of Tadahira and a younger brother of Lord Ononomiya (*Senjūshō* 8-16). His writings include the *Morosukeshū* 師輔集.
100. Nakatsukasa 中務 (912–989?), a daughter of the poetess Ise. Both mother and daughter were included in the list of Thirty-Six Renowned Poets (see note 4 of story 8-11). Nakatsukasa's anthology is titled the *Nakatsukasashū* 中務集.
101. The poem appears in *Shūi wakashū* 17, no. 1088; *Shūishō* 3, no. 98; *Nakatsukasashū* no. 125; and *Hyakuninshu hitoyogatari*, Kiyohara Motosuke.
102. Motosuke 元輔 (908–990) was one of the Thirty-Six Renowned Poets and an editor of the *Gesenshū*. The governor of Higo province with Upper Junior Fifth Rank, he was the father of Lady Sei Shōnagon (author of the *Pillow Book*). Motosuke's poetic anthology is the *Motosukeshū*.

Kasasagi no hashi[103]

Heavenly River,
The sky is so clear
Thanks to the fan's breeze
You can see
The Kasasagi Bridge.

The participants found his poem very interesting as well. So the poems by Lady Nakatsukawa and Motosuke won the contest, and the rest of the fine verses were completely disregarded as if they were [mere] trees on a deep mountain rather than blossoming flowers.

8-19 Sanekata

Long ago some courtiers went to Higashiyama to view the blossoms,[104] but suddenly it began to rain. The people were very confused by the violent shower, but Sanekata[105] remained calm as he stood under a tree and recited:

Sakuragari
Ame wa furi kinu
Onajiku wa
Nuru tomo hana no
Kage ni yadoran[106]

While we view the blossoms
In this shower,
I will get wet in any case

---

103. The poem is included in *Wakan rōeishū* I, Ōgi, no. 202; *Motosukeshū*, no. 73; *Shūi wakashū* 17, no. 1089; and *Hyakuninshu hitoyogatari*, Kiyohara Motosuke.

104. *Hana* 花 (flowers or blossoms) and *hanami* (flower viewing) usually mean to enjoy the viewing of cherry blossoms.

105. Fujiwara Sanekata 藤原実方 (?–998) was a son of Sadatoki. He became Lieutenant General of the Imperial Guard of the Left in 994 and was appointed Governor of Mutsu province in the following year with Lower Fourth Rank.

106. The poem appears in *Wakan rōeishū* I, Ame, no. 85; *Shūishō* 1, 31; *Shūi wakashū* 1, 50; and *Hyakuninshu hitoyogatari*, Fujiwara Sanekata Ason.

So I prefer to take shelter
Under the shade of the flowers.

Since Sanekata did not try to avoid the shower, he was so soaked by the rain dripping from the blossoms that it was quite impossible for him to keep his robes dry.[107] Nevertheless, people thought his attitude was very tasteful.

Some time later, Great Councilor Tadanobu[108] mentioned the incident to the emperor, saying, "This was indeed interesting." But when Yukinari,[109] the director of the imperial secretariat office[110] learned what had happened, he declared, "Sanekata's poem is interesting, but he was a fool." Sanekata indirectly heard[111] about this and was said to have held a strong grudge against Yukinari.[112]

---

107. *Shiborikane*: "hard to wring out."
108. Tadanobu, or Narinobu 斉信 (967–1035), was a son of Tamemitsu and a grandson of Lord Kujō (see *Senjūshō* 8-10, 8-18).
109. Fujiwara Yukinari, or Gyōsei 藤原行成 (972–1027), a son of Yoshitaka (*Senjūshō* 8-5), was a provisional great councilor and excelled in many artistic fields including poetry.
110. *Kurōdo*, or *kurando* 蔵人: "imperial secretary." Yukinari became director of the office in 995.
111. *Morekiku* is a compound expression: *more*, "leaking," and *kiku*, "hearing"; to hear something leaked indirectly.
112. For the dispute between Sanekata and Yukinari, see *Kojitan*, or *Kojidan*, 2-33; *Jukkinshō* 8-1; and *Hyakuninshu hitoyogatari*, Fujiwara Sanekata Ason.

8-20 [Untitled]

In the spring of the year following Lady Taikenmon'in's[113] passing, one of her former attendants, Kanekata,[114] visited her palace. He saw that the people there were still grieving and not enjoying the blossoms.[115] The flowers were in full bloom just as they had been in the previous year; it was as if they thought of nothing else. Kanekata recited a poem:

Kozo mishi ni
Iro mo kawarazu
Sakini keru
Hana koso mono wa
Omowazari kere[116]

Without changing
Their color from last year
The flowers are
In full bloom
And think of nothing.

When Shunzei[117] heard the verses, he criticized them, saying, "I think the first part of the poem[118] is very fine, but I don't like the last part starting with *Hana koso*,[119] for it sounds like a butterfly flitting through the air."[120]

---

113. Taikenmon'in 待賢門院, or Fujiwara Akiko (1101–1145), a daughter of Fujiwara Kimizane, was the wife of Emperor Toba and the mother of the emperors Sutoku and Goshirakawa. In 1124 she received the official title Taikenmon'in and built Enshōji and Hōkongōin temples.

114. Kanekata 兼方, or Hata Kanekata (1036–1113), was an officer of the Imperial Guard of the Left. He was not alive when Taikenmon'in died and so it would have been impossible for him to compose a poem after her death.

115. *Genryō* 元亮; the expression is used here to mean "leisurely enjoying blossoms."

116. The poem appears in *Kin'yō wakashū* 9, Zatsubu, no. 524; *Fukurozōshi* 1; *Hōbutsushū* 1; and *Ujishūi monogatari* 1-10.

117. Shunzei 俊成 (1114–1204), a son of Fujiwara Toshitada 藤原俊忠 and the father of Fujiwara Teika, was known as a celebrated poet. He edited the *Senzai wakashū*. His writings include the *Korai fūtaishō* and the *Shunzei kashū*.

118. The first three lines of the seventeen syllables of a *waka* poem are called *uenoku* 上の句 (upper or top verse), while the last two lines of fourteen syllables are called *shimonoku* 下の句 (lower verse).

119. *Hana koso* 花こそ: *Hana* (flowers) and *koso*, an emphatic term; i.e., the very flowers.

120. *Hichō* 飛蝶; the verse gives an unsettling impression like that of a butterfly in flight (*hichō*).

When Kanekata heard Shunzei's criticism, he dressed himself in formal attire and went to Shunzei's mansion. There he said to a servant, "Tell your master that although it may be inconvenient for him, I have come to tell him something." When Shunzei received this message, he concluded that Kanekata must have come to discuss his poem *Kozo mishi ni,* so he told the servant, "I am rather busy now. I wonder what this is all about?" When the servant reported back to Kanekata, he simply said, "Tell your master that there is a famous poem, *Hana koso yado no aruji narikeri.*"[121] Then he left. When Shunzei heard this, he said to himself, "Well, it is just as I thought."

Kanekata understood Shunzei's criticism of his poem to mean: "The verse starting with *Hana koso* is not so good." Thus he confronted him with: "How about your father's famous *hana koso* poem?"[122] But this is what Shunzei actually meant: "Any tasteful verse could follow the poem's fine first part, but the ending lines *Hana koso mono wa omowazari kere,* 'the flowers think of nothing,' sound terribly weak." Shunzei did not mean to criticize the *koso* of *hana koso*.[123] In such a situation, how could Kanekata compare his poem to Toshitada's?

8-21 Tadamine

Long ago, a poet named Tadamine[124] went north[125] about the time of the second month. The clouds he saw rising above the mountains were hardly distinguishable from the trees because the latter were completely covered in snow. He composed this poem:

---

121. The verse means "The very blossoms are the hosts [of my shelter for] tonight." It is the last portion of a very popular poem by Fujiwara Kintō: *Haru kitezo hito mo toikeru yamazato wa hana koso yado no aruji narikere,* "For a visitor to a mountain village in the spring, the blossom is the host of his night's shelter"; see *Shūi wakashū* 16, no. 1015.

122. The poem is here erroneously attributed to Shunzei's father, Toshitada, in the *Senjūshō* text. It was a common practice to use the poems of a critic's father's to rebuke his criticism, as may be seen in *Jikkinnshō* 4-11 and *Kokon chomonjū* no. 188.

123. The sentence suggests that Kanekata misunderstood Shunzei's criticism of his poem. According to Shunzei, nothing is wrong with the last part (starting with *Hana koso*) of the poem by Kintō (by Toshitada in the text), but the lines starting with *Hana koso* by Kanekata are not well suited to the refined first part of his poem.

124. Tadamine 忠峰, birth date unknown, was one of the Thirty-Six Renowned Poets and an editor of the *Kokin wakashū*. His anthology of poetry is the *Tadamineshū* 忠峰集.

125. *Koshi no kata,* or *Koshiji* 越路, is the old name for the northern region including the central part of present-day Niigata prefecture.

Kumo no iru
Koshi no shirayama[126]
Oinikeri
Ookuno toshi no
Yuki tsumori[127] *tsutsu*

Clouds are rising
Above the white mountain of Koshi
Which seems to have aged
With the snow piled on it
For so many years.

This poem is most tasteful.

8-22 Ise

Long ago the renowned poetess Ise[128] lived in the capital. She had become very poor and could find no means to support herself in the city, so she wandered about here and there. One day she visited [Kōryōji Temple] in Uzumasa[129] and stood before the image of Yakushi Medicine Buddha, composing a poem:

Namu Yakushi
Awaremi tamae
Yono naka ni
Ari wazurau mo

....

126. *Koshi no shirayama*, "the white mountain of Koshi," i.e., Mount Haku of Kaga.
127. *Tsumori*, "piling up," here also means aging or piling up years. The poem appears in *Wakan rōeishū* 11, Yama, no. 497; *Shūishō* 4, no. 159; and *Shūi wakashū* 4, no. 249.
128. Ise 伊勢 (877–939), a daughter of Fujiwara no Tsugukage, served Lady Atsuko, a consort of Emperor Uda, and gave birth to a son who died young. She was one of the Thirty-Six Renowned Poets, and 180 poems by her appear in the imperial anthologies, including the *Kokin wakashū*, and in her private collection, the *Iseshū*. Similar stories about Ise appear in the *Ima monogatari*; *Genpei seisuiki* 17 (Chūsei no bungaku, pp. 159–160); *Zōzōshū* 17; *Ominaeshi monogatari* (Koten bunko, pp. 17–18); and *Hyakuninshu hitoyogatari* II, Ise (Iwanami bunko, pp. 166–167).
129. The principal image of the Kōryūji Temple in Uzumasa (in Kyoto) is Prince Shōtoku. The temple is known for other statues including the seated Amida and Miroku as well as Yakushi Medicine Buddha.

Onaji yamai zo

Show me your mercy,
O Yakushi Buddha
For in this life
Suffering from poverty
Is the same as suffering from illness.

As soon as she had finished reciting her poem, she felt the hall move for a moment.

Toward dawn, a noble monk appeared to her in a dream and said, "The Buddha is deeply moved by your poem, and he will help you survive this life. Quickly leave this place, and do not hesitate regardless of what happens on your journey."

Feeling blessed, Ise immediately left Uzumasa, but soon she felt ill and was forced to rest in an old empty hall. Presently, a party of mounted travelers with a fine carriage passed in front. A man dressed like a monk, who appeared to be the master of the party, entered. Feeling embarrassed, Ise retired to the back of the hall, but the man followed her and said to her kindly, "I am very sorry to speak to you like this. I received a revelation from the Buddha, so I am asking you to come and see where I live." Remembering her dream and trying to comply with the Yakushi Buddha's wish, Ise decided to follow the monk. Pleased, he

took Ise to his home, and there she learned that he was the chief administrator[130] of Iwashimizu Hachiman Shrine[131] in Otokoyama. From that time forth, Ise was well treated and eventually blessed with many children. Since the man had lost his dear wife, he had been looking for someone with good looks and a good disposition to wed, so he was happy to have Ise [as his wife] and greatly appreciated her.

8-23 Mitsune and a Poem

Long ago there was a celebrated poet called Mitsune.[132] When the cherry blossoms were in full bloom in his garden, many courtiers and nobles visited his home to admire the splendid view and all lamented the coming of sunset. The blossoms usually lasted for seven days. Mitsune composed a poem when he thought he would have no more visitors after the flowers had scattered away:

Waga yado no
Hanami gatera ni
Kuru hito wa,
Chirinan atozo
Koishi karu beki

I will miss the people
Who visited my home
To admire the blossoms
After they leave me
The flowers scatter away.

 This poem deeply touches our hearts. Truly, blossoms are the hosts [at a flower-viewing party] in a mountain village, and these verses remind us of a similar poem.[133]

---

130. Unidentified. Chief administrators of major shrines are called *kengyō* 検校.

131. The Iwashimizu Hachimangū 岩清水八幡宮 is in Otokoyama, Yahata (Yawata) city, Kyoto.

132. Ōshikōchi Mitsune 凡河内身恒 (?–925), one of the Thirty-Six Renowned Poets, served as a judge for the imperial anthology *Kokin wakashū*; he was as celebrated as Ki no Tsurayuki (868–945). A similar story appears in the *Hayakuninshu hitoyogatari* (maki 3, Iwanami bunko, p. 242).

133. This refers to Kintō's poem; see note 9 of story 8-20.

8-24 Hanayamain and a Poem

When Emperor Hanayama[134] received the tonsure, Lord Midō's consort[135] sent him an especially fine plum branch with fragrant and red-colored blossoms. The retired emperor composed a poem in reply:

Iroka o ba[136]
Omoi mo irezu
Ume no hana
Tsune naranu yo ni
Yosoete zo miru[137]

I will not dwell
Either on the color
Or on the scent
Of the plum blossoms,
Received in this transient life.

His poem is very tasteful. In this transient life, he would think of neither the color nor the fragrance [of the blossoms]. But if the flowers and this life could last forever, he would no doubt pay attention to both the blossoms and their scent. It was most noble that the emperor truly understood the transience of life and showed this [in his poem]. Likewise, Lord Midō was said to have been deeply moved by the poem and wet his sleeves with tears.

---

134. Because of a political plot by Fujiwara Kaneie, Emperor Hanayama (968–1008) was forced to take the tonsure in 986 at the Gankyōji Temple (also called Hanayamadera). He was subsequently given the title *in* 院, the tonsured and retired emperor; thus he became known as Hanayamain 花山院. He enjoyed music and poetry and edited the *Shūi wakashū*.
135. Lord Midō 御堂 was Fujiwara Michinaga (966–1027), a son of Kaneie. He was also called Midō Kanpaku 御堂関白, or Regent Midō. He married Rinko, a daughter of Minamoto Masanobu, in 987 and then married Akiko, a daughter of Minamoto Takaaki, in 988. The term *okata* 御方 refers to a wife or consort. The lady in the text may be either Rinko or Akiko; see Imai Gen, *Hanayama-in no shōgai* (Tokyo: Ōfusha) 103.
136. *Iro* 色 (color) and *ka* 香 (scent or fragrance) also imply sexual desire.
137. The poem is included in *Wakan rōeishū* I, Kōbai, no. 101, and *Kokin wakashū* 16, no. 1445. A similar story is included in *Kokon chomonjū* 5.

8-25 A Breeze over an Ogi Plant[138]

Long ago people gathered at Regent Ichijō's[139] mansion to enjoy linked-verse parties. One of them composed these opening lines:

Aki wa nao
Yuu magure koso
Tada naranu

An autumn twilight
Most elegant
And unusual

The other guests tried in vain to add the last two lines to complete the poem. Yoshitaka,[140] the regent's thirteen-year-old son, succeeded, reciting:

Ogi no uwa kaze
Hagi no shita tsuyu

A breeze passing over the *ogi*,
The dew below the *hagi*.[141]

Greatly impressed by his son's verses, Regent Ichijō thought his talents would be wasted unless they were recognized by someone of higher status. So he went to Lord Midō[142] and said, "My young son composed such and such verses." The lord replied rather offhandedly, "Parents usually favor their children," and made no particular comments on the boy's verses except to say, "They sound fine."

---

138. *Ogi* plants like Japanese pampas grass grow as high as 1.5 meters in the summer and autumn. They appear in old poems as do *hagi*, which also grow in the fall as tall as 1.5 meters. *Hagi* have small reddish purple or white flowers and are one of the Seven Autumn Plants or Grasses, *aki no nanakusa*.
139. Fujiwara Koremasa, or Koretada (924–972), the eldest son of Morosuke (see *Senjūshō* 8-18) and the brother of Kaneie and Takamitsu (see *Senjūshō* 8-14). He became regent and one of five poets who edited the poetry anthology *Gosen wakashū*.
140. Yoshitaka Shōshō (954–974), a lieutenant general of the Imperial Guard of the Right, died of smallpox at a young age.
141. Yoshitaka's poem appears in the *Wakan rōeishū* 1, Autumn, 229.
142. Fujiwara Michinaga (966–1027); see note 2 of story 8-24.

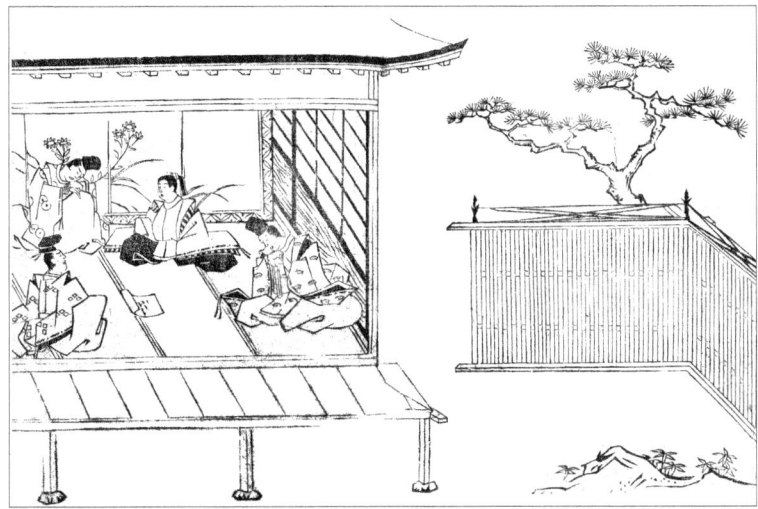

The regent had expected something more from Lord Midō, such as, "For his age, your son shows great skill, composing these last two lines to complete the poem." He later informed Lady Jōtōmon'in [Lord Midō's daughter][143] about his son. The famous poetess Nakatsukasa,[144] who was in her ladyship's service, relayed the regent's message to her mistress. Lady Jōtōmon'in sent him a detailed reply in writing: "Your son did very well with the last two lines; they left me feeling as if poets of the past such as Hitomaro and Akahito[145] had been reborn." Nakatsukasa also added a poem of her own to express her feelings:

Ogi no ha ni
Kaze otozururu
Yūbe niwa
Hagi no shita tsuyu
Okite zo mashi nuru

---

143. Jōtōmon'in 上東門院, or Fujiwara Akiko (988–1074), was a daughter of Michinaga, an imperial consort of Emperor Ichijō, and the mother of emperors Goichijō and Gosuzaku; see *Senjūshō* 8-26. She received the tonsure at the age of 39.

144. See *Senjūshō* 8-11, 8-18, and 8-26.

145. Both Kakinomoto no Hitomaro (d. 710) and Yamabe no Akahito (d. 736) were the most celebrated ancient poets included in the *Man'yōshū*, the oldest Japanese poetry anthology; see note 64 of story 8-11.

A breeze passing over
The *ogi* leaves,
And the dew below
The *hagi*,
Add more taste to the evening.

Her poem also is very fine, and people said the party was the most elegant event of its day.

8-26 Henjō

Long ago when Abbot Henjō[146] visited Lady Jōtōmon'in,[147] she invited him through Lady Uma[148] to spend the night at her palace. Henjō replied, "Your ladyship, since I have something else to do, I would prefer to leave." Lady Nakatsukasa[149] jokingly asked Henjō, "Are you leaving without seeing the *ominaeshi* flowers[150] in the field in front of our ladyship?" Henjō replied with his poem:

Ominaeshi
Ookaru nobe ni
Yadorise ba
Ayanaku adana no
Na o ya tatsubeki

Lingering among
So many *ominaeshi*
In the field,
I may falsely gain

---

146. Henjō 遍昭, or Yoshimine Munesada (816–890), was a grandson of Emperor Kanmu and received the tonsure in 850. He built the Gangyōji Temple at Hanayama in the capital and was promoted to *sōjō* (abbot or director) of the temple. He was also one of the Six Poet Saints, or Six Renowned Poets (*rokkasen* 六歌仙).

147. See note 6 of story 8-25.

148. *Naishi* 内侍 (court lady) Uma served Imperial Consort Sadako around 990, and her poems in the *Umano naishishū* are dated from 970 to 999.

149. See *Senjūshō* 8-11, 8-18, and 8-25.

150. The *ominaeshi* 女郎花, a one-meter-high bush with small yellow flowers, is one of the Seven Autumn Plants. Here the flowers are compared to the ladies-in-waiting at the palace.

An amorous name.

Immediately, Lady Nakatsukasa recited a poem in reply:

Hana yue mo
Adanaru na o ba
Nagasaji to
Kikeba tamoto o
Hikimo todomezu

I will not stop the man
By holding his sleeve,
As I hear he would not
Allow a false charge to be made
On account of the flowers.

Lady Jōtōmon'in heard this exchange from behind a screen and felt both poems were incomparably splendid.

8-27 Great Councilor Shijō

Great Councilor Kyoshin[151] lived near Hachijō.[152] While gazing at the bright moon around the ninth month, he heard the faint sound of someone pounding cloth with a *kinuta*.[153] He recited a poem by Great Councilor Shijō:[154]

---

151. Minamoto Kyōshin 源経信 (1016–1097) was a son of Michikata and the father of Minamoto Toshiyori. He held Second Rank and was appointed in 1040 to the post of *gonnosochi* 権師, or provisional director of police, in Kyushu in 1094 and died there. A scholar of Chinese and Japanese literature, he was called Great Councilor Katsura as he founded the Katsura style of *biwa* music while living in Katsura. He wrote a diary, the *Sochiki* 帥記. A story about him appears in *Jikkinshō* 10-4.
152. Many mansions of noblemen were located in the Hachijō area of Kyoto during the Heian period; see Tsunoda Bun'e, *Heiankyō teiyō* (Tokyo: Kadokawa shoten), 348.
153. *Kinuta* 砧: a wooden or stone stand used to pound fabric to soften it and increase its luster.
154. Fujiwara Kintō 藤原公任 (966–1041), a son of Yoritada, held Second Rank and was popularly called Great Councilor Shijō; he was very skilled in Chinese and Japanese poetry.

Karakoromo[155]
Utsu koe kikeba
Tsuki kiyomi
Mada nenu hito o
Sora ni shirukana[156]

By the sound of
Pounding robes,
I know someone
Is not yet sleeping
In the clear moonlit night.

Then he heard a voice by a bush in the front garden recite a Chinese-style poem: "A line of geese flying across the bright North Stars.[157] And the sound of pounding cold robes in the South Palace[158] under the moon."

The voice was very loud and awesome. The surprised councilor looked in the direction of the voice and saw a creature standing one *jō*[159] and several feet in height with [unkempt] hair that looked as if it were growing upside down. "What has happened? O Great Bodhisattva of Hachiman, please help me!" the councilor prayed. The creature said, "Why would I harm you?" and disappeared.

Later, the councilor said [to his attendants], "I am not exactly sure of its appearance." It might have been the demon living at Suzaku Gate.[160] Indeed, a creature with such good taste might have lived in those days.

....

155. *Karakoromo* 唐衣: a Chinese robe; the word is often used in poems to refer to robes in general.
156. The poem appears in *Wakan rōeishū* I, *Ei*, no. 352, and is attributed to Ki no Tsurayuki. The word *sora* 空, "sky," in *Sora ni shirukana* in the poem, has another meaning ("presumably" or "probably") and is an *engo* 縁語, or a poetic term related to *tsuki*, "moon."
157. Hokutosei 北斗星: the Plough.
158. Nanrō, South Palace (see *Senjūshō* 8-15), contrasts with the North Star and cold robes (winter clothes). This poem, with its mention of geese flying south across the North Star and the pounding of cold robes, suggests seasonal change, the coming of winter. It is included in *Wakan rōeishū* I, *Ei*, no. 346.
159. One *jō* equals ten *shaku*, or one foot.
160. Suzakumon 朱雀門, a large gate facing Suzaku Avenue to the south of the imperial palace. For the demon at the gate, see *Senjūshō* 8-3.

8-28 Gyōson

Sōjō Gyōson of Byōdōin[161] lived during the reign of Emperor Ichijōin.[162] In his long ascetic career, he visited many holy places related to the Law. When he practiced Zen meditation in the rock chamber at Shō,[163] incense was produced by his concentrated mind and [fragrant] smoke rose incessantly although there was no fire. Before spring arrived, flowers blossomed from his hands joined in prayer. Gyōson spent three years at Shō and three more years as an ascetic on Mount Kago in Ama.[164] His practice and virtue were so great that he received many revelations of incarnated buddhas of all directions in his hut, which was filled with incense smoke.

---

161. Abbot Gyōson 僧正行尊 (1055–1135) of Byōdōin was a son of Minamoto Motohira, received the tonsure in 1066 at Onjōji (Miidera) Temple, and studied the Tendai and Shingon teachings under Myōgyō of Byōdōin Temple. In 1125 he became a senior abbot (daisōjō) and served emperors Shirakawa, Toba, and Sutokuin.

162. The reign of Emperor Ichijōin (r. 986–1011) did not correspond with the life of Gyōson.

163. Many ascetics, including Gyōson and Gyōkei, confined themselves to Shō no Iwaya 笙の岩屋, one of the rock chambers on Mount Ōmine in Yoshino (Nara prefecture).

164. This refers to Ama no Kaguyama 天香具山, or Mount Kaguyama of Ama (in Nara prefecture), which has long been a poetic site (utamakura).

Gyōson wrote a poem on a *sotoba* stupa in the rock chamber at Shō:

Kusa no io
Nani tsuyukeshi[165] *to*
Omoiken
Moranu iwaya mo
Sode wa nure keri[166]

In a grass hut
I wondered
Why is there so much dew [on my sleeves]?
In a rock chamber where no dew leaks
My sleeves are still wet [with tears].

The *stupa* decayed as time passed and the ink faded. I am moved to tears when I think that the author of this poem may have been reborn somewhere in the Pure Land of the Buddha, while his poem remains in this world after so many years.

When Sōjō Gyōkei[167] of Sakurai, a disciple of Gyōson, confined himself to practice in the rock chamber at Shō, he saw his master's poem. Gyōkei missed him very much and added a verse: "Truly, the dew cannot leak in, yet my sleeves are wet." Later, when I [visited the rock chamber and] saw the lines written [by Gyōkei],[168] I was greatly moved at the thought of these verses being written by a man of such taste.

It may have been disrespectful for someone ignorant like me, whose poetic style and language are not yet sufficiently developed, to inscribe a poem after such accomplished verses. Moreover, I was afraid that my writing might be criticized, but I could not leave the place

---

165. *Tsuyu* 露, "dew," also means tears; thus *tsuyukeshi*, "much dew," means "many tears."
166. *Sode wa nure keri*: "sleeves wet (by tears)." The poem suggests that whether in a grass hut or a rock chamber, where no dew could form, his sleeves were wet with tears. This expresses the poet's lonesome and tearful feelings during his solitary ascetic practice. The poem is included in *Kin'yō wakashū* 9, no. 533. *Kokon chomonjū* 2-53 tells of Gyōson composing a poem in the rock chamber of Shō.
167. Sōjō Gyōkei 僧正行慶 (1101-1165), a son of Emperor Shirakawa, received the tonsure, lived in Onjōji Temple, and became Gyōson's disciple.
168. The *Saigyō monogatari* narrates how Saigyō visited the rock chamber of Shō and missed meeting Gyōson.

without expressing my feelings, and I wished to establish a Buddhist relationship with Gyōson. I composed this poem:

Tsuyu mora nu
Iwaya mo sode wa
Nure keri to
Kikazu wa ika ni
Ayashi kara mashi[169]

If I had not learned
About his wet sleeves
In the rock chamber
Where no dew leaked in,
I would have wondered [about my own wet sleeves].

After I finished my poem, I left the cave elated. It is my hope that the dew in my poem will become the dew in Gyōson's poem on a lotus leaf[170] and that I will not be ignored after my death.

8-29 [Untitled]

Someone who saw Abbot Byōdōin[171] and was much impressed by him told this story. Once when the abbot met Monk Kōya at court,[172] he noticed his crooked left hand and asked, "What happened to your hand?" Kōya replied, "I fell from a veranda when I was young and broke it." The abbot said, "If that is so, then I will pray for you. Would you like me to do that?" Kōya answered, "If you can do anything for my hand, that would be wonderful." The abbot began to recite the incantations

---

169. The poem is attributed to Saigyō in his poetic anthology the *Sankashū* (II, no. 917).
170. The expression reveals the protagonist's wish to be reborn in the Pure Land through Gyōson.
171. For Abbot Gyōson, see *Senjūshō* 8-28.
172. The term *nai*, or *dai* 内, refers to the imperial court. Kōya, or Kūya shōnin 空也上人, is Monk Kūya (903–972), who was popularly called Amida Hijiri, Holy Man of Amida. His lineage is not known. After traveling through many provinces he came to Kyoto and built Saikōji Temple (also called Rokuhara Mitsuji Temple); see *Senjūshō* 1-6.

of Fukūkensaku,[173] and before he finished the third recitation, Kōya's hand was healed. He felt most ennobled by the abbot and his marvelous revelation.

During the reign of Emperor Ichijōin,[174] many melons were delivered from Yamato province. Doctor Masatada,[175] who was at court at the time, announced, "One of these melons is very poisonous and anyone who eats it will soon die."

When this was reported to the emperor, he said, "This sounds strange. Seimei[176] may know something about it. Call him." As soon as Yin-Yang Master Seimei appeared before the emperor, he was told, "Something is wrong with these melons. Check them and tell us if there is anything strange." After a while, Seimei reported, "There is an evil spirit[177] [in these melons]." "In that case, call Gyōson[178] and have him pray," ordered the emperor.

As soon as Gyōson recited some incantations, the largest melon sprang up a few feet from the wooden floor several times. Then it split open and a snake, a foot long, crawled out and died on the spot. It was a most unusual occurrence. Something like this had not happened since ancient times and it is possible that it will never happen again. The event reflected great credit on Masatada, Seimei, and Gyōson. Much time has passed since then and such superior men are no longer among us. This is most regrettable, even to someone like me who has abandoned the secular world.

---

173. Fukūkensaku Kannon 不空羂策観音, who helps all sentient beings by the mercy of *kensaku* 羂策, the cords or ropes of the Kannon.
174. Refers to Emperor Ichijō, who reigned from 986 to 1011; his time did not coincide with that of Masatada and Gyōson; see *Senjūshō* 8-28.
175. Tanba Masatada 丹波雅忠 (1021–1088), a son of Tadaaki, was a director of medicine with Lower Junior Fourth Rank and a renowned doctor.
176. Abe Seimei 安部清明 (921–1005) was a Yin-Yang master and a doctor of astronomy.
177. Here, *ryōge* 霊気 (spirit) has a negative meaning like *mononoke* 物の怪, an evil spirit possessing someone or something. The story of the melon appears in other collections including the *Kokon chomonjū* (no. 295) and the *Genkō shakusho* (4, Kanshū).
178. See *Senjūshō* 8-28.

8-30 Narimichi and the Ball

Jijū Great Councilor Narimichi[179] had loved *kemari*[180] since his youth and enjoyed playing it everyday, either alone or with others.

Once when he was playing *kemari* at Saishōkōin Temple,[181] he noticed a small, odd, but noble-looking man crouching [near him]. Thinking this was odd, Narimichi asked him, "Who are you?" The man replied, "I am the spirit of the ball. Since you kick it so well, I am showing you my true nature." He then vanished. Afterward, the little man often appeared [when Narimichi was kicking a ball], watching it without blinking his eyes. This was truly mysterious.

At another time, Great Councilor Munemichi,[182] Narimichi's father, saw his son wearing a pair of special shoes and kicking a ball against a railing at Kiyomizu Temple. Munemichi was most upset and felt as if he were dreaming; he tried to call out to his son to stop him. But when he saw that his son was suspended five inches above the *tatami* floor as if floating, he thought Narimichi had become a *kenin*, or a possessed man, and so he left him, joining his hands in prayer. Narimichi was elated [after hearing about this from his father].

According to Narimichi, *kemari* was created during the reign of Emperor Yōmei.[183] The game was played by his courtiers,[184] who were trying to entertain Prince Shōtoku during his leisure time. The prince was very skilled in the game and spent two hours on his own every

---

179. Jijū Dainagon Narimichi 侍従大納言成通 (1092–1162), a son of Munemichi, held Second Rank and was talented in poetry, horsemanship, and *kemari* (see the following note).

180. *Kemari* 蹴鞠 was a game popular among courtiers and noblemen in the Heian period. A ball, made of deer skin, was hung from a tree branch and kicked as high as possible to keep it from touching the ground. Participants wore special leather shoes with the toes tapered upward. The play area (*maritsubo*, or *mariniwa*, "ball yard") was seven and a half *ken* square with a tree planted at each of the four corners: cherry in the northeast, willow in the southeast, maple in the southwest, and pine in the northwest. The tree chosen for play depended on the season.

181. Saishōkōin 最勝光院 was built in 1173 in keeping with a vow of Emperor Go-Shirakawa; it is located in present-day Imakumano, in Kyoto.

182. Fujiwara Munemichi 藤原宗通 (1071–1120) was the father of Narimichi. According to a *Kokon chomonjū* tale (11, Kemari 17), he scolded his son for kicking a ball in Kiyomizu Temple.

183. Emperor Yōmei (r. 585–587) was the father of Shotoku Taishi 聖徳太子, or Prince Shōtoku (574–622).

184. *Gekkeiunkaku* 月卿雲閣 refers to noblemen and courtiers.

morning kicking a ball wherever he was. People heard voices and believed that all the sages of the three generations of past, present, and future and the spirits of the *kemari* ball joined the prince whenever he was practicing. No one knew exactly who they were. The *Fusōki*[185] states that a pleasant fragrance always filled the air after Narimichi kicked a ball. The buddhas of the three generations must have joined him in his games. This was truly wonderful.

8-31 [Untitled]

Great Councilor Tsunenobu[186] and Middle Councilor Toshitada[187] excelled at poetry and *kemari*. According to them: "When you present the *kemari* ball to a lord, you draw it closely to the middle of the three divided branches of either the pine or willow tree.[188] You should walk under the branch to the third tree[189] and drop your right knee with your hands stretched out. In general, you should maintain proper form in *kemari* just as you would make an effort to keep the collar of your robes from becoming loose. With a shout, you should forcefully attack the ball as it comes toward you. Attempting to maintain your form is useless when you are trying to keep the ball from falling to the ground. Keeping the ball for a long time is permitted in China but not in our country. Kicking it three to five times is fine, but not more than that. Isn't it unsightly to receive the ball without maintaining good form? A ball coming from the pine usually falls onto a larger place after running on the upper branches. In this case, it is better to drop your left knee while stretching the right one. A ball coming through a supple willow branch falls quickly. In this case, you should keep your body flexible with your hips bending and try to embrace the ball."

---

185. Unidentified.
186. Tsunenobu Dainagon 経信大納言 (1016–1097) was a son of Minamoto Michikata and the father of Toshiyori. He was talented not only in poetry but in *biwa* music. Stories about him are included in *Senjūshō* 2-4, 7-2, 8-27, and 8-32.
187. Toshitada 俊忠 (1073–1123) was a son of Fujiwara Tadaie, the father of Shunzei, and the grandfather of Teika. He attained Junior Third Rank and was known as a poet. Stories about him appear in *Senjūshō* 2-8, 8-20, and 8-32.
188. For the four trees used in *kemari*, see note 2 of story 8-30.
189. That is, the tree from which the ball is hung.

How would these two gentlemen have felt if they had seen the spirit of the *kemari* ball? They were most unusual in this degenerate age. Narimichi, Great Councilor Jijū,[190] was said to have praised them as his equals.

8-32 [Untitled]

In the beginning of Emperor Toba's[191] reign, a *kemari* match was held at court. Great Councilor Narimichi's[192] role was to look after all the arrangements, including presenting the ball to the emperor. But on that day Narimichi was not present for some reason, even after the sun had risen high in the sky. The ball was about to be presented with a pine branch according to Lord Tsunenobu's[193] suggestion, but just then Narimichi appeared and declared, "This is not correct. The ball should be presented with a willow branch during the first spring of an emperor's reign." And so he changed the branch. Since pine is an evergreen, it is difficult to detect the color of spring in it. But the green of the willow is superior to all the others when representing spring.

Many years later, in the beginning of Emperor Nijō's[194] reign, when Lord Narimichi was sixty years of age, Middle Councilor Shunzei[195] presented the ball with a bamboo branch at a *kemari* game. When Narimichi heard this, he praised Shunzei, saying, "He is superior to his father, Middle Councilor Toshitada." How can we learn about such things unless we ask about them?

---

190. See *Senjūshō* 8-30.
191. Emperor Tobain (r. 1107-1123) was a son of Emperor Horikawa. The previous story took place while he was alive; the present tale tells of events after his demise, when he was called Tobain 鳥羽院 (ex-emperor Toba) after his retirement in 1123. He died at the age of fifty-four in 1156, but his dates do not correspond with those of Tsunenobu.
192. See *Senjūshō* 8-30.
193. Minamoto Tsunenobu 源経信 (1016-1097) was a son of Michikata and held Second Rank. He was the father of Toshiyori and called Sochi Great Councilor; see *Senjūshō* 8-27 and 8-31. Since he died the year Narimichi was born, it is impossible that the two could have met. Moreover, Emperor Toba reigned in 1107, after Tsunenobu's death.
194. Nijō 二条 (r. 1158-1165) was a son of Emperor Goshirakawa.
195. Fujiwara Shunzei 藤原俊成 (1141-1204), a renowned poet, was a son of Toshitada. He supposedly held Third Rank and was middle councilor but never reached this rank in fact.

8-33 Emperor Toba and the Biwa

When Emperor Toba[196] passed away, the imperial court became a sorrowful place. Some courtiers exchanged their colorful robes for dark mourning dress,[197] while others felt the cries of insects lamented the clear autumn moon. The mourners, including the lords Mitsuyori[198] and Nariyori,[199] gathered at court to observe the *chūin* mourning period.[200] Even when night deepened, the mourners could not sleep because of their sadness. Then they heard the noble sound of a *biwa* lute from the late emperor's quarters. Excitedly, they asked each other, "Who is playing so loudly at this time of mourning?" Playing a lute then seemed unfitting. But it was certainly the voice of the deceased emperor that was heard loudly chanting and thrice repeating Hakurakuten's poems.[201]

The first and the second strings of the [lute] sounded as bleak and lonely as the wind passing through the pine leaves.

The third and the fourth strings sounded as pure as a caged crane crying for her young one.

The fifth string sounded as subdued as a frozen waterfall, unable to flow.

The *biwa* played continuously until near dawn.

The mourners all wondered, "What has our late emperor become after death? Is he like the Chinese courtesan[202] who was so attached to *koto* music that she continued playing it night after night even after her bones were left in a field? Or has he fallen into the Demon's Way?"

---

196. See *Senjūshō* 8-32.
197. *Sumizome* 墨染: "a robe dyed in the soot," meaning a dark colored robe often used by priests. The dark robes are here contrasted with *hana no tamoto* 花の袂, the flowery sleeves of colorful robes.
198. Fujiwara Mitsuyori 藤原光頼 (1124–1173) was a son of Akiyori and the older brother of Nariyori. He held Second Rank and received the tonsure in 1164.
199. Fujiwara Nariyori 藤原成頼 (1136–1202) held Third Rank and received the tonsure in 1174. For another tale about him, see *Senjūshō* 7-9.
200. *Chūin* 中陰, or *chūu* 中有, is the period between a person's death and rebirth in a future existence; it generally lasts forty-nine days.
201. See *Senjūshō* 8-7
202. See *Senjūshō* 7-1.

Some said that Emperor Toba had become the deity of Kamo Shrine.[203] Just as Lady Nii of Hachijō[204] received the miraculous jewel ball,[205] they wondered if the emperor had been given the miraculous abilities to speak the Koma[206] language and play the *biwa* as well as an incarnation of a deity.[207]

8-34 [Untitled]

Sōzu Eshin[208] was so learned and talented that he could rid himself of worldly delusions in his mind by gazing at the clear moon.[209] However, owing to the fate of this life that all living beings must perish, he died at the age of seventy in Yokawa.[210] It was most noble and awesome to see three blue lotus flowers emerge[211] from his bosom after his death.

The emperor[212] asked to have the flowers, but the monks of Mount

---

203. Kamojinja 加茂神社, or Kamo Shrine, in Kyoto has two shrines: Kamikamo Jinja, the Upper Shrine; and Shimokamo Jinja, the Lower Shrine.
204. This is a reference to Taira Tokiko (1126–1185), the wife of Taira Kiyomori, who lived in Nishi-hachijō. Her last moments are related in *Heike monogatari* 11; see the following note.
205. The *tama* 玉, a jewel ball, was one of the three imperial regalia in the possession of the infant Emperor Antoku, who died during the defeat of the Taira clan in 1185. Lady Nii of Hachijō, the emperor's grandmother, held him in her arms with the jewel ball and threw herself into the sea; see *Heike monogatari* 11. The association of Lady Nijō with the jewel ball and the deceased Emperor Toba is not clear in the text, but it may suggest that both possessed some miraculous power: the former, the jewel ball; the latter, his unusual ability to speak a foreign language and to play the *biwa* so well as an incarnation of the Kamo Shrine deity.
206. The Korean language, meaning here a foreign language.
207. *Kenin* 化人 refers to an incarnation of a buddha or bodhisattva appearing in this life as a human being (like Emperor Toba) to benefit sentient beings.
208. Eshin 恵心, or Genshin 源信 (942–1017), founded the Pure Land Sect in Japan. Because he lived in the Eshin'in Hall of Yokawa on Mount Hiei, he was popularly called Sōzu Eshin or Yokawa. His writings include the *Ōjōyōshū*.
209. *Makoto no tsuki* 実の月, the true or clear moon, refers to a clear heart and an enlightened mind.
210. Yokawa 横川, one of the Three Pagodas, or Towers, along with the Saitō (Western Pagoda) and the Tōtō (Eastern Pagoda) on Mount Hiei.
211. *Shōrenge* 青蓮華; when born from the mouth or bosom of a deceased person, the flowers suggest enlightenment.
212. Emperor Go-Ichijō (1008–1036) was a son of Emperor Ichijō and Lady Akiko, a daughter of Fujiwara Michinaga, or Lord Midō.

Hiei[213] discussed the matter and firmly refused the imperial request. So the emperor asked for just one of the flowers and the monks agreed. They stored the remaining two flowers in Monju Hall[214] [in the mountains]. The lotus given to the emperor was soon transferred to the Fujiwara clan because Lord Midō[215] [of the Fujiwara] was the emperor's grandfather. It was taken to the treasure house of the Byōdōin[216] at the time of Lord Uji.[217]

When the lotus was enshrined in the treasure house, Lord Midō and many noblemen attended the ceremony, which included dancing and music. It was held in the middle of the second month, when the plum blossoms, looking like snowflakes, had fallen and were scattered on the stage. When the blossoms on the dancers' crowns dropped onto their sleeves, they looked like the falling snow. People found this most tasteful and very interesting.

8-35 [Untitled]

In the time of Lord Uji,[218] a peasant named Kinoshirō Tomonari[219] lived in Nukafuta in the Naga district of Ki province.[220] Commoners generally think only of their daily activities, such as obtaining food in the morning and evening, and they never consider their future lives. But probably thanks to a karmic relationship in his former life, Tomonari [realized his future life] and had deep faith in the Kannon of

---

213. *Shūto* 衆徒: the monks and the students of Enryakuji Temple on Mount Hiei. They decided matters by discussion in meetings.
214. Monjurō 文殊楼 in the Eastern Pagoda of Mount Hiei was built in 861 by Ennin (Master Jikaku), who introduced belief in Monju, or Mañjuśri, from China.
215. Lord Midō Kanpaku 御堂関白, or Fujiwara Michinaga (966–1027), was a son of Kaneie and grandfather of Emperor Goichijō; see *Senjūshō* 8-24.
216. Byōdōin 平等院 was built in 1052 by Fujiwara Yorimichi by converting his father's villa into a temple. In 1053 other halls were built, including Amida Hall (commonly called Hōōdō, Phoenix Hall), Hokkedō Hall, and Hōzō (Treasure House).
217. Lord Uji, or Fujiwara Yorimichi (992–1074), a son of Michinaga, served as regent to three emperors: Ichijō, Go-Suzaku, and Go-Reizei.
218. Fujiwara Yorimichi; see note 10 of story 8-34.
219. Unidentified.
220. Present-day Naga district in Wakayama prefecture.

Kokawa.²²¹ Whenever he cultivated the fields in the mountains and gathered leaves in the mulberry groves, he thought of the Kannon and recited the Kannon's name.

Unable to escape sickness, Tomonari fell ill toward the end of the spring when he was fifty years of age. He remained ill in bed throughout the summer until the beginning of the ninth month. Meanwhile, his stomach became swollen and gave him terrible pain. He now thought, "I have believed in the Kannon since the time I heard a preacher in the capital say, 'The Kannon will discard his vows to save all sentient beings if he has spoken falsely and cannot save even one devotee in the two generations of the present and future. His devotees shall be saved from the sufferings of birth, illness, aging, and death.'²²² Since I took a vow to depend on the Kannon forever, I have recited his name five hundred times every day during the thirty years of my devotion. Among the Kannon of various places, I have especially believed in the one of Kokawa and have never neglected my monthly visits to the temple. But now I am suffering from this illness on account of a former karmic existence.²²³ O Kannon, if your vows to save your devotees are true, how can you fail to help me? Even though I am to die and succumb to the limits of human life, you can mercifully take this pain away from me.²²⁴ Why am I suffering so much? Please quickly help me and make me feel well again."²²⁵ Thus he prayed devotedly to the Kannon.

A noble monk appeared to him in a dream that night and said to him, "What you have said is quite correct. I have brought you some medicine. Take it without delay." The monk handed him three small, round pills. Tomonari took them and swallowed two of them but dropped the third on the floor. When he tried to pick it up, he awoke

---

221. Kokawa Kannon 粉川観音 is a one-thousand-arm Kannon enshrined in Kokawa Temple in present-day Wakayama prefecture. A similar story appears in *Kokawadera engi* 粉河寺縁起, no. 22.

222. This sentence appears in the eighth chapter of the Lotus Sutra.

223. *Jōgō* 定業: negative karma from a person's previous existence, such as illness and other suffering.

224. *Daijuku* 代受苦: receiving or accepting pain on behalf of sufferers, thus showing the great mercy of bodhisattvas.

225. *Shōnen* 正念: correct feelings, that is, usual and normal feelings as opposed to suffering and torment.

from his dream. He now felt refreshed and light as his belly was no longer swollen and the pain had subsided. He awoke his wife and child sleeping beside him and told them everything. They were most pleased and looked for the third pill and found it. It was a small, hard lotus seed and gave off a fragrance more pleasant than daphne and musk.[226] They sewed it into a brocade bag and kept it as an amulet.

Seven days later, they opened the bag and found a small blue lotus flower[227] blooming from the seed, which had split in two. Believing this was strange, they mentioned it to other people, and soon Lord Uji heard about it. He immediately summoned Tomonari. After listening to his detailed explanation about the lotus flower, the lord was overwhelmed by so many tears that he could not wipe them all away. He wanted to worship the flower to establish a Buddhist relationship, so he asked Tomonari to bring the lotus to him behind the screen. As soon he saw the flower, Lord Uji told Tomonari to give it to him in exchange for some rice paddies, saying, "You and your descendants can

---

226. *Jinja* 沈麝.

227. *Shōrenge* 青蓮華: a blue lotus flower; also refers to the bud of the lotus. Stories about a lotus flower blooming from the mouth of a devotee after his death as a sign of enlightenment are found in *Hosshinshū* 3-4; *Konjaku monogatarishū* 19-14; and *Shishū hyaku innenshū* 9-20.

spend the rest of your lives there." The lord had the flower stored in the treasure house of Byōdōin Temple.

So Tomonari not only was cured of his illness, but also obtained land. Thereafter, he spent his life in comfort and continued to worship the Kannon with even greater faith.

This was a most wondrous event. If the Kannon's benefits in this life are so efficacious, how can we doubt them in our future life? There was nothing strange about Eshin's obtaining a blue lotus flower.[228] Does anyone wonder if this is just a parable? Tomonari swallowed the two pills to cure his illness and used the third to make the Kannon's benefits more widely known, and this was most remarkable. He also encouraged people to believe in the Kannon to establish a relationship with the deity. This was most extraordinary.

We are very much interested in Tomonari. He may have been reborn somewhere and received the Kannon's deep mercy.

---

228. See *Senjūshō* 8-34.

9-1 The Naishi Office and Kashima

Our country is the country of the gods. Divine power has protected the Way of the Buddha and the Way of the Ruler.[1] Our emperors, venerated as Masters of Heaven with the Jeweled Ranks and Ten Thousand Vehicles,[2] are graciously related to the Great Deity of Ise.[3] The lords of the Fujiwara clan, revered as regents, were also the descendants of the Kasuga Deity.[4] Who among the hundreds of court officials is not related to a deity?

In ancient times when the Great Deity Tenshō[5] hid herself in a rock chamber, everything became dark and eight million deities grieved. They made a bonfire in front of the chamber and played *kagura* music.[6] The great deity was drawn to the music and dance, and as soon as she opened the door of the chamber, the whole country was illuminated again and has remained so ever since. The great deity made a vow, declaring, "My descendants will be the emperors under heaven and will rule this county." To Prince Amenokoyane, she said, "Your descendants will control political affairs." The prince readily accepted this order, and her vow has been faithfully obeyed to this day.

The great deity announced, "I will protect future generations of emperors. What do you say to that?" All the deities present, including Prince Amenokoyane, prostrated themselves, their crowns touching the earth, and offered no objection. She continued, "Make a mirror to reflect my likeness and place it in the keeping of the ruler of this country." So the deities made a mirror but failed to produce a perfect one on their first attempt. They succeeded on their second attempt and

---

1. *Buppō* 仏法, *ōhō* 王法.
2. Manjō no hōi 万乗の宝位: a bejeweled rank of Ten Thousand Vehicles. A jeweled rank refers to the position of the emperor and the Ten Thousand Vehicles; the ancient Chinese emperors sent many military vehicles into battle.
3. Great Deity Tenshō 天照大神 enshrined in Ise Shrine 伊勢神宮 is the ancestor of the emperors.
4. The third deity, Prince Amenokoyane 天小屋根, is the ancestor of the Fujiwara clan; see *Senjūshō* 6-3.
5. This account is based on the legend recorded in the *Nihon shoki*. The conversation between the great deity and Prince Amenokoyane also appears in *Sangoku denki* 三国伝記 2-15.
6. *Kagura* 神楽: the music and dance annually offered to the divine mirror since the time of Emperor Go-Shirakawa (r. 1074–1077) in the garden in front of Naishidokoro Palace.

this perfect mirror was called Naishidokoro.[7] The first imperfect mirror was called Hinokumano-miya and is now enshrined in Hinokuma Shrine in Kii province.[8] The perfect mirror was kept in the emperor's residence hall in accordance with the great deity's vow. But Emperor Sujin[9] felt it too unseemly to enshrine it there and later transferred it to another hall. It has been enshrined in Unmei Hall since the time of Emperor Uda.[10]

At the end of the ninth month of Tentoku 4,[11] in the time of Tenreki,[12] a fire broke out in the quarters of the Imperial Guards of the Left and destroyed the entire main palace. Because this happened at

---

7. Naishidokoro 内侍所 here means "divine mirror," but later the term refers to the place or office where the mirror was kept; the women who served in the office were called *naishi nyokan* 内侍女官.
8. Hinokumanomiya 日前宮 is in present-day Akitsuki in Wakayama city.
9. Emperor Sujin 崇神 (r. 97–30 B.C.). *Gokeshidai* 11 and *Jingū zōreishū* 神宮雑例集 2 state that the mirror was moved to Unmei Hall 温明殿 during the time of Emperor Suinin 垂仁 (r. 29 B.C.–A.D. 70).
10. Emperor Uda reigned from 887 to 897.
11. The date corresponds to 960. The incident is mentioned in *Fusō ryakki* 26.
12. Tenreki was the reign of Emperor Murakami (r. 946–967). Both Tenreki and Tenroku refer to the reign of Emperor Murakami.

midnight, the Naishi ladies did remove the mirror from Unmei Hall, which was located near the main palace. As he hurried there, Lord Seishin[13] tearfully cried, "The hall must have burnt down and this is the end of the world!" But he then saw the mirror hanging from the top branch of the cherry tree in the South Palace. It shone brighter than the sun rising from the mountainside. The lord worshipped it and could not stop his joyful tears. Quickly kneeling on his right knee and spreading out his left sleeve, he said to the mirror, "Long ago, Deity Tenshō vowed to protect our emperors. If this vow remains unchanged, please come into my sleeve!" Immediately, the mirror flew into his sleeve. The lord himself carried it to the Kashikodokoro.[14]

In our degenerate times, no one would think of receiving a mirror into his sleeve and no mirror would ever fly there. The gods are the same and remain unchanged since ancient times, but men's hearts have become darkened [with delusions] and can never become as clear as the moon.

Some time later, Lord Kujō[15] fell ill and no one, even those with superior knowledge and virtues, could cure him. Feeling sorry for him, Lord Seishin gave him the sleeve that had received the imperial mirror and said to him, "Please use this sleeve to cure your sickness." As soon as Lord Kujō placed the sleeve by his pillow, he was cured. Were evil spirits overcome by the power of the mirror? This was truly amazing.

Later, the robe [with the sleeve] was given to Great Councilor Kintō,[16] then to Lord Dainijō.[17] When Lord Kyōgoku[18] inherited it, he

---

13. Seishinkō 清慎公 was Fujiwara Saneyori 藤原実頼, also referred to as Lord Ononomiya (900–970), a regent and the founder of the Ononomiya style of imperial ceremonies. His writings include his diary, the *Seishin kōki* 清慎公記. His acquiring of the mirror appears in *Gōkeshidai* 11 and *Kokon chomonjū* 1-2.
14. Kashikodokoro 賢所 of Dajōkan 太政官, the great political office where the divine mirror was stored.
15. Fujiwara Morosuke (908–960) was a younger brother of Lord Seishin. Since he died before the fire occurred in the imperial palace, his recovery from sickness after the fire is historically incorrect.
16. Fujiwara Kintō (966–1041) was a grandson of Lord Seishin; see *Senjūshō* 5-15, 8-10, 8-11, 8-15, and 8-27.
17. Fujiwara Norimichi (996–1075) was a great grandson of Lord Kujō; see *Senjūshō* 6-2.
18. Fujiwara Morozane (1042–1101), a nephew of Lord Dainijō, was a regent and a prime minister; see *Senjūshō* 3-7 and 6-6.

had a history compiled about the robe, and his descendants kept this for a while. The robe is presently with Lord Konoe.[19]

The Great Bright Deity of Kasuga is the ancestor of the Fujiwara clan and protects the Hossō School. During the reign of Empress Shōtoku,[20] the image was transferred from Kashima of Hitachi province and Hiraoka of Kawachi province to the foot of Mount Miwa in Yamato.[21] In the following year, it was transferred to Mount Mikasa.

9-2 Sadamoto

Long ago Doctor Ōe Sadamoto,[22] while serving at court, began to feel the futility of the secular world's glory. He had always longed for the serene and pure life in a forest. However, because he was presented with no other opportunities, he remained as he was. Later, the woman[23] whom he could not leave for years died, and he finally decided to renounce secular life. Sadamoto went to Jōkō[24] of Kiyomizu Temple and received the tonsure.

At some point Sadamoto visited Naiki Yasutane[25] and said to him, "I have finally left the secular world, where I was held back by someone and suffered shame and slanderous remarks." Yasutane envied him because he also wished to receive the tonsure and wet his colorful sleeves with tears. After that, Yasutane sequestered himself in a quiet place on Mount Hiei, studied the *shikan* teaching with Monk Zōga,[26] and finally became a man of much virtue.

Sadamoto met more wise men, deepened his faith in the Way, and

---

19. Fujiwara Motozane (1143–1166), a son of Tadamichi, became Minister of the Left in 1160 and was an ancestor of the Konoe family.
20. Empress Shōtoku (r. 764–770) is also known as Empress Kōken.
21. Mount Miwa is in present-day Sakurai city.
22. Ōe Sadamoto 大江定基 (962–1034), a grandson of Koretoki, was a scholar and a director of the imperial library with Lower Junior Fifth Rank. He received the tonsure in 988 and in 1003 went to China, where he died. He was called Great Master Entsū 円通大師.
23. This woman was not Sadamoto's formal wife and came from the capital; see *Konjaku monogatarishū* 19-2; *Hosshinshū* 2-4; and *Ujishūi monogatari* 4-7.
24. Kiyonori 清範 (962–999) was a high administrator (*jōkō*) of Kiyomizu Temple; see *Kojidan* 3-34 and *Konjaku monogatarishū* 17-38.
25. Naiki Yasutane 内記保胤 was Yoshishige Yasutane 慶滋保胤 (931–1002); see *Senjūshō* 5-3.
26. For Monk Zōga, see *Senjūshō* 1-1.

came to dislike secular affairs even more. He wanted to go to China and asked a few men who had the same desire [if they would accompany him]. But there was one person he was much concerned about and that was his old mother, who, if she had learned her son was leaving for China, would have grieved so much that she would have fallen ill and died.

Distressed by this anxiety, Sadamoto visited his mother to bid her farewell. She said to him, "The sadness of separation between a parent and child is unbearably painful and cannot be compared to anything else. Indeed, even the Buddha compares the grief in this life to a sad mother who is separated from her child. How can I say that I won't grieve? But shouldn't I be pleased by your wish to pursue the Way?[27] It is truly worthy of a disciple of the Buddha."

Hearing this, Sadamoto was greatly pleased and made a vow to practice virtue for the sake of his mother. He declared, "She is not an ordinary mother in this life, but thanks to the good karma from a previous life, she is my mother. If people had gently warned me against going to China, I would not necessarily have listened to them. But [though she did not do so,] if my mother were to express her opposition in words and appearance, how could I ignore her? Going to China is to pursue the Way. Isn't she a most wonderful mother to encourage me to do this?" None of the people who read his written vow failed to shed tears.

However, Sadamoto was still concerned about his mother, so he invited Monk Jōgen[28] to deliver the Eight Lectures on the Lotus Sutra [for her] at Takaradera Temple.[29] This was most touching. The mother's wish for her son was likewise very commendable. Generally, a mother would find it unbearable to be separated from her child even for a little while, but Sadamoto's mother endured the separation [from her son] across hundreds and thousands of waves to China. Perhaps she would not see her son again, but she encouraged him to pursue the Way. She surely possessed a remarkable heart. We no longer see such examples as this. All the buddhas must have been impressed by Sadamoto's pure heart and softened [consoled] his mother's sad feelings.

---

27. *Guhōdenju* 求法伝授: seeking the Law and transmitting it.
28. Unidentified.
29. Hōshakuji Temple is in present-day Ochikun in Kyoto.

Sadamoto finally went to China and showed so many remarkable revelations of the Law that he impressed the emperor. He received a title and was called Great Master Entsū.[30]

When I read these records, I shed many tears. Since I could not ignore them, I wrote them down, hoping that anyone who read my humble writings would join the wise men of the past on the same lotus seat.[31] I feel most embarrassed that the superior words of men of olden days have been replaced by my humble writings. But after my death, I hope the people of later generations will understand my sincere intention and not blame me for my sinful deeds.

9-3 Nun An'yō

Long ago Sōzu Eshin[32] had a young sister, Nun An'yō.[33] After her beloved husband died, Nun An'yō immediately cut her hair, sequestered herself in a mountain village in Ono,[34] and spent day and night worshipping Bodhisattva Jizō.[35]

One night she was single-mindedly reciting a sutra, praying, "Please deliver me in my future life." When she fell asleep, her principal image, Bodhisattva Jizō, appeared to her in a dream and said, "I will certainly help you. Meanwhile, do not neglect your practice." As soon as he finished speaking, the nun awoke. From then on she practiced the Way even more fervently. Thanks to her efforts, she passed away one evening with the heavenly flowers falling and the purple clouds appearing in the sky as symbols of her deliverance. This was most noble.

Prior to her death, the nun had urged her brother, Eshin, "When I

---

30. For Sadamoto's attainments in China, see *Hosshinshū* 2-4.
31. *Ichiren no tane* 一蓮のたね, a lotus seat, means rebirth in Amida's paradise to sit on the same lotus seat with other enlightened ones.
32. Genshin 源信 (942–1017) studied with Master Jikei on Mount Hiei and was popularly called Sōzu Eshin because he retired to Eshin Hall of Yokawa on Mount Hiei. He is the author of the *Ōjōyōshū* 往生要集.
33. An'yōni 安養尼, Nun An'yō (953–1034), a younger sister of Monk Genshin, suffered from illness for seven days before her death; see the *Kōfukujiryaku nendaiki*, in *Zokugunshoruijū*, 29, II, p. 137. For a story about her belief in Jizō, see *Kojidan* 3-28.
34. The site is near present-day Ichijōji Temple and the Yase-Ōhara area in Kyoto.
35. Jizō Bosatsu 地蔵菩薩 helps sinners in the Land after Death before Bodhisattva Miroku, Buddha's successor, appears; see Yoshiko Dykstra, "Jizō, the Most Merciful: Tales from *Jizō Bosatsu Reigenki*."

fall sick, be sure to come to me in my last moments and help to deliver me to the next world." Eshin promised to do so. When she suddenly fell ill, Eshin had retreated to Mount Hiei, but he remembered his promise. He sent someone to her with a message: "Since I am in the midst of confinement, I cannot leave the mountain. Ask someone to help you to get a carriage and come to West Sakamoto.[36] I will pray for your future life." Exhausted, the nun barely managed to secure a ride to Sakamoto, and she died on the way. Eshin hurried to Sakamoto only to see her perish. His grief was indescribable. He carried her into the room of Abbot Shōzan[37] of Shūgakuin,[38] saying, "Please, pray for her recovery." This was very difficult, but the abbot immediately chanted the incantation of Fudō[39] while Eshin prayed to Jizō. After they repeated their recitations several times, the nun was revived and told them, "Both Fudō and Jizō took my hands and helped me out of the Land after Death." Six years later, just as she had wished, the nun was delivered thanks to the help of Eshin.

Wasn't it an extraordinary revelation that the nun returned to this world from Enma's[40] office in the Land after Death? No one knew whether it was due to karma in her previous life or to some coincidence unrelated to her past karma. Because she had a close relationship with a superior person [Eshin], she could not fail to be delivered to a better place. It would be of no use [to us] to wish for something like that to happen without cultivating a superior relationship. Wishing to have a wise and virtuous monk [like Eshin] as an older or younger brother would be as futile as shooting at an imaginary flower with a bow made from a rabbit's horn[41] and an arrow made from hair grown on a turtle's shell. Ignorant and untalented people should at least concentrate on the Way by reciting the Buddha's name, but instead they spend their time in futility until they are old. It is most sad and regrettable. I feel

---

36. Nishi Sakamoto is in the area of present-day Ichijōji Temple in Sakyō-ku, Kyoto.
37. Shōzan Sōjō 勝算僧正 (939–1011) was an eminent monk and popularly called Abbot Shūgakuin; see *Senjūshō* 5-8.
38. Shūgakuin in Sakyō-ku, Kyoto, was one of the three thousand Buddhist temple quarters on Mount Hiei. Presently, Shūgakuin Detached Palace is on the site.
39. Fudō Myōō 不動明王.
40. Enma 閻魔, ruler of the Land after Death who judges sinners.
41. The expression emphasizes something impossible.

very envious when I hear the story of Nun An'yō and think of her pure heart.

The Shikan teaching of the Tendai Sect says: "They should live by the sea and purify their hearts with the sound of the waves or live in a deep valley and calm their minds with the sound of the wind passing over the pines on the summit." Hardly anyone could have visited the nun, tramping up the snow-covered path [to her dwelling]. Dressed in a shabby hemp robe, she sometimes heard the voice of a guest in a rain shower passing by her window. At other times she considered the strong winds blowing over the summit as her friends arriving for a visit. All the while she quietly recited the name of the Buddha because she realized the futility of life. It was most noble of her to practice virtue to become a buddha[42] while she was still in this life.

As Master Shōan[43] said, "A quiet place is a great teacher of the Way."[44] Our minds are just like water. Doesn't water become pure or

....

42. *Hotoke no tane* 仏の種, the seeds of the Buddha, means practicing virtue, which will result in becoming a buddha.
43. Great Master Shōan 章安大師, a disciple of Master Chi-i.
44. *Dainaru chishiki* 大なる知識, a great master who leads others to the Way. The term *chishiki*, "wisdom," refers to a teacher or someone who leads others to the Way.

muddy depending on its container?[45] Even lowly people like us can purify our minds by living deep in the mountains, where we can be changed from what we were in the secular world. We should know that [living in a quiet place] is our true teacher. It is indeed fitting that the wind from a summit wakes us from our [illusory] dreams and the sound of a waterfall overwhelms us with tears.

9-4 Great Virtuous Master Kanri

Long ago a man and a woman lived in the capital of Heian.[46] They did not seem to be of lowly status. [The husband] associated with courtiers because he served at court,[47] handling documents and letters. But owing to his poverty, he was often absent from his job and stayed at home.

His wife gave birth to a baby boy whose features and appearance were most attractive. The couple had the child late in their lives and loved him so much that they constantly kept him by their side. Their love for the baby consoled them during their sad days of poverty.

One day, the husband suddenly fell ill[48] and died. It was only natural that his wife grieved so much that she wanted to die with him. As time passed, her grief subsided. When her life became more difficult, however, she wept day and night and felt barely alive.

When the child reached the age of eleven, he tearfully said to his mother, "I have been feeling very sad because you have to raise me under such difficult conditions. Since we have no future here, if you allow me to leave, I will throw myself into the water or go far away where I will survive by begging." At this his mother became even sadder and replied, "When your father passed away, I felt like dying, but I have endured because you have consoled my sad heart. Poverty makes life very difficult, but you should not throw away your life." She and her son both shed many tears.

With his pure heart the child always prayed to the Buddha, "Please

---

45. *Utsuwa:* "container," "capacity," "ability." The text here means just as water changes its shape depending on its container, so do our minds depending on our capacities.
46. Another expression for Kyoto.
47. The terms *shizan* 芝山, *hōko* 蓬壺, and *chikuen* 竹園 in the text all refer to courtiers and the imperial palace. It must have been difficult for the protagonist, who was not rich, to keep up with the expensive tastes of the courtiers with whom he had to associate.
48. *Yogokochi* 世心地, refers to an epidemic.

let me have some reward so I can be a good son to my mother." Perhaps the buddhas in this life pitied him: Lord Sadanobu[49] summoned the boy and favored him greatly; he even visited his poor mother [whose life became easier].

After the boy learned that he might be affected by the curse of the Bright Deity of Kasuga, he immediately went to Yamashina Temple,[50] received the tonsure, and called himself Kanri.[51] He excelled in learning and had many talents, and he eventually became the lecturer of the Three Meetings.[52] In time he was promoted to the position of *sōzu* administrator. Among many past superiors, he was known as Great Virtuous Kanri. His knowledge and faith in the Way were truly profound.

Kanri's deep filial feeling truly touches our foolish hearts. If we have any feelings at all, who in this life does not have filial feelings? But only a few people retain a sense of obligation and are motivated by it. Weren't Kanri's dutiful feelings toward his mother most noble?

Conceived in her body, he burdened her for ten [nine] months, tortured her body by turning and kicking thirty-eight times, and drank 188 *koku*[53] of her milk [while sitting] on her lap. How many times did he cause his mother pain from the day of his birth? How often was she concerned about her child in good times and bad? Even the Buddha would be unable to count the times she felt anxious about her child. She would offer to die in his place and lament not being buried with him. Those are a mother's true feelings. That is why the *Shinji kangyō*[54] says, "A mother's affection [for her child] is so profound that I [the Buddha] cannot explain it even though I have lived in this life for one *kalpa*."[55]

It is said: "A peacock becomes pregnant[56] when it hears the rolling

---

49. Sadanobu 貞信, or Fujiwara Tadahira (880–949), a son of Mototsune, was a regent and a prime minister.
50. Kōfukuji Temple in Nara.
51. Kanri 観理 (894–973) was a monk of the Shingon Sect who became *betto* (director) of Tōdaiji Temple. He served Tadahira and later received the tonsure at Kōfukuji Temple.
52. The Three Meetings include the Yuimae Meeting at Kōfukuji Temple, the Saishōe Meeting at Yakushiji Temple, and the Gosaie Meeting at the imperial palace.
53. One *koku* 石 equals 180 liters.
54. *Shinji kangyō* 心地観経 (*Daizōkyō*, 3, p. 301).
55. A reference to a long period of time in Buddhist cosmology.
56. See *Ōjōyōshū* 2 (*Shisō taikei*, p. 290).

thunder, a *kuramushi* insect[57] when it is blown by the wind, and a rabbit when it watches the moonlight." Although some people are not blessed with fatherly love, everyone receives motherly love. When we quietly reflect on this matter, we want to reward our parents, but it is quite rare to sustain such filial feelings for long. I wish the Buddha would help me to preserve filial feelings just as Kanri did and to think solely of rewarding my parents.

9-5 Umanokami Akinaga's Tonsure

The second son of Great Lord Midō[58] was Umanokami Akinaga of Takamatsubara.[59] He excelled not only in knowledge of Buddhist and non-Buddhist writings, but also in talents and personality. As a son of Lord Midō, he was undoubtedly treated well by others.

Lord Midō was so impressed by Tajimanokami Takamasa,[60] who had been diligently serving him from morning to night, that he urged his son Akinaga to marry Takamasa's daughter. But Akinaga hesitated, saying, "Although I am not yet so superior, I was born the son of my lord and some day I wish to be head of the clan. So I wonder if I should depend on a local governor[61] as my father-in-law." Thus he repeatedly declined his father's recommendation, but Lord Midō would not listen to him, and so Akinaga spent many days and months feeling helpless.

One day he quietly pondered, "If I obey my father, I will waste my life. If I pursue my wish, I will not be filial. So I should cut off my hair and singularly devote myself to attain the Way for my future life." Akinaga went to Mount Hiei and visited Monk Zōga,[62] who happened to be on the mountain. Monk Zōga at first hesitated to grant him his

---

57. *Kuramushi* 求羅虫 is a small imaginary insect that becomes enlarged when blown by the wind; see *Daichi doron* 大知度論 7 (*Daizōkyō*, 25, p. 13).
58. Fujiwara Michinaga 藤原道長 (966–1027), the most powerful member of the Fujiwara clan, a son of Kaneie, was also called Midō Kanpaku. After taking the posts of Minister of the Left and the Right, he became regent, then prime minister with Junior First Rank. He received the tonsure in 1019. His daughter, Akiko, was the mother of emperors Go-Ichijō and Go-Suzaku.
59. Unidentified. Michinaga did not have a son named Akinaga.
60. Unidentified.
61. *Zuryō* 受領, a local governor, referring here to Takamasa.
62. See *Senjūshō* 1-1.

wish, but when it became clear that Akinaga's decision was firm, he shaved his head and granted him the tonsure.

When Lord Midō heard about this, he was so surprised that he immediately went to Mount Hiei to ascertain the situation. He saw Akinaga becoming a fine monk, so he said nothing and instead shed many tears. It was only natural that some of the lord's close attendants stood up and lamented loudly, while some turned their faces to the wall and others hid their tearful faces in their sleeves. The lord tearfully said to Akinaga, "I never thought that your decision was so firm. Nothing is so regrettable as being ignorant. If I had known your determination, I would not have insisted on having my way. Is this a dream?" Seeing his father grieving so, the new monk was overwhelmed by tears and remained silent. "It's no use saying anything. By what name do you call yourself now?" "I call myself Gyōshin," replied Akinaga. "I never expected to hear such a name,"[63] the lord said, lowering his head as he shed more bitter tears. The people around him could not suppress their tearful voices. After a while, Lord Midō realized there was nothing further he could do, so he promised to visit his son again and left.

The way Akinaga received the tonsure truly touches our hearts. Wasn't it wise that he refused to accept a lower status,[64] even for a short while? He was a descendant[65] of a family as celebrated as the Fujiwara of Mikasayama,[66] which had closely served the imperial court. Moreover, he was only sixteen years old at the time. I am tearfully overwhelmed when I imagine the bright future he could have had in his later years. Because he eventually accumulated many merits in his practice, he showed marvelous revelations of the Law.

Following Monk Zōga, Akinaga went to Tamunomine[67] and also climbed Mount Hiei to propagate the Law. He gathered around him

---

63. Michinaga did not expect to hear his son's Buddhist name.
64. *Iyashiki kusa no shitaba niha tsuyu ha okaji*: literally, "I will not place my dew under the lower leaves of the lowly grass."
65. *Fuji no uraba no sue* 藤のうらばの末: *Fuji* (wisteria) alludes to the Fujiwara clan; *uraba* (the back of a leaf); *sue* (the tip of a leaf); thus a distant descendant of the Fujiwara.
66. Mikasayama, or Mount Mikasa, in Nara also implies an imperial hat or umbrella, referring to the fact that Fujiwara men closely served many emperors. Kumoi 雲居: the place of clouds, meaning a place as high as clouds, i.e., the imperial palace.
67. Tamunomine is in present-day Sakurai city. Monk Zōga in Tamunomine is mentioned in various writings, such as *Honchō hokke genki* 3-82 and *Konjaku monogatarishū* 12-33.

people both related and unrelated to the Law, including the high and low who wished to seek the Way; he taught the noble doctrines, such as the *shikan* concept.[68] This was most extraordinary.

Many ascetics avoid others, confining themselves to quiet mountains and valleys. This is because they cannot empty their minds when they are among people. But an accomplished person such as Monk Kūya[69] deliberately chose to live in towns, declaring that he could remain calm even in the midst of others. Once his mind was completely clear, how could he be distracted even in the presence of ignorant folk? His mind was still and clear when he preached and explained the profound Law among the masses. This was truly noble.

9-6 Monk Dōki

Some time ago, I read in the *Kōsōden* how Monk Dōki[70] of China went to India to transmit the Buddhist Law. He met Master Kabenron,[71] from whom he learned profound teachings. He confined himself alone to Baradai Temple[72] and translated various sutras into Chinese. He then passed away as is our fate in this futile life.

Six years later Monk Tō,[73] a disciple of Dōki, went [to India] to translate [Buddhist texts into Chinese]. He was not sure of his master's route but finally arrived at the Baradai Temple, which by then had become a ruin. He saw no monks residing there, only some standing Buddhist images. Tall autumn weeds hid the doors, and insects made a forlorn sound. The wind blew through the top branches of the pines and quails cried all day long. On seeing the temple in such wretched condition, Tō wet his sleeves with his tears. Finally, he managed to enter the temple; Dōki was not there, but Tō discovered sutras transcribed in Chinese. He tearfully examined them and took them back to China.

---

68. See *Senjūshō* 1-1.
69. See *Senjūshō* 1-6, 5-13, 7-4, and 8-29.
70. Dōkihōshi 道希法師 in the *Kōsōden* 高僧伝 *(Biographies of Eminent Monks)* also appears in the *Daitōseiiki guhō kōsōden* 大唐西域求法高僧伝, *Daizōkyō*, 51, pp. 2, 4.
71. Kabenronshi 火弁論師, or Seshin 世親, refers to Vasubandhu, a monk of northern India. He was one of the ten masters who commented on the *Yuishiki sanjūshō* 唯識三十頌.
72. Dōki stayed and studied in Nālanda Temple, not in Baradai Temple (see *Daizōkyō* 51, p. 2).
73. Tohōshi 登法師, or Tōhōshi 燈法師, received the precepts from Xuan Zhuang (*Daizōkyō* 51, p. 4).

It is truly heartbreaking that [Dōki], who overcame much hardship traveling through the desert[74] and later faced wild beasts such as tigers and wolves, arrived in India only to die there before he could return to China with his transcribed sutras. His grief and sadness must have been great, but there were a few consolations: He met someone related to the Law [Vasubandhu] and discovered traces of the Buddha along the way. It is especially noble that he remained alone in that dilapidated temple, quietly reading sutras.

It is a pity that common and ignorant people like us cannot take the place of a [superior] man such as Dōki when he is faced with heartless death in this futile life.[75] When I saw the summary of this story in the *Yūshinshū*,[76] I could not ignore it and thus have recorded it here.

---

74. *Ryūsa* 流砂 refers to the Taklamakan Desert.

75. The sentence means it is regrettable that superior men like Dōki must die while ignorant people like us remain alive.

76. The work is unidentified, but it appears in *Kankyonotomo* 1-10; *Senjūshō* 1-8, 2-1, 4-5, and 9-6. Minobe Shigekatsu thinks that it must have been similar to a Buddhist tale collection such as the *Senjūshō* and the *Kankyonotomo* (*Kankyonotomo*, in *Chūsei no bungaku*, p. 34).

9-7 Kūkanbō

Before receiving the tonsure, Kūkanbō of Kōya[77] was called Nariyori or Prime Minister of Bōjō.[78] Since leaving secular life around the end of Eiryaku,[79] he had confined himself to the mountain.[80] When I heard of this distinguished ascetic, I became interested in him and visited him.

In his ten-foot-square grass hut,[81] Kūkanbō had beautifully arranged three statues of Amida[82] with flowers and incense. He quietly sat in front of them, reciting the Buddha's name. Everything appeared very pleasant.

When I asked him, "What devotion should we practice for our future life?" he replied, "I have the buddha nature,[83] which is forever clear and serene. Because of this, whatever I do comes from the buddha world. So all my actions, including thinking, sitting, and standing, are within the Law. I have never neglected daily meditation. Since I observe the teaching of Non-Discrimination of the Three,[84] I do not hate or slander others. Whatever I practice, by its very nature, benefits both myself and others and leads us to the buddha world."[85] As I heard Kūkanbō speak, I thought he exceeded his reputation for nobility, and I wet my sleeves with my joyful tears.

On my way home, I concluded that what Kūkanbō had told me

---

77. Kōya no Kūkanbō 高野の空観房, or Fujiwara Nariyori 藤原成頼 (1136–1202), was a son of Akiyori, became a *sangi* minister in 1161, and received the tonsure in 1174; see *Senjūshō* 8-33.
78. *Bōjō* 防城 means a capital city.
79. The last year of Eiryaku (1161) does not correspond to the time when Nariyori took the tonsure in 1174.
80. Mount Kōya in the northeast of Wakayama prefecture is the headquarters of the Shingon Sect.
81. *Hōjō no iori* 方丈のいおり: one *jō* (ten feet) square *iori* (a hut made of branches and grasses).
82. *Amidabutsu no sanzon* 阿弥陀仏の三尊: three images of Amida Buddha, flanked by the bodhisattvas Kannon 観音 on the right and Seishi 勢至 on the left.
83. *Busshō* 仏性: the buddha nature in all sentient beings, which makes it possible for us to become buddhas.
84. *Shinbutsugyūshujō* 心仏及衆生: mind, Buddha, and sentient beings. *Zesanmusabetsu* 是三無差別: no discrimination of the mind, Buddha, and sentient beings.
85. *Hōkai* 法界 refers to all the objects of consciousness, the entire universe.

was correct. I wonder if it was Master Shōan[86] who said, "Every night, I sleep with the Buddha and every morning, I wake up with the Buddha." Sōzu Eshin[87] commented thus, "This is exactly the same as the idea of the Thirty-Seven Buddhas and Bodhisattvas Living in My Mind.[88] I am originally a buddha. My waking and sleeping are the Buddha's waking and sleeping, although Master Shōan did not say this." What Eshin wrote corresponds exactly to what Kūkanbō told me.

If we practice any merits with the thought of Non-Discrimination of the Three, then we benefit ourselves as well as others in attaining future deliverance. This is most noble. Good and evil are within ourselves, so there is no discrepancy between good and evil. All sentient beings are related to us, and the Buddha's mercy for all living beings is strong. Because the buddhas know all living beings are related to them, they show their mercy equally to everything and everyone.

Indeed, I understand the saying, "The thought of benefiting oneself is the same as benefiting others, and this is the true service for buddhas."[89] Alas, although I do not truly understand Non-Discrimination of the Three, I wish buddhas would help me accept the idea so that I will not dislike others and feel just as Kūkanbō felt. With this desire, I am somehow tearfully overwhelmed.

Indeed, if mind, buddhas, and sentient beings were different, then even the buddhas would not show mercy to everything so easily. A Buddhist text tells us, "The great mercy of buddhas and bodhisattvas is not unrelated to us.[90] If a buddha is in the flames of the Mugen Hell,[91] he grieves, and this shows his mercy is related to us."[92] Kūkanbō, having left the secular world and quietly concentrating on his deep thoughts, was most extraordinary.

As I calmly think of mind, [in my former existences] I might have

---

86. Master Shōan 章安 took the tonsure at the age of seven and became a disciple of Great Master Chi-I at twenty-three.

87. Eshin 惠心, or Genshin 源信 (942–1017); see *Senjūshō* 2-5, 6-7, 8-34, 8-35, and 9-3.

88. *Sanjūshichison jūshinjō* 卅七尊住心城; the concept appears in various writings such as the *Kanshin ryakuyōshu* 観心略要集 by Genshin; *Hōbutsushū* 6; and *Senjūshō* 5-4.

89. A similar passage appears in *Senjūshō* 7-14 and in the *Myōgyō shin'yōshū* 妙行心要集 by Genshin (*Dainihon bukkyō zensho* 39, p. 247).

90. *Muen* 無縁: no relation to buddhas and bodhisattvas in obtaining enlightenment.

91. *Mugen jigoku*: one of the Eight Hells where sinners undergo incessant suffering.

92. *Uen* 有縁: a relationship to Buddha and bodhisattvas for future deliverance.

been a horse enjoying grass in the woods, a cow cultivating a poor man's rice paddies, a buck living on a summit and missing his mate, or a pheasant wandering the fields and losing her life to protect her eggs. Sometimes we are born as animals on mountains and at other times as fishes.[93] Repeating hardship and sadness, continually hurting and harming each other, we create more reasons to fall into the bad realms.[94]

Here is a woman: A coquette[95] who bathes herself in perfume. Gazing into a beautiful rain bird mirror[96] in the morning, she draws her eyebrows as thin as willow leaves to please; in the evening, she fills her robes with enticing scent to enchant. But she never pays attention to the moon in her heart.[97] This woman, to whom you are utterly attracted,[98] might have been one of your parents in a former life, which would be most unbecoming. Or she might have been a snake hiding in a bush, frightening people. Or perhaps [that fish] in your mouth. Such beings are created out of human love and obligation.[99]

A buddha equally bestows his mercy on all living beings. Although I try not to dislike anything, I would be frightened and run away if a snake suddenly appeared out of a bush. This is most sad. From now on, I will have a stronger conviction and not be disturbed even if a snake falls on my head. Besides, because I have now learned the meaning of Non-Discrimination of the Three, how could I, even for a moment, dislike[100] other beings?

---

93. *Irokuzu* includes scaly beings like fish.
94. *Akushu* includes the three lower realms of hungry ghosts, animals, and hell.
95. *Akikaze no nagori o okuru*, literally, "sending the traces (*nagori*) of autumn breezes," or coquetry; see *Senjūshō* 1-1.
96. A mirror with the imaginary Chinese rain bird carved on its back.
97. *Mune no naka no tsuki*: "a moon in one's chest," i.e., an enlightened mind like the moon.
98. *Onna no iro, joshoku* 女色: a woman's color. *Iro* 色 here refers to sex and the term means a sexual affair with a woman.
99. *On'ai* 恩愛.
100. *Sobamu*: to avoid something or someone with a feeling of dislike or hatred.

9-8 The Courtesan of Eguchi

Some time ago, around the twentieth day of the ninth month, I passed through a place called Eguchi.[101] A courtesan's house was located between the northern and southern banks of two rivers. I could not help but feel sorry for this woman, who had to depend on travelers to make a living.

A cold rain, as cold as any in winter, began to fall, so I decided to take shelter at the courtesan's house for a short while. But the woman of the house did not appear willing, so I composed a poem for her:

Yononaka o
Itou made koso
Katakarame
Karino yado o
Oshimu kimi kana

Avoiding worldly life
May be difficult,
But alas, you begrudge
My temporary stay
At your place.

Slightly smiling, the woman replied:

Ie o izuru
Hito toshi kikaba
Kari no yado ni
Kokoro tomu na to
Omou bakarizo

I only thought
Someone like you
With the tonsure

---

101. Eguchi 江口 was in present-day Osaka city. It was a river port town where the Yodo and Kanzaki rivers met and many courtesans gathered to entertain travelers. This story is related to *Senjūshō* 5-11, which narrates how the protagonist met a nun in Eguchi who was skilled at composing linked verse.

Should not stay at a place
As worldly as this.

After she had finished, she quickly let me into the house. I thought to remain there only until the rain had stopped, but I spent the entire night there thanks to her elegant poems.

The woman looked to be about forty years of age and was quite graceful in her appearance and manners. Throughout the night, we talked about various matters. She began to tell me her story.

"I have been a courtesan since I was young. I think my profession is most lamentable. I hear women in general are sinful, but especially those who work as courtesans. A past karmic relationship must have caused me to lead this shameful life. During these last few years, as I have grown older, I became more regretful and finally stopped being a courtesan.

"Now the temple bell sounds mournful in the evening. I wonder how long this transient life will last; I feel everything is so futile. Toward dawn, my mind becomes clearer and the cries of departing birds deeply touch my heart. In the evening, I feel as though anything could happen, and then in the morning, I wonder if I should cut my hair and leave this mundane life. Alas, abandoning long-accustomed ways is not so easy; I am like the birds that constantly suffer during the cold nights in the Himalayas.[102] So I have not yet been able to renounce this life. How sad it is," she wept. Her unusual story quite overwhelmed me, and the sleeves of my black robe became wet with tears and were difficult to dry. At daybreak, I reluctantly left her, promising to see her again.

On my way home, I shed many tears as I thought of her. Merely looking at the trees and grasses, my heart was tearfully touched. Truly, the Way of Poetry was leading me to the Way of the Law. Had I not recited my poem to her, she would not have let me remain and I would not have known such a wonderful person. Thanks to her, my yearning for the Way increased. I felt most grateful that our meeting had helped me obtain a deeper enlightenment.

In spite of the promise I had made to visit her in a month, I was unable to fulfill it because I was busy attending a high-ranking monk

---

102. An imaginary bird in the Himalayas was said to forget the coldness of mountain nights while enjoying sunny days. The bird is like those who wish to change their lives to enter the Way but have not yet done so because they are still attached to secular life.

from the capital. I deeply regretted this, so I sent her a message with a poem:

Karisome no
Yo ni wa omoi o
Nokosu na to
Kikishi kotonoha
Wasure mo sezu

I never forget
Your words
Which tell me
Not to attach to anything
In this temporary world.

The woman entrusted her reply to my messenger. I quickly opened her message and found a poem written in an elegant hand:

Wasurezu to
Mazu kiku karani
Sode nure te
Wagami wa itou
Yume no yononaka

Hearing that you have
Not forgotten my words,
My sleeves become wet with tears
As I am still left amidst
This futile dream world.

She wrote another poem as a postscript, saying that she had finally changed her life although her heart was not yet completely in accordance with the Way:

Kami oroshi
Koromo no iro wa
Somenuru ni

Nao tsurenaki wa
Kokoro narikeri

By cutting my hair,
Dyeing the color of my robe,[103]
I have left the world,
But only my heart
Is not yet in the Way.[104]

For no reason, her poem moved me to tears. She was indeed a fine woman.

It is quite natural for a courtesan to desire the favor of a man she is attracted to, but it is rare for such a woman to abandon this desire and long for the life after death. The good deeds in her previous lives must have been remarkable; the accumulated good karma must have purified her heart near the waters of Eguchi. Her poems were very tasteful.

I recall her saying that in the evening she was unsure of herself but

---

103. This is a reference to a black priestly robe.
104. The poem implies that, despite her efforts to leave the secular world, she still has some difficulties.

in the morning she thought of receiving the tonsure. She fulfilled her wish and finally left secular life behind. Sometime later, I wanted to visit her, but since I heard that she had left Eguchi after receiving the tonsure, I have done nothing about it. But I often think of her, wondering what her last moments will be like.

Why does it seem natural that one's heart becomes pure in the evening and at dawn? I grow melancholy when night falls and I hear the autumn wind blowing across the pampas grass. The leaves of the mountain trees disturbed by stormy winds and scattered by winter showers wet my sleeves like tears under the evening sky. The lonesome cries of monkeys in the tall pines and of flying geese from the northern lakes at dawn purify my heart, and somehow tears fall.

9-9 The Buddhist Service for the Wife of Lord Sanjō

Some time ago Great Lord Sanjō[105] held the third memorial service for his late wife.[106] Monk Myōhen[107] of the Sanron Sect was the officiating monk. Because I heard that he was a promising young scholar, I attended the service, hoping to hear something meaningful from the scriptures.

Various *fuju*[108] messages were read at the service, including one prepared by Goryō Sanefusa,[109] the eleven-year-old son of the deceased. Monk Myōhen read the boy's message, which was written in Japanese *kana* mixed with Chinese characters:

"Three years, or more than one thousand days, have passed since Mother passed away. I have shed so many tears that my sleeves cannot absorb them, and the color of my mourning sash has washed away. How many more years will it take to ease my sorrow? How many more months will it take to appease my grief? Shinju[110] was buried near my

---

105. Fujiwara Saneyuki 藤原実行 (1080–1162) was a prime minister, father of Kiminori, and grandfather of Sanefusa.
106. The wife of Saneyuki was also a daughter of Akisue.
107. Myōhen 明遍 (1142–1224) studied the Sanron Sect teachings in Tōdaiji Temple.
108. *Fuju* 諷誦: dedicatory messages for memorial services.
109. Sanefusa 実房 (1147–1225), a son of Kiminori, received Junior Third Rank at the age of fourteen and later became Minister of the Left.
110. Unidentified.

mother's grave for ten years[111] to protect her from thunder; Shōjaku[112] was buried with my father in the same casket.[113] Although I grieve, I have neither laid down on the moss of Mother's grave for a single night nor spent a single moment by Father's casket. But not even the tears of Shinju can extinguish the Mugen Hell's flames for Mother. In vain Shōjaku was buried with Father under the moss, for he cannot accompany him on the mountain path to death.[114] Crouching alone on the path where the demon messengers of hell pass, I grieve while King Ma's[115] reprimands reach my ears alone. But now I should immediately stop my lamentation and practice virtue [for my future life]."

At the end of the message, all the listeners—behind and beyond the screens,[116] the thoughtful and the heartless, shed tears like rain. After a while, the officiating monk wiped his tears away and said, "I have heard a little about the writer of this message. I understand he is only some ten years of age, but he is familiar with Chinese and Japanese learning. Truly, all the buddhas of the Three Generations must be impressed, and his deceased mother must be moved." Everyone agreed with his words and shed more tears.

Few people—even those with wrinkles on their foreheads and frostlike eyebrows[117]—understand the feelings of others. Few can express their feelings in writing. Just as sandalwood is said to release its scent from its second leaves[118] and plum blossoms are most fragrant while they are still buds, outstanding individuals [like Sanefusa] display their talents when young.

I was so impressed by Monk Myōhen, who exhorted us to avoid the

---

111. This does not accord with the occasion of a third memorial service, which would have been held not ten years after the mother's death but three.
112. Unidentified.
113. Earlier the story states that the father, Lord Sanjō, is still alive.
114. *Shide no yamaji* 死での山路.
115. Maō 魔王, or King Yama (Enma), is the judge in hell.
116. Noblemen and women usually stayed behind screens.
117. *Hitai ni* (on the forehead) *ihin* (Wei Beach in China [where Tai Gong-wang used to fish]) *no nami* (waves) *o tatami* (to fold): "the waves of Wei Beach are folded," refers to the wrinkles on the forehead. *Mayu* (eyebrows) *ni shōzan* (Mount Shang in China [where the four celebrated recluses sequestered]) *no shimo* (frost) *o tare* (to place): "to place the frost of Mount Shang on the eyebrows," refers to white eyebrows.
118. *Sendan wa futaba yori kanbashi* 栴檀は二葉より香ばし is an expression often used for someone who shows talent at a young age.

Six Dusts,[119] that I am no longer attached to secular matters. Isn't the concept of Everything Is Void[120] in various sutras such as the *Hannya*[121] the same as avoiding the Six Dusts? Myōhen's preaching [that day] exceeded his reputation for nobility. I felt his inner virtues were superior and his ability to understand the truth of life most distinguished.

As I walk about the capital, I see many families in mourning and smoke endlessly rising from Mount Toribe because death occurs constantly in Funaoka.[122] How pitiful it is to expose our bones there, leaving behind only futile names. How sad to be buried under firewood and produce smoke and clouds that cause rain to obscure the sky. Our life is as short as the morning dew and the dream of a spring night. All the pleasures in such a short life lead to future suffering. Isn't it tragic that we pay no heed to the futility of life and death[123] while attached to secular affairs?

We try not to dwell on the Six Dusts of secular life, but we are easily attached to things familiar to us. When we open our eyes, the world of the Six Dusts appears so attractive that it moves our hearts. When we listen to songs and music, they sound so beautiful that they excite our minds. Thus leaving these attractions behind is most difficult. But we must remember that everything is created in our minds. Without our minds, there would be neither color[124] nor the sound of music. They are the products of our minds and are not real. So attaching ourselves to color and music is completely futile. Where do our hearts and minds dwell? According to a sermon, our sins are as numerous as the dew on the grass, which will vanish when the blessed [Buddha's] sun shines. Since we all equally receive the blessings of the sun, we should raise our minds to the truth and use our deep knowledge to avoid the Six Dusts and thus erase our sins.

---

119. *Rokujin* 六塵 is a reference to the six roots 六根 (eye, ear, nose, tongue, body, will), which cause delusions in our minds like dust.
120. *Manpō kūjaku* 万法空寂: all the laws are empty and silent.
121. The *Hannya* (*Hannyakyō* 般若経, *Prajñāpāramitā-sūtra*, or the Wisdom Sutra) teaches the doctrine of *śūnyatā* (*kū* 空, nothingness).
122. Toribeyama and Funaoka were burial grounds in Kyoto.
123. *Shōji no mujō* 生死の無常.
124. Here, *iro* 色 (color) refers to carnal desire.

9-10 A Reunion at Hasedera Temple

Some years ago, after receiving the tonsure, I[125] visited various famous temples. Around the beginning of the tenth month, I arrived at Hasedera Temple.[126] At sunset I heard the evening bell sound mournfully and saw the lonesome sight of autumn leaves blown by the wind.

After reciting a sutra at the Kannon Hall, I looked around and saw a nun quietly praying near me, fingering her rosary beads. Moved by the sight, I recited a poem:

Omoirete
Suru zuzu oto no
Koe sumite
Oboezu tamaru
Waga namida kana

Pure sounds
Of devout
Prayer and the
Rosary beads
Moved me to tears.

Hearing my poem, the nun looked up and quickly caught my sleeve, asking, "Oh, how are you?" It was my former wife with whom I was once very close.[127] Surprised, I asked her, "Why did you take the tonsure?" At first she was too tearful to speak, but eventually she began to tell her story.

"When you left me after receiving the tonsure, I didn't know what to do and wandered from one place to another. The sound of the evening bells made me tearful and the birds crying at dawn deepened my loneliness. My sadness increased and became intolerable. I finally cut my hair and became a nun around the third month of last

---

125. Although the text mentions no name, the protagonist is regarded as Saigyō.
126. Hasedera 長谷寺, or Hatsusedera Temple, in Nara was regarded among the Heian nobles as a special place for meeting people and reunions.
127. The *Hosshinshū* (6-5) mentions that Saigyō's wife was related to Lady Reizei, a daughter of Fujiwara Akiyori, Lord Minbu of Kujō.

year.[128] Since leaving my daughter with her aunt,[129] I have been living in Amano village on Mount Kōya.[130]

"After you left me I vainly held a grudge against you, thinking you may have associated with another woman. But now that I see you pursuing the Way, I bear no such grudge. On the contrary, I am grateful that you gave me a chance to enter the Way. When we separated, my wish was to see you in the Pure Land after our deaths, so unexpectedly meeting you here like this seems like a dream." While she spoke, the nun could not stop her tears.

I was overwhelmed to learn that she had received the tonsure and wept when I heard that she bore no grudge against me. However, unable to remain there any longer, I instructed her about some teachings from a sutra and then left, promising to visit her at her home.

When I lived with her, I considered my wife to be a wise person,

---

128. The wife received the tonsure on the same day as Saigyō received his, and she spent a few years in the capital with her daughter; see *Saigyō monogatari*, in *Saigyō zenshū*, Nihon koten bungakukai, p. 990.

129. The daughter was adopted by Lady Reizei in the *Saigyō monogatari*, in *Saigyō zenshū*, Nihon koten bungakukai, p. 966.

130. There was a village for ascetics in Nishitani on Mount Kōya located in the northeast of Wakayama prefecture; see *Saigyō monogatari* II, *in Saigyō zenshū,* Nihon koten bungakukai, pp. 990–992.

but that was all. A woman usually holds a grudge for a trifling reason, when things do not turn out well for her. She is constantly annoyed by unbearable feelings rising one after another, and she spends her life in a futile way. My wife was able to turn the sadness caused by our separation into an opportunity to enter the Way; she even left her cherished daughter behind. Wasn't this most noble of her?

Although embarrassed and ashamed by some of the details in this story and regardless of any criticism I may receive, I could not resist writing it down.

9-11 Sōzu Kakuei

Long ago, while wandering in parts of northeast Michinoku, I came to a remote place called Kuzu no Matsubara, or Kuzu Pine Grove, in the Shinobu district.[131] It was neither a mountain nor a level field, but a pleasant hill with attractive trees and plants, and there were fresh water streams flowing everywhere. Anyone secretly wishing to escape the secular world would be glad to live there.

As I went further on, I came to a thick grove of pines under which a bamboo basket and hemp robe had been left without any sign of their owner. I felt sad, wondering what had happened to him. I found an inscription carved on the trunk of one of the trees: "As a student of the Hossō Sect, I used to take part in Buddhist services for aristocrats, but lately I have been wandering through many provinces as a mendicant monk and will end my life in the Kuzu Pine Grove."

Yono naka no
Hito niwa kuzu no
Matsubara to
Yobaruru na koso
Ureshi karikere

People in the world
Call me Kuzu no Matsubara,

---

131. Present-day Fukushima city. Matsubara is now called Kōrichō.

Kuzu[132] Pine Grove,
I am pleased
To be called by that name.

On the seventeenth day of the second month of Hōgen 2 (1157), Assistant Sōzu[133] Kakuei ends his life at the age of forty-one.[134]

Kakuei, a son of Lord Gonijō,[135] was a younger brother of Lord Monk Fuke.[136] He composed the famous poem:

Hana o nomi
Oshimi naretaru
Miyoshino no
Konoma ni otsuru
Ariake no tsuki

People usually begrudge
The fallen blossoms,
Likewise, the dawn moon
Sinking among the trees
Of Miyoshino Field.[137]

Kakuei was a disciple of Abbot Ichijōin Kakushin,[138] but at the age of twenty, he decided one night to renounce the world. During the cold season, he removed his lined *kosode*,[139] donned a one-layer kimono,

---

132. *Kuzu* 葛, one of the Seven Plants of Autumn (*aki no nanakusa*), plays on *kuzu* 屑 (trash or something useless).
133. *Shōsōzu* 小僧都: an assistant to a great *sōzu*, which is ranked below a *sōjō* 僧正, or abbot.
134. If Kakuei 覚英 died in 1157, he could not have been a son of Lord Gonijō (1062–1099).
135. Gonijō 後二条, or Fujiwara Moromichi (1062–1099), a son of Morozane. Gonijō became a *kanpaku* regent and received Junior First Rank; see *Senjūshō* 6-6.
136. Fuke 富家 was Fujiwara Tadazane (1078–1162), a son of Moromichi. He was popularly known as Lord Fuke because he lived in the Fuke district of Uji.
137. Miyoshino 三善野, the Yoshino 吉野 district in Nara prefecture, is famous for its cherry blossoms.
138. Ichijōin Kakushin Daisōjō 一乗院覚信大僧正 (1065–1121), a *bettō* director of Kōfukuji Temple, was a son of Fujiwara Morozane and a younger brother of Lord Gonijō.
139. The *kosode* 小袖, a lined kimono with short sleeves, was generally worn by women in later times.

and quietly left. No one knew where to look for him. Over the next ten years, Kakuei wandered across many provinces before dying in this place. It was most sad.

Although he could have been served by three thousand monks as the abbot of a temple, he abandoned both title and wealth and ended his life, content with the name Kuzu no Matsubara. Wasn't he indeed most noble? When we study the lives of the distinguished monks recorded in the *Biographies of High Monks*,[140] our minds are purified by the story of Sōzu Genpin, who composed a poem: "*Kegasaji*, not to soil."[141] Kakuei seems nobler than Genpin; if we are to renounce the world, we should imitate Kakuei. Alas, it is sad that, ignoring the hearts of Genpin and Kakuei, our minds are attached to futile titles and profit.

Postscript

Vainly spending our time [not practicing the Way], how would we recall this human life? While traveling through the Six Realms,[142] we experience a variety of conditions and stages. The human world is listed after that of the buddhas, and only those living in the human world can learn the Buddhist teachings.

Once we are born in the human world, we should do our best to gain merit for our future lives by observing the Five Precepts[143] and practicing the Ten Good Deeds.[144] But instead, we pass our days frivolously until our hair becomes white and we sadly face death like sheep approaching [the slaughter house].

Here I have recorded in nine rolls[145] what I heard about ancient and modern sages and my experiences with distinguished people I

---

140. *Kōsōden* 高僧伝.
141. The *Hosshinshū* (1-1) narrates how Genpin declined the position of great *sōzu* by reciting a poem: "I will not soil the sleeves of my robe, which were washed by the pure water of Mount Miwa." For more references to Genpin, see *Senjūshō* 1-8, 2-4, and 2-8.
142. *Rokushu* 六趣: the realms of heaven (Buddhist), humans, *ashura*, animals, hungry ghosts, and hell.
143. *Gokai* 五戒: the five precepts prohibiting killing, stealing, adultery, false words, and drinking.
144. *Jūzen* 十善: the ten good deeds (not to kill, steal, commit adultery, speak false testimony, utter strange words, speak ill of others, be talkative, be avaricious, be angry, and have evil views).
145. *Maki* 巻: rolls or chapters.

met, hoping that I may become like them and have them as future friends when I retire to the quiet life.[146] I have included casual remarks, poems, and miscellaneous tales. While reminiscing about the past, I have added random notes and small details, hoping they might provide additional insight.

Monk Gengyō of Silla[147] said, "There is no reason why we should be affected by the *karma* of others, but there is an unfathomable power in karmic relations."[148] I hope that what I have recorded here may earn the merits [of Amida Buddha], and so I have arranged these many tales into nine chapters.

I completed this work in the latter part of the first month of Juei 2 (1183)[149] in the *hōjō* hut[150] of Zentsūji Temple in Sanuki province.[151]

---

146. *Kankyo* 閑居 refers to life after renouncing the world.
147. Gengyō 元暁 (617–686) was a most distinguished monk of Shiragi (in ancient Korea). His influence on ancient Japanese Buddhism was great since more than sixty of the eighty rolls of his writings (the *Sōshōin* documents) were brought to Japan from Korea.
148. *Engi* 縁起, a relationship caused by associating with others. The same expression is found in various *Senjūshō* tales, e.g., 3-8, 5-2, and 6-11.
149. The colophon of the Matsudaira text states that the work was copied in Shōwa 4 (1315) and Chōroku 3 (1459); these dates are the same in the Hashimoto text.
150. *Hōjō no iho* 方丈のいほ: a one *jō* (ten feet) square hut. Saigyō lived in a hut in the compound of Zentsūji Temple at the age of fifty (*Sankashū* no. 1366).
151. Zentsūji is in present-day Kagawa prefecture.

SELECTED BIBLIOGRAPHY

Primary Sources

Iwamoto Yutaka, ed. *Hokekyō* 法華経. Tokyo: Iwanami shoten, 1962.
Kobayashi Yasuharu, ed. *Kojidan* 古事談. Tokyo: Gendai shichōsha, 1981.
Minobe Shigekatsu, ed. *Kankyonotomo* 閑居友. *Chūsei no bungaku*. Tokyo: Miyai shoten, 1974.
Sekiguchi Shindai, ed. *Makashikan* 摩訶止観. Tokyo: Iwanami shoten, 1966.
Yoshida Kōichi, and Koizumi Hiroshi, eds. *Hōbutsushū* 宝物集. Tokyo: Kotenbunko, 1969.

Secondary Sources

Brower, Robert H., and Earl Miner. *Japanese Court Poetry*. Stanford: Stanford University Press, 1967.
Dykstra, Yoshiko. "Jizō, the Most Merciful: Tales from *Jizō Bosatsu Reigenki*." *Monumenta Nipponica* 33, no. 2 (1978): 179–200.
———. *The Konjaku Tales*. Japanese Sections. 3 vols. Intercultural Research Institute Monograph Series 25, 27–28. Osaka: Kansai Gaidai University, 1998–2003.
———. *Miraculous Tales of the Lotus Sutra from Ancient Japan*. Honolulu: University of Hawai'i Press, 1987.
———. "Shintō Tales." *Journal of Intercultural Studies* 5 (1978): 67–88.
———. "Tales of the Compassionate Kannon: The *Hasedera Kannon Genki*." *Monumenta Nipponica* 31, no. 2 (1976): 113–143.
Fujioka Sakutaro. *Kamakura Muromachi jidai bungakushi*. Tokyo: Ōkura shoten, 1915.
Haga Yaichi, ed. *Senjūshō* (Meicho bunko). Tokyo: Fuzanbō, 1927.
Itō Hiroyuki. *Inton no bungaku*. Tokyo: Kasama shoin, 1975.

Kawada Jun, ed. *Sanetomoshū, Saigyōshū, Ryōkanshū*. Volume 21 of *Nihon koten bungaku zenshū*. Tokyo: Shōgakkan, 1967.
Kazamaki Keijirō. *Saigyō to Kenkō*. Volume 15 of *Kadokawa sensho*. Tokyo: Kadokawa, 1970.
Kojima Takayuki, and Asami Kazuhiko, eds. *Senjūshō*. Kyoto: Ōfūsha, 1985.
Kubota Jun, ed. *Saigyō zenshū*. Tokyo: Nihon koten bungakukai, 1962.
Kuroda Shōichirō. *Saigyō no kenkyū*. Tokyo: Tōkyōdō, 1961.
Mezaki Tokue. *Saigyō no shisōteki kenkyū*. Tokyo: Yoshikawa kōbunkan, 1978.
Mills, D. E. *Collection of Tales of Uji: A Study and Translation of Uji shūi monogatari*. Cambridge: Cambrige University Press, 1970.
Minobe Shigekatsu. *Kankyonotomo*. Tokyo: Miyai shoten, 1974.
Moore, Jean. "Senjūshō: Buddhist Tales of Renunciation." *Monumenta Nipponica* 41, no. 2 (1986): 127–174.
Morell, R. E. "Shasekishū." PhD diss., Stanford University, 1966.
Nagai Yoshinori. *Nihon Bukkyōbungaku kenkyū*. Tokyo: Koten bunko, 1957.
Nagano Jōichi, ed. *Setsuwa bungaku jiten*. Tokyo: Tōkyōdō, 1969.
Nishida Masayoshi. *Bukkō to bungaku: Senjūshō*. Kyoto: Ōfūsha, 1967.
Nishio Kōchi. *Chūsei setsuwa bungakuron*. Tokyo: Shimashobō, 1963.
———. *Senjūshō* (Iwanami bunko). Tokyo: Iwanami shoten, 1970
Nomura Hachirō. *Kamakura jidai bungaku shiron*. Tokyo: Meiji shoin, 1926.
———. *Kinko bungakushiron* (Setsuwa bungaku). Tokyo: Meiji shoin, 1942.
Sasaki Nobuetsuna, ed. *Saigyō zenshū*. Tokyo: Bumeisha, 1941.
Ury, Marion Bloom. "The Hosshinshū: A Patial Translation with Notes." MA thesis, University of California, Berkeley, 1965.
Yasuda Takako, ed. *Senjūshō kankei bunken mokuroku*. Tokyo: Kasama shoin, 1980.
Yasuda Takako, Umeno Kimiko, Nozaki Noriko, Kawano Keiko, and Morise Yoshie, eds. *Senjūshō kōhonhen*. Tokyo: Kasama shoin, 1974.
Yasuda Takako, Umeno Kimiko, Nozaki Noriko, Kōno Keiko, and Morise Yoshie, eds. *Senjūshō*. 2 vols. Tokyo: Gendai shichōsha, 2006.
Yasuda Takako, Umeno Kimiko, Nozaki Noriko, and Morise Yoshie, eds. *Senjūshō zenchūshaku*. 2 vols. Tokyo: Kasama shoin, 2003.
Yoshizawa Yoshinori. *Kamakura bungakushi*. Tokyo: Tōkyōdō, 1942.

www.ingramcontent.com/pod-product-compliance
Lightning Source LLC
Chambersburg PA
CBHW061934220426
43662CB00012B/1900